COUNTING THE DAYS

‖‖ ‖‖ ‖‖

POWs, Internees,
and Stragglers
of World War II
in the Pacific

COUNTING THE DAYS

POWs, Internees,
and Stragglers
of World War II
in the Pacific

CRAIG B. SMITH

Smithsonian Books
WASHINGTON, DC

This book may be purchased for educational, business,
or sales promotional use. For information, please write:
Special Markets Department
Smithsonian Books
P. O. Box 37012, MRC 513
Washington, DC 20013

Published by Smithsonian Books
Director: Carolyn Gleason
Production Editor: Christina Wiginton

Edited by Lise Sajewski
Designed by Mary Parsons
Maps by XNR Productions, Inc.

Library of Congress Cataloging-in-Publication Data
Smith, Craig B.
Counting the Days : POWs, Internees, and Stragglers of World
War II in the Pacific / by Craig B. Smith.
p. cm.
Includes bibliographical references and index.
ISBN 978-1-58834-355-0
1. World War, 1939–1945—Prisoners and prisons,
Japanese.   2. World War, 1939–1945—Prisoners and
prisons, American.   3. World War, 1939-1945—Personal
narratives.   4. Prisoners of war—Japan—Biography.
5. Prisoners of war—United States—Biography.
6. World War, 1939-1945—Pacific Area.   I. Title.
D805.A2S64 2012
940.54'72091823—dc23
2011047583

Manufactured in the United States of America

16 15 14 13 12   1 2 3 4 5

Dedicated to the United States Marines
who served on Guam

CONTENTS

卌 卌 卌

MAPS AND PLATES

‖‖ ‖‖ ‖‖

MAPS

PLATES

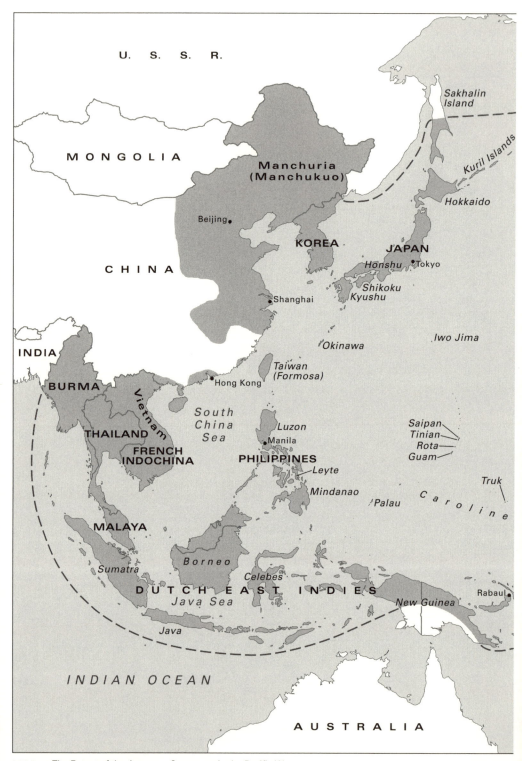

MAP 1: The Extent of the Japanese Conquests in the Pacific War

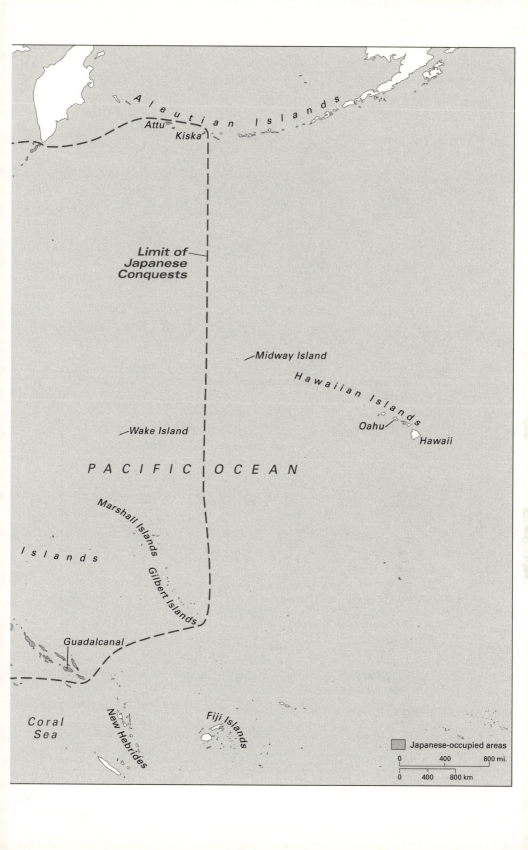

Aleutian Islands

Attu
Kiska

Limit of
Japanese
Conquests

Midway Island

Hawaiian Islands

Oahu
Hawaii

Wake Island

PACIFIC OCEAN

Marshall Islands

Islands

Gilbert Islands

Guadalcanal

Coral
Sea

New Hebrides

Fiji Islands

Japanese-occupied areas

0	400	800 mi.

0	400	800 km

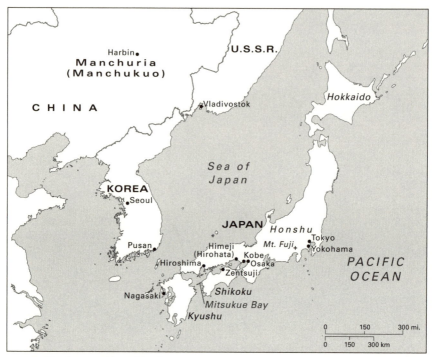

MAP 2: The Japanese Home Islands

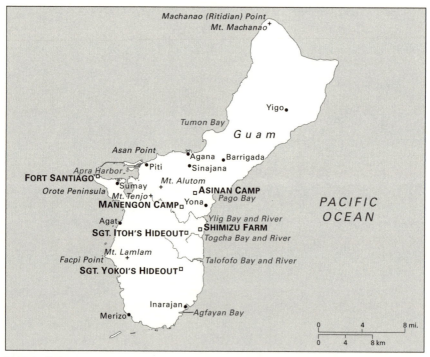

MAP 3: Guam

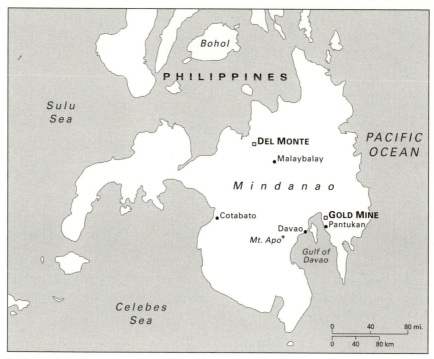

MAP 4: Mindanao

MAP 5: Manzanar

AUTHOR'S PREFACE

〲〲〲

eas were calm that early morning in the Gulf of Davao, at the southern end
of the Philippine island of Mindanao. I was traveling by *banca*, a small
wooden boat used by Filipino fishermen. The boatmen, a taciturn Muslim and
his son, spoke little English but had been recommended to me by someone I
trusted. September 1985 was not a good time to be in Mindanao. The Inter-
Continental Hotel where I was staying was nearly empty because terrorist activity had sharply curtailed tourism. The guerrillas were aggressively killing local
mayors, police officers, and school principals. Since I fit none of those categories,
I felt reasonably safe. Tourists were kidnapped only for ransom.

I would have preferred to drive around the gulf, through small villages like
Mabini, to the eastern side, where an old gold-mine mill was located. However,
no one would drive me there—too dangerous to enter an area controlled by
guerrillas who used illicit gold to buy weapons—therefore, the boat. I reasoned
that a snorkeling expedition in the gulf would provide an innocent enough cover
for the trip. The snorkel, mask, and fins were props and never got wet. Once we
were well out in the gulf, the older boatman looked at me as if to ask, "Where
to?" When I pointed to the east, he let me know by signs and words that he didn't
want to take his boat too far that way. I told him to go as far as he could. As we
motored east for several hours, I reflected on what had brought me to the Philippines in the first place.

From work and through family, I knew several people who were prisoners of
the Japanese during World War II, the conflict the Japanese called the Pacific
War. The stories of these former prisoners were so amazing that I felt compelled
to interview these people to document how they had survived. They were not
alone; thousands of others shared their fate, not only in Asia but in Europe as
well. Many POWs—or *horyo* as the Japanese called them—simply had the bad
luck to be in the wrong place at the wrong time.

Simon and Lydia Peters, for example. Civilian noncombatants during World War II, they were nonetheless rounded up by the Japanese invaders and thrown into separate prison camps in Davao. Later, they fled from the city in a banca similar to the one in which I was sitting. They made their way across the gulf to hide in the jungle for the duration of the war, and nearly died during those desperate years. The story of their remarkable struggle to survive had drawn me to Mindanao.

In the early afternoon, the banca turned back. We'd reached the point where the opposite shore stood green on the horizon—palm trees and an inviting beach, still more than a rifle shot away, were visible. But I could tell by my captain's body language that he was getting nervous, so we gave it up and returned to Davao. I took some satisfaction in the fact that I had at least retraced part of the journey Simon and Lydia had made in 1942, when they escaped from the Japanese into that same distant, foreboding jungle.

On the return to Davao, there was little breeze and the sun beat down on the open boat. The trip was uneventful except when we passed by one other banca filled with rough-looking characters. They were "fishing" by tossing sticks of dynamite in the water, scooping up their catch of stunned fish, and fortunately, paying no attention to us. I returned to the hotel without incident.

Once I'd heard the former prisoners' stories, I was not content to just record them. To the extent possible, I wanted to relive them myself—to physically see and immerse myself in the settings where they experienced the struggle to stay alive. I traveled to Japan and the Philippines, went into the jungle in Guam, visited war memorials and battlegrounds. I retraced the routes taken by the prisoners, visited the old camps where possible—or the sites if the camps no longer existed—and spoke with guerrillas, freedom fighters, and others who witnessed or took part in these events.

Privately, I had another reason for understanding how these prisoners had survived. As part of my job, I frequently traveled internationally. During the 1980s, kidnapping and hostage taking were often on the news. For the innocent victims, it was another case of someone simply in the wrong place at the wrong time. Some survived captivity that stretched into years; others died in captivity or were killed. These incidents worried me; I realized that I too could become a victim. Would I be a survivor?

From my discussions with the horyo, I found that the survivors shared some common traits. They came from strong, closely knit families. They were determined and resourceful. They had a sense of humor, laughing at themselves and their circumstance, no matter how desperate; a spirit of resistance and courage (never surrender!); a degree of cleverness or ingenuity in making tools essential for survival; an established routine to occupy the mind; the discipline to maintain personal hygiene and physical conditioning no matter how harsh the conditions; a close relationship for mutual help with other prisoners; a secret means of communicating; contingency plans for escape or for hiding from threats and attacks; the daring to explore confines and barriers of camps to steal food or find means of escape; a positive outlook—and most important—an enduring hope for eventual release and freedom.

They tried to learn and understand the culture, language, and behavior patterns of the enemy to better cope with demands and not make breaches of etiquette that could prove fatal. When guarded, they cultivated relations with those guards who seemed more sympathetic or less competent, without collaborating. They were creative in discovering unfamiliar foods to keep from starving and in building or improving shelters. Communications with other prisoners and the outside world, when possible, were important. All prisoners reported the tremendous benefit they received from messages to and from home—whether by radio broadcast, letter, or confiding in and reminiscing with other prisoners.

Prisoners also sought to maintain their spirit of resistance: by sabotage, sarcastic or insulting comments to the guards, violating petty rules, pretending to not understand, or being slow to follow directions. Resistance could lead to punishment, solitary confinement, or even death, so it required careful judgment.

The Japanese camps had a high death rate for both their military and civilian prisoners. Due to their cultural and militaristic views concerning POWs, the Japanese treatment of prisoners differed significantly from their Western counterparts. The Allied Nations generally treated prisoners humanely. However, the United States singled out its Japanese-American citizens for internment during the war. German-American and Italian-American citizens did not suffer mass imprisonment. In the spirit of objectivity, I have included the experiences of prisoners from both sides of the Pacific War.

I tape-recorded and transcribed the stories, which were at once both chilling and heartwarming. They told of horrors beyond imagining—starvation, harassment, humiliation, beatings, torture, forced labor, sickness in the absence of medical care, extended separation from families and loved ones, and the overarching fear of execution and an unmarked grave. But they also told of human kindness, sacrifice, friends taking great risks, love, marriages, and new beginnings. People responded differently: some prisoners got the "thousand yard stare," refused to eat, and simply willed themselves to die, while in others a fierce spirit of resistance arose, enabling them to endure the unbearable and ultimately to survive. Even so, the survivors were deeply and permanently scarred by their ordeals; years later, the memories exist, and there are times when the pain and fear return. Post-traumatic stress disorder has real significance for them.

The events recounted in this book are all true. This assertion, simple enough on the surface, must be hedged by several practical considerations. Memories dim with time, and with a few exceptions, the prisoners were not allowed to keep written records. Personal belongings were lost, confiscated, or destroyed. No one was around to record exact conversations.

In some cases, I changed or deleted names to protect the privacy of individuals, either at their request or because I was unable to locate them and give them an opportunity to review the manuscript. Wherever possible, I have corroborated the facts through independent research or by speaking to other observers or witnesses. I visited the sites myself, insofar as visits were feasible.

I constructed the central elements of the book from extensive tape-recorded interviews with the Peters, Garth Dunn, Mitzi Yoshinaga, and Masashi Itoh. In Itoh's case, I also drew upon his lost diary that I'd discovered forty years after the war. Interviews were transcribed and then given to the participants for their review. Once we reached agreement on the correct interpretation and chronology of the events, I wrote the story, and they reviewed the manuscripts in various drafts. I was unable to meet Kazuo Sakamaki and based his story on his book. Every effort has been made to accurately reflect the sense of events that took place during and following World War II. For certain historical facts and dates, I have consulted the extensive literature of the Pacific War. I have listed these references and sources, which may be of interest to readers, in the Annotated Bibliography.

I have great admiration for the horyo—they overcame suffering and succeeded in almost miraculous survival against the odds. If you asked them, they would say that they were no different from anyone else. They simply did what they had to do.

—Craig B. Smith
Balboa, California
2011

INTRODUCTION

|||| |||| ||||

After World War I, a series of international meetings was held in Geneva to establish uniform protocols for humanitarian treatment of civilians, wounded military personnel, and other prisoners of war (POWs). The third meeting, held in 1929, specifically dealt with policies for the treatment of POWs. The 1929 agreement was signed by forty-seven nations, including Japan. All of the participants in World War II were signatories to the agreement except the Union of Soviet Socialist Republics (USSR). The Third Geneva Convention contained a number of provisions dealing with the humane treatment of prisoners. Officers were not required to work; enlisted men could be forced to work, although not on projects related to the war. They were to be paid for their labor and were not required to give information to the enemy beyond their name, rank, and service identification number. The convention recognized the prisoner's obligation to attempt to escape.

During World War II, the Geneva Convention did not apply on the Eastern Front, since the USSR had not signed the treaty. On the Western Front, the German treatment of Allied military prisoners was generally acceptable. The Allied treatment of German, Italian, and Japanese POWs was equally free of problems. During the First World War, the Japanese treatment of Russian POWs had been exemplary. But by the time of the Second World War, the Japanese government had failed to ratify the Third Geneva Convention, stating that it would comply with the convention *except* in circumstances in which the agreement ran counter to Japanese policies. By the end of the war, the Japanese held the worst record for the treatment of prisoners.

There were several reasons why this was the case. The Imperial Japanese army believed in the samurai code of *bushido*—"the way of the warrior." This philosophy permeated down to the lowest ranks of the military. Bushido taught that to become a prisoner was the greatest disgrace, that a soldier's life belonged to the emperor, that martial courage was respected above all else, that suicide was preferable to capture or defeat, and that it was a duty to kill one's own wounded rather than have them fall prisoner to the enemy. Soldiers memorized this maxim: "Honor is heavier than mountains, and death is lighter than a feather." It was the soldier's duty to fight to the death, or to "eat stones," meaning to fall dead, face down on the battlefield.[1]

In January 1941, Japanese war minister Hideki Tojo introduced a new field service code of conduct *(senjinkun)* for Imperial Japanese Army and Navy personnel. This code stipulated that Japanese were not allowed to surrender. Captured officers were expected to commit suicide. Any military person who was captured and then repatriated could expect to return to a life of shame and dishonor.[2] There can be little doubt that the existence of this policy toward their own troops had considerable influence on how Japanese prison camp commanders and guards treated Allied POWs.

During World War I, the Japanese army had a high degree of well-trained, professional soldiers, capable of practicing bushido in an enlightened manner. During World War II, however—particularly the later stages—the education level, training, and professionalism of the vast number of new recruits fed into the army declined significantly, and with this decline the brutality increased proportionally. The army also put military priorities ahead of civilian needs and dealt harshly with subjugated populations to ensure that its directives were promptly carried out.[3]

To add to the problem, Japan was not prepared for the magnitude of victories achieved early in the war. At the beginning of the war, the Japanese had only one POW camp—Zentsuji, on Shikoku Island. Japan captured a total of approximately 320,000 Allied soldiers. More than 140,000 of these prisoners were Western soldiers and another 180,000 were Allied Asian troops.[4] Initially the POWs were kept in improvised camps in Asia where they were forced to work as slave laborers. Food was inadequate and medical care almost nonexistent. Death rates were high—13,000 Allied military personnel died during forced labor on the Burma-Thailand railroad; more than 2,000 American troops died during the Bataan Death March and at Camp O' Donnell. Later, most of the surviving Asian troops were released; the surviving Western troops (approximately 47,000) were gradually transported to Japan to supplement the workforce there. Approximately 11,000 of these Western prisoners never made it to Japan, either dying from terrible conditions on the "hell ships" that transported them, or dying when the transports were sunk by enemy fire. Overall, nearly one-third of the prisoners of war died during captivity, either in the conquered territories or later in Japan.[5] For Western military personnel, the odds of dying as a Japanese POW (30 percent) were ten times greater than the odds of dying in combat (3 percent). The death rate among the Asian troops will never be known but was probably higher. There is no accounting of the civilian deaths that occurred in camps.

The events that ultimately led to the Pacific War and were responsible for the attack on Pearl Harbor and the fighting in the Philippines, Guam, and elsewhere, originated in the early 1900s. Following their astonishing defeat of the Russian army and navy in the Russo-Japanese War of 1904–1905, the Japanese diverted their attention away from their islands to other Pacific Rim countries where they could find additional resources and raw materials. In a limited way, Japan opened its doors to Western influences, and at the same time, Japanese left their homeland for foreign countries and new opportunities.

In migrations to countries rimming the Pacific Ocean, some Japanese arrived as contract laborers, and then decided to remain where they found work; others came as immigrants who planned to seek permanent residence. Some came as officials who took part in governmental or military missions. The result was a growing Japanese presence. Agricultural workers came to Hawaii and California, while in the Philippines, laborers worked on road construction and sugar plantations; others served as carpenters.

Imperial Japan's leaders knew that their nation needed additional land and resources to continue expansion. During the power vacuum created by World War I, the Japanese seized the opportunity to make inroads into China. The Open Door treaty, signed in Washington, D.C., in 1922, legitimatized Japan's "special rights" in China and led to settlers and industrial development in Manchuria. In 1931—on the basis of a trumped-up rationale—Japanese forces invaded Manchuria and established the puppet state of Manchukuo. In addition to Manchukuo's fertile farmland, Japan needed its resources of oil shale, coal, iron, and other minerals. When no serious international opposition arose, Japan annexed additional parts of northeast China and Mongolia.

Full-scale war broke out with China on July 7, 1937, following an event known as the Marco Polo Bridge Incident. The bridge—located in Fengtai—straddled the Yongding River and was the southern entrance to the city of Beijing. Japan had surrounded the city. Following military exercises near the bridge, Japan claimed a Japanese soldier was in the city and demanded permission for troops to enter and retrieve him. When the Chinese forces denied permission, the Japanese attacked. Beijing was captured several days later, and the two countries were officially at war.[6]

Throughout the period prior to Pearl Harbor, the United States failed to recognize the extent of Japanese ambitions—and then it was too late. Early U.S. war planning considered the Philippines "indefensible." Congress, which did not want to provoke the Japanese with militaristic actions in the Pacific, rejected proposed efforts, even minimal ones, to strengthen Guam and other strategic U.S. Pacific bases.

In 1940, in response to Japanese aggression in Asia, the United States instituted an embargo on the shipment of iron and steel to Japan. By April 1941, the situation in the Pacific was growing tenser each day. In the summer of 1941, President Franklin D. Roosevelt extended the embargo to include petroleum, and the United States froze Japanese assets in the U.S. This action placed great pressure on the Japanese government.

The Japanese were caught in a vise. Without oil, iron, steel, and other essential strategic materials, they could not continue their campaign in China. Instead, they would face a long war of attrition that they knew they could not withstand. But the Japanese politically could not accept the United States' terms for turning on the flow of oil and steel. The Americans insisted on nothing less than withdrawal of Japanese forces from China, Vietnam, and other Southeast Asian territories.

An alternative was to buy oil from the British and Dutch possessions of Burma and the Dutch East Indies (Indonesia and Malaysia), but upon the United States' urging, these governments were equally uncooperative. The Japanese recognized that any effort to seize oil by military force would probably provoke a response from the United States. Yet if they waited too long, they would not have even enough oil to fuel the ships needed to attack the U.S. Their options were blocked at each juncture by the United States.

World War II began on September 3, 1939, when Britain and France officially declared war on Germany following its invasion of Poland. Although the United States was ostensibly neutral, in the spring of 1941, meetings were held between British and American planners. On June 2, 1941, the U.K.-U.S. "Basic War Plan" stipulated that Germany and Italy would be conquered first; the position in the Pacific would be a defensive one.

The Japanese recognized that the time to move was while the Allies were occupied in Europe, and they began to make preparations. By the summer of 1941, U.S. scout planes and merchant marine vessels frequently sighted Japanese naval transports moving south.[7] Despite ample warnings obtained via intelligence and other means, the United States did little to prepare any U.S. possessions for the possibility of war. Defenses were not placed in a ready status until it was too late.

Meanwhile, the Japanese dispatched a special diplomatic mission to Washington, D.C., to negotiate with President Roosevelt and Secretary of State Cordell Hull. The U.S. response to these efforts was to inform the Japanese that they first had to withdraw their forces from China and Indochina and recognize the Chinese national government at Chungking.

Rejection of the Japanese diplomatic position enabled Prime Minister Hideki Tojo and the Ministry of War to convince Emperor Hirohito that war with the United States was inevitable. Secretary of State Hull reached the same conclusion when he learned that Roosevelt's conditions had been rejected by the Japanese—as he knew they would be. He told the secretaries of the army and navy, "Now it's in your hands."[8]

General Douglas MacArthur—at that time in the Philippines—was recalled to active duty. He was 61 years old. Late in November 1941, the American military finally began some last-minute actions. On November 21, MacArthur was urged to move the B-17s—bombers that would be essential to defend against an invasion—south from Clark Field near Manila to Del Monte Field in Mindanao. Unfortunately, only some of them were moved. On November 24, Washington radioed all Pacific commanders that "An attack on the Philippines or Guam is possible." Still, little was done—possibly because there was little that could be done over the vast distances of the Pacific Ocean. However, on Sunday, November 30, MacArthur placed Corregidor Island on full alert and ordered air patrols and other defensive measures. By this point the general's instincts told him that there was trouble ahead.[9]

In Japan the situation was quite different. Planning for an attack on Pearl Harbor and other U.S. possessions in the Pacific had gone on for more than a year. Special shallow-water torpedoes that could be dropped from low-flying aircraft were tested and perfected. Midget submarines, shrouded in canvas to conceal their existence, were towed to sea by fishing boats. They practiced maneuvers entering the mouth of Mitsukue Bay, which had a narrow entrance like Pearl Harbor. The carriers and other ships that would attack over the vast regions of the Pacific were prepared, dispersed, and made ready for a coordinated attack.[10]

On November 26, a conference was held on board Vice Admiral Ibo Takahashi's flagship *Ashigara* to make final preparations for the invasion of the Philippines. The Japanese plan called for a series of cautious amphibious landings from both the north and south. This plan was modified when the invaders met little resistance.

The defenders on Guam, Wake Island, Hawaii, and the Philippines had a typical Thanksgiving holiday. Only a slight feeling of uneasiness was in the air. Few believed that the Japanese would dare attack U.S. possessions.

At this moment, the Japanese players in the drama were assembling on a Pacific Ocean stage. Vice Admiral Chuichi Nagumo's attack force steamed at flank speed toward the Hawaiian Islands, even as the Japanese special envoys met with Roosevelt and Hull to discuss "peace." On November 18, a "Special Attack Force" of five submarines, each carrying a midget submarine piggyback behind the conning tower, left Japan along with a number of other submarines to get in position for the attack on Pearl Harbor. Vice Admiral Shigeyoshi Inoue's invasion force prepared to move on Guam. Two fleets converged on the Philippines: Vice Admiral Takahashi led the largest armada against the northern islands while Rear Admiral Takeo Takagi sailed with another force from Palau. From there he would strike at Davao on the southern island of Mindanao. Other forces moved even farther south to attack and eventually occupy Shanghai, Singapore, and Hong Kong as well as other British, Dutch, and French possessions in Indochina, Indonesia, Burma, and Borneo.

The stage was set for a Pacific War that would last almost four years and bring untold destruction. It was a war that would become noted for inherent savagery—no quarter asked; none given. Prisoners and wounded were mistreated and frequently killed by both sides. Racial stereotyping was one of the root causes, with both sides misjudging the fighting qualities of the other. An atrocity by one side hardened the resolve to respond in kind by the other.[11] The forces unleashed by the Japanese attacks in the Pacific affected millions of people before the war ended. In this book, I have chosen to tell the stories of a handful of people from both sides of the Pacific War to explain how they survived the conflict and its aftermath.

First is Garth G. Dunn, who was a twenty-year-old U.S. marine stationed on the island of Guam. He was among the American military personnel taken prisoner by the Japanese in the first days of the war. Ensign Kazuo Sakamaki was the sole survivor from the crews of the five midget submarines that attempted to sneak into Pearl Harbor on the eve of the aerial attack. On the day following the attack on Pearl Harbor, he became the first Japanese POW captured by American forces. Simon and Lydia Solomaniuck were civilians, European expatriates living in the Philippines. After immigrating to the United States when the war ended, they changed their last name to Peters. Their story is typical of the thousands of noncombatants put in prison camps by the Japanese. Mitsuye Yoshinaga was a U.S. citizen of Japanese descent living in Malibu, California. She symbolizes the 110,000 Japanese Americans imprisoned by the United

States for the duration of the war. Finally, there is the remarkable story of Masashi Itoh, a Japanese farm boy who enlisted in the Imperial Japanese Army shortly after Pearl Harbor and came to Guam near the end of the war. After the Japanese defeat, he remained hidden in the jungles of Guam, held captive by his own conscience and beliefs until 1960, fifteen years after the end of the war.

CHAPTER 1

DECEMBER 1941

B y November 1941, Japan had taken over a third of China and occupied
French Indochina. Europe had fallen to the Germans; Britain had suffered
through Dunkirk and now stood alone. The Germans had turned on the Soviet
Union and were approaching Moscow. As the clock ticked down to December
1941, momentous events were about to occur that would transform the world in
ways impossible to imagine. Even forty-five years later, when I started my interviews, the drama of the first week in December 1941 remained vivid in the memory of the people in this narrative. Their lives were irrevocably altered by what
transpired; unknowingly, they were about to become prisoners of that age, a
condition that would stay with them for the rest of their lives.

The following pages describe that fateful first week in December when the
world as they knew it suddenly changed.

MONDAY, DECEMBER 1, 1941
(Tuesday, December 2, in Japan, the Philippines, and Guam)

WASHINGTON, D.C. A strange quiet settled over Washington after the
Thanksgiving week meeting between Secretary of State Cordell Hull and special
Japanese envoy Saburo Kurusu. The United States' trade embargo of the previous summer was having a devastating impact. The Japanese military leaders
knew they could not sustain their war machine without alternate sources of raw
materials and petroleum. Hull already believed, from intercepted dispatches, that
war was coming, and he knew the Japanese could not accept his last proposals.
A few days earlier, warnings had been sent to American outposts in the Pacific
advising them to destroy codebooks and ciphers.[12]

Despite all of the ominous signs, the Japanese ambassador and special envoy arrived at the State Department for still another meeting with Secretary of State Hull. It was to prove fruitless.

MANILA. All B-17 bombers based at Hickham Field in Hawaii were flown to the Philippines to reinforce General Douglas MacArthur's ability to defend against an invasion by sea. There were reports of unidentified aircraft sighted over Clark Field.

DAVAO. Simon Peters was a mining engineer at the Davao gold mine, on the southern Philippine island of Mindanao. He recalled the momentous days of December: "Things were going along in their normal way at the mine. There we were somewhat isolated, so we did not know all the events that were taking place in the world, but we did listen to the radio, and we knew there was tension with Japan. We probably would have been more concerned if we'd had a better picture."[13]

GUAM. Private First Class Garth Dunn was a young recruit who had been in the U.S. Marines for a year and a half. His first posting was to Guam, where he became an Insular Patrolman, part of the island's police force. In December he was stationed in the village of Inarajan. He recalled: "It was a quiet day in the village. Nothing much was going on. We didn't expect much on a Tuesday. I finished my rounds, laid around, wrote some letters home, slept. If there was anything on my mind in particular, it was being away from home on Christmas for the first time."

CENTRAL PACIFIC OCEAN. On December 1, the submarines of the Special Attack Force were five days out from the Hawaiian Islands. They sailed submerged during the day and cruised on the surface at night. Passing between Wake and Midway Islands, they set course directly for Oahu.

On board the "mother ship," submarine I-24 under command of Lieutenant Commander Hiroshi Hanabusa, Ensign Kazuo Sakamaki was thinking back to those last hectic days in Japan. On November 16, 1941, crew members of the Special Attack Force had been called to a meeting at the Kure Naval Base. Vice Admiral Mitsumi Shimizu, commander of the Japanese Sixth Fleet, informed them that they would soon be sailing to take up positions in preparation for an attack on the United States. The young sailors were silent as they absorbed this news and thought about what it meant to them. The next day Sakamaki and one of his classmates took a final walk through the town of Kure—one last look at Japan. In town they each bought a small bottle of perfume, to be used before going into battle—an old samurai tradition.

On November 18—his twenty-third birthday—Sakamaki wrote a final letter to his parents. That evening the submarine group sailed from Japan.

LOS ANGELES. Mitsuye (Mitzi) Takahashi was an American citizen, a high school graduate, and had completed a year of business school training. Even so, racial prejudice made it difficult for her to get a job. In 1941, she secured a position with the Yokohama Bank. She has vivid recollections of the frenetic pace of activity at the bank: "We were terribly busy then. We didn't think much about war—no one discussed such things at the bank anyway. Personally, I was looking forward to the new year, hoping that things might settle down a little bit and I'd have some time for myself."

TUESDAY, DECEMBER 2, 1941
(Wednesday, December 3, in Japan, the Philippines, and Guam)

HONOLULU. Nagao Kika, the Japanese consul general in Honolulu, received another coded request for information on naval ships in Pearl Harbor. He had been sending reports every two days. The latest message directed him to report on a daily basis and to provide information on the presence of "observation" balloons above Pearl Harbor and anti-mine nets protecting warships. This message was intercepted by U.S. naval intelligence and mailed to Washington. Unfortunately, it would not be translated until December 30.

TOKYO. Messages were sent to all Japanese diplomatic officials stationed in U.S. territories, British and Dutch possessions, and the South Seas instructing them to destroy codes and secret documents "in preparation for an emergency." This message was also intercepted and translated by the U.S. Office of Naval Intelligence, which had broken the Japanese secret codes. Due to bureaucratic bungling, however, it was not brought to the attention of the proper authorities.

On the same day, a message was sent to the Japanese fleet confirming that Japan intended to go to war against the United States, England, and Holland—the date and time "in early December" to be specified later. Subsequently a message was sent to the combined fleet which read, "Climb Mount Nitaka, 1208." This code indicated to the commanders that the date of the attack was to be December 8th (Japan time).

MANILA. More strange planes were tracked by radar off the Luzon coast. MacArthur's staff believed that they were Formosa-based planes establishing range and navigational data.

GUAM. Garth recalled: "One cloudy day, when I was patrolling at Inarajan, I heard the sound of an aircraft flying over the island. I called into Agana and reported that I'd heard planes. They told me I was crazy—that I must be hearing things. Then, maybe two or three days later—I think it was December 3rd—the clouds were up there again. It really wasn't overcast, just kind of blowing clouds like you see in the tropics all the time. I heard the planes again and called in and reported them. They told me again that I must he hearing things. If they believed me, they never gave any indication. Hell, we all knew there were no planes on Guam. They had to be from Saipan."

WEDNESDAY, DECEMBER 3, 1941

(Thursday, December 4, in Japan, the Philippines, and Guam)

MANILA. Air Force P-40s began nightly patrols over Luzon. A large Japanese bomber formation was sighted a few dozen miles away from the Lingayen Gulf beaches. MacArthur's staff postulated that these were trial flights by the Japanese to familiarize themselves with the air route in the event war broke out.

THURSDAY, DECEMBER 4, 1941

(Friday, December 5, in Japan, the Philippines, and Guam)

MANILA. More air contacts in the northern Philippines, this time a flight of Japanese Zeros that turned back to the north after being sighted.

GUAM. Garth recalled: "The captain called me and Dick Ballinger back to Agana to walk 'Beat One.' This beat included the Service Club, which was right across the street from a local hangout we called 'Chong's Bar.' The reason we were recalled was that a marine patrolman had lost his pistol to a sailor in the Service Club the night before. This was the worst thing that could happen to a marine—lose his weapon to a sailor! The captain thought that we could deal with the problem.

"Dick Ballinger was a patrolman at the Merizo Outstation. Merizo is on the southern end of Guam, just a little farther down the coast from Inarajan. He was one of the champion boxers of the Asiatic Fleet, and a hell of a nice guy.

Private First Class Garth Dunn, Guam, 1941

"When we reported for duty in Agana, the two of us were told to walk the beat from midnight to 6 a.m. We were informed about what happened to the other patrolman, and were told to be alert if the sailors started raising hell again. Sure enough, as we came down the street that night, we could hear them in the Service Club, raising all kinds of hell. Curfew time was twelve o'clock. The Service Club had been trying to close, and these sailors wouldn't leave. When we arrived, they'd started to break up the furniture.

"Ballinger said, 'I'll go in the front, and you go around to the back.'

"I took off and went around, while he waited a few minutes for me to get in position. Then, about the same time that he entered the front door, they saw him and started running for the back door, just as I stepped in.

"I yelled at them to stop. They didn't, so I drew the .45 and threw a slug in the slot. I told them to stop again, quieter this time. In fact, the whole place got quiet. They stopped for just a second, trying to make up their minds. Then, Navy Chief H. L. Townsend (we called him 'Boats'), who was one of the ringleaders, started inching toward me. With him was a big sailor named L. E. Bluma—who was one of the wrestling champs of the Asiatic Fleet. They were the same two sailors who'd taken the other patrolman's gun.

"Real calmly I said, 'Chief, stand still or I'll shoot you.' But the two of them kept edging forward, sort of half-assed grinning as they came, figuring they'd bluff me. At that point I fired a round through the wooden floor right in front of the chief's foot. Then they believed me and both of them froze. No one was smiling any longer. In a moment Ballinger came up behind them, and we walked them out of the club and into the paddy wagon.

"The night before, the other patrolman had gone into the Service Club alone. They tackled him, took away his gun, and tossed him out on his ear. Now he was up for a summary court-martial for losing his weapon, and they were on their way to jail.

"Of course two days later all crimes were forgiven because the war started."

FRIDAY, DECEMBER 5, 1941
(Saturday, December 6, in Japan, the Philippines, and Guam)

WASHINGTON, D.C. U.S. naval offices and facilities in Japan, China, Guam, Wake, and other Pacific possessions were ordered to destroy codes and secret documents.

MANILA. MacArthur ordered more guards at airfields, more coastal patrols by pursuit aircraft, and the manning of all military installations on a twenty-four–hour basis.

GUAM. Garth recalled: "I spent a quiet Saturday doing some Christmas shopping. Since we'd gotten paid on the 5th, and since I was in Agana anyway, I bought some teakwood carvings and some Aga-Aga weavings for the folks back home. I took the gifts to the post office so they'd arrive in time for Christmas."

TEN MILES SOUTHEAST OF PEARL HARBOR. Sakamaki saw the lights of Hawaii. The submarine crew could hear jazz music coming over the radio from the islands. As he carried out last-minute preparations, Sakamaki made a horrifying discovery: the gyro compass on his submarine was malfunctioning. Without this critical instrument, navigating the midget sub underwater was a problem. Nonetheless, he resolved to proceed with the mission. His target was the U.S. battleship *Pennsylvania*.

LOS ANGELES. Mitzi recalled: "We'd been so busy, and I was looking forward to going home to the ranch for the weekend. I wanted to rest up, buy a few Christmas gifts for my friends."

SATURDAY, DECEMBER 6, 1941

(Sunday, December 7, in Japan, the Philippines, and Guam)

PACIFIC OCEAN, APPROXIMATELY 600 MILES NORTH OF OAHU.
Vice Admiral Chuichi Nagumo's fleet began refueling operations. Due to calm seas these were completed without complications. Just before noon the task force turned south and increased speed to twenty knots, heading toward Hawaii. A signal was sent to the ships of the fleet: "The rise and fall of the Empire depends on this battle. Every man will do his duty."

WASHINGTON, D.C. President Franklin D. Roosevelt sent a personal message to Emperor Hirohito calling on Japan to withdraw from Indochina and reduce tensions in the Pacific. He offered assurances that the United States had no intention of invading Indochina, and appealed to Hirohito to find "ways of dispelling the dark clouds." Due to internal Japanese machinations, this message did not reach the emperor until after the attack on Pearl Harbor.

DAVAO. Simon recalled: "Lydia and I spent a quiet weekend. Our biggest concern at the time was trying to decide what we would do for the Christmas holidays. We considered having some of our friends from the mine for a small party because we knew they would be planning similar get-togethers and would include us."

GUAM. Garth recalled: "I still had the duty. At least on a Sunday night we expected no more problems with the goddam sailors. By then they'd spent most of their money, or they were too hungover to raise more hell. One of the patrol's chores was to take care of the street lights. A patrolman would turn them on at dusk, and the guy with the 6 a.m. shift would turn them off. They all had to be turned on by hand. There was a switch on the bottom of each lamppost.

"So we went out and walked the beat, watched a few drunken Chamorros stagger home, then turned off the street lights, and otherwise had a quiet Sunday night. Too quiet, as it turned out."

APPROACHING PEARL HARBOR. Ensign Sakamaki wrote a final letter to his parents, changed into his submariner's uniform, and sprayed it with perfume. With his faulty equipment, he did not expect to survive the mission. As midget sub HA-19 was released from the mother submarine underwater, it began to list. Sakamaki and his aide, Kiyoshi Inagaki, scrambled to move ballast and trim the craft. Finally underway near midnight, he raised the periscope to see where he was and discovered that he was headed in the wrong direction, away from the harbor.

LOS ANGELES. Mitzi recalled: "Twice a year the Yokohama Bank had a party for its employees and their families—in the summer and winter. In 1941, the party was scheduled for December 7. This was another reason why I went home for the weekend, so I could get some other clothes for the party. I did a few chores and made arrangements with my brother to take me to the party on Sunday. Mostly I spent a lazy day because I was so tired from work."

SUNDAY, DECEMBER 7, 1941
(Monday, December 8, in Japan, the Philippines, and Guam)

PACIFIC OCEAN, NORTH OF HAWAIIAN ISLANDS. At 0615 hours Vice Admiral Nagumo—the commander of the Japanese fleet consisting of 6 aircraft carriers, 2 battleships, 3 cruisers, and assorted support vessels—launched an attack of 183 planes against American bases on Hawaii.[14] Elsewhere, 25 Japanese submarines—5 of which carried midget submarines—were in position.

WASHINGTON, D.C. The Department of Defense learned that Japanese carrier-based aircraft had attacked Pearl Harbor, Kaneohe Marine Air Station, Hickham Field, and other military facilities in Hawaii. In a far-ranging series of attacks spread out across the Pacific, Guam was bombed, as was Davao on the island of Mindanao, and Clark Field and Camp John Hay in northern Luzon. Despite early warnings, half of the American heavy bombers and fighter aircraft were destroyed on the ground. Japanese troops landed in some parts of the Philippines. Japanese submarines in the Pacific Ocean sank an American transport carrying lumber, and distress signals were heard from another ship. President Roosevelt immediately ordered the country and the army and navy into a state of full preparedness for war.

YAMANASHI PREFECTURE, JAPAN. "The Imperial Army and Navy, before dawn this day, December 8th, entered into a state of hostility in the Western Pacific with British and American forces." This broadcast came over Japanese radios at seven o'clock in the morning and was repeated a number of times. Later that morning, an Imperial edict was issued that gave the official declaration of war. Masashi Itoh recalled that he "listened, absorbed—my whole being concentrated on the words coming from the brown loudspeaker on the table. I remember vividly how my mother's and father's eyes remained riveted on my face as I listened."[15]

A month later, Itoh and other conscripts from his village were inducted into the Imperial Japanese Army.

DAVAO. Simon recalled: "I went home from the mine a little earlier than usual, because we were having company for dinner that night, an Italian married to a Russian woman. He lived in Davao. We were listening to the radio, and we heard about the attack at Pearl Harbor. But we never knew how serious the damage there was. At the same time, we started hearing about some attacks in the Philippines.

"At first, we were actually happy that the Japanese started the war, because we were so sure that America would come and beat the hell out of them, and then things would be better than they had been—less tension. Nobody worried. The Americans working at the mine thought that all they had to do was pack up their things and someone would come and pick them up. Nobody thought the war would last long—maybe two, three months at most."

GUAM. Garth recalled: "My duty ended at 6 a.m. At the end of the shift we returned to the Insular Patrol base and checked in. I went into the galley—why I did this, I don't know—and ordered a whopping breakfast. I never ate as much as I did that particular morning. I finished it all off and then went upstairs to sleep.

"We slept in a large screened-in room above the mess hall. I think there were about twelve guys sleeping there when I walked in. I stripped to my shorts, switched on a fan at the foot of the bed, and went quickly to sleep. It was around 7:30 a.m.

"The war started for us at 8:25 a.m. I remember opening my eyes and seeing another patrolman, my friend Hollis Smalling, shaking me. He was screaming, 'Get up, get up! The goddam Japs are bombing the island!'

"My first reaction was that he was playing a joke on me. We had done that lots of times when someone was asleep. So I told him, go the hell away and let me sleep. He ran off somewhere. In a few minutes he was back.

"Get up, goddam it, get up! The captain's on the phone and he wants to talk to you. If you don't believe me about the bombing, look out the goddam screen."

"On the way to the phone, I looked out the window. The street down below was jammed with people carrying things and running every which way, trying to get out of the city. It was complete chaos and pandemonium. I couldn't believe my eyes.

"Yes, sir," I heard myself saying into the phone, still not comprehending what was happening. The captain told me to get dressed on the double—my best khakis and shoes—then grab two other guys and take them on a patrol downtown, see what the damage was, and then report back to him.

"I located two other patrolmen—Carl Redenbaugh and Bill Burt—and we headed for the city. About halfway there, some more bombers came over. I wouldn't call them 'dive' bombers, they were more like 'glide' bombers. They swung in over the city and then let go with whatever it was they were carrying.

"The three of us ducked under a house—one of those up on stilts. Redenbaugh decided he'd be better off running down the street, and we had to restrain him so he didn't run out in the open and get himself killed. After the planes left, we looked around and made our way back to the jailhouse to make a report. All of the patrolmen were meeting there to get assignments and to assess the damage.

"By night we had watches all around the island. But hell, we knew there wasn't much we could do if the Japanese were serious about taking over Guam. We had no artillery, no planes, no heavy weapons. There were three miserable .30-caliber machine guns, and one .50, but no pin to hold it in its mount. Half the rifles were smeared with a protective coating of Cosmoline, and they were mostly 1900 Springfields—World War I vintage. The rest of the marines down at the marine barracks at Sumay had a similar array of weapons—nothing suitable for fighting off an invasion.

"Our one piece of artillery—the three-inch gun on the minesweeper *Penguin*—was now on the bottom of the harbor. To defend the island, we had about 150 marines, about 250 sailors, and the Insular Guard, a native militia of about 250 men with minimal training—a force of about 650 against more than 5,000 Japanese. That was it. Of course, we all hoped for and expected reinforcements from the Philippines or Hawaii, until we learned that they were having their own problems."

AT THE ENTRANCE TO PEARL HARBOR. By the time that daybreak arrived, Sakamaki still had not been able to enter Pearl Harbor. He was bitterly frustrated by his failure to accomplish the mission. He could see two boats patrolling near the entrance to the harbor. He submerged his midget submarine to a depth of thirty-five feet and moved blindly toward them. Getting closer he saw they were destroyers. Suddenly there was a loud crash and he hit his head and was knocked unconscious. The midget submarine was fired on by a destroyer and depth charges were dropped.

When Sakamaki came to, the submarine and torpedoes were intact. Through the periscope he could see pillars of black smoke rising over Pearl Harbor and realized the air attack was underway. He decided to surface and run directly into the harbor through the gauntlet of destroyers patrolling the entrance. On the way in, he ran aground on a reef near the entrance to the harbor, but managed to back the submarine off the reef. On his next attempt, he ran aground again, and then was stuck for some time until he and Inagaki were able to shift ballast and float free. They submerged and found that the torpedo-firing mechanism was damaged. It was now past noon.

During the afternoon they struggled to get their errant submarine headed into the harbor, thinking they would ram the battleship, but all of their efforts failed. Once darkness fell, totally exhausted, with both torpedoes inoperable, they abandoned the mission and decided to sail to Lanai Island, which was the designated recovery point to pick up the midget-sub crews. On the way, Sakamaki recalled seeing Diamond Head pass on his port side before he collapsed from exhaustion.

LOS ANGELES. Mitzi recalled: "I'd stayed in Malibu all weekend, and we had no communication with anyone that morning. In the afternoon my brother drove me to the bank; he was going to the party with me. We were both dressed up in our good clothes. When we got to the bank, it was closed and dark. No one was around, there was no party. We couldn't understand what had happened. After waiting for someone else to come, we returned to Malibu. When we got back to the house, we found out that the United States was at war with Japan. Everyone was sad."

MONDAY, DECEMBER 8, 1941

(Tuesday, December 9, in Japan, the Philippines, and Guam)

WAIMANALO BEACH, EAST COAST OF OAHU. With first light, Sakamaki awoke and saw a small island ahead. Thinking it was Lanai, he tried to increase speed, hoping to arrive before it became too light and they were spotted, but the motor failed because the ship's batteries were completely discharged by all the violent maneuvers of the last twenty-four hours. Once again helpless, the submarine wallowed in the rough seas and then ran aground. Realizing that further attempts were futile, Sakamaki gave the order to abandon ship

Sakamaki's Midget Submarine on Waimanalo Beach, Oahu

and set the fuse on an explosive charge to destroy the submarine. Both Sakamaki and Inagaki slipped overboard into breaking waves and tried to make it to shore.

Unfortunately, Inagaki drowned, but Sakamaki made it ashore on Waimanalo Beach where he collapsed and passed out. Shortly thereafter, Corporal David M. Akui, patrolling Waimanalo Beach, found an Asian man lying unconscious on the sand. When Sakamaki came to, he looked up to see Corporal Akui standing over him with a pistol drawn to take him into custody.

The explosive charge failed to go off and midget submarine HA-19 washed up on the beach and was recovered by the Americans. All of the other midget submarines sank and their crews were lost without sinking any American ships. Ensign Sakamaki thus had the good luck to be the only survivor of the five midget submarine crews, and the bad luck to become the first Japanese POW of World War II.

DAVAO. Simon recalled: "We made a big mistake. We arrested all the Japanese who worked at the mine — maybe 200 of them. They were gardeners, carpenters, blacksmiths, electricians, and laborers. They were good employees, but we were so enthusiastic to do something for America, to take some action. All of their furniture and belongings were put in one of the warehouses, and the people were sent to Davao with just a suitcase and put in some kind of a stockade. Naturally they were hurt by this treatment, and later on they were anxious to come back to the mine to get their belongings."

GUAM. Garth recalled: "The watch on the north end of the island called in a report that they'd seen two guys approach from the direction of Saipan in an outrigger canoe and land on the north shore, near Machanao Point. The captain sent four of us out there. I was driving. Another patrolman, Harris Chuck, was with me in the cab, and Corporal Oscar Thoren and another guy were in the back. The corporal had a Thompson submachine gun.

"As we approached the spot, there was some shooting, and one shot knocked out the windshield of the truck. We stopped and everybody bailed out—me out the driver's side, Harris out the passenger side, and the other two off the back. We sprayed the bushes with the submachine gun. One of the patrolmen spotted two guys hiding in some bushes. They were Saipan Japanese, unarmed, and out of uniform. We guessed that they were trying to infiltrate—maybe had brought a radio ashore, although we couldn't find anything. We loaded them up and hauled them back to the jailhouse, where we tossed them in a cell.

"After we'd jailed them, the bombers came over again. A bomb hit on or near the patrol headquarters, causing part of the roof to cave in. There was general panic. About then I went a little crazy. I stepped back to the cell where we'd put the two infiltrators, drew my .45, and cocked it. I pulled a bead on the face of the closest guy and told him, 'If a bomb hits this building, you're a dead sonofabitch.'

"He stared right back, never blinking, not saying a word, but I knew he knew what I meant. A few minutes later I was sent out on another patrol, so my bluff wasn't called. Later on, that little exercise in bravado damn near got me killed. Anyway, that was our excitement for the day. The rest of the time we just tried to stay under cover while the Japanese flew over and plastered everything at will.

"Obviously, we were pretty rattled, having to sit there and get the shit kicked out of us, and unable to do much to fight back. At one point a bomb hit the patrol headquarters. A big timber and lots of plaster crashed down into the room, creating a panic among the men and officers assembled there. The assistant chief of police, Sergeant George Shane, sort of snapped—went crazy for a moment. It wasn't long before order was restored, but everyone was real jittery.

"I'm not criticizing anyone. By and large the U.S. troops were all good men and proved it many times over during our long captivity in Japan. Their actions during the Japanese attack reflected their frustration, hopelessness, and terrible sense of betrayal—of being abandoned and sacrificed to the enemy. We had no way of knowing that the people we thought could help us had also been attacked and were having their own desperate struggle. Not knowing the true circumstances, we could only curse their lazy dead asses and promise ourselves that we'd kick the shit out of those fat soft barflies in Hawaii and the Philippines once the war was over.

"The only resistance we could offer to the bombings came from those fools who would stick their heads out and blaze away with a rifle or a .45 at the planes as they went over—which only wasted ammunition. I suppose it gave them some personal satisfaction, but it didn't hinder the Japanese. The other thing we did was try to organize our defenses. We knew there would be a landing. The question was where and when?

"In the afternoon an invasion fleet, consisting of dozens of ships, was sighted moving toward Guam. The defensive plan was to defend the marine headquarters and barracks at Sumay, where the main body of marines was located. The navy was supposed to take care of the shipyard at Piti. Our duties—the Insular Guard and those marines assigned to the Insular Patrol—were centered around the Plaza de Espana and the Governor's Palace.

"Our officers figured that the Japanese would have to come down through some narrow streets to reach the palace. Consequently three squads of Insular Guard personnel were set up with machine guns at various points around the plaza where they could rake the approaches to the palace. Riflemen were hidden behind hedges at other points. Our small group of marines (twelve in all) was stationed around the palace, behind it, and inside it. Then we waited."

LOS ANGELES. Mitzi recalled: "I came to work Monday morning and found the bank closed. There were police and FBI men everywhere. They had already arrested some of the alien employees of the bank, but we did not know that. Those of us who were U.S. citizens were told to continue working to put the bank's affairs in order. There was a man there, from the state bank examiner's office, who was directing things. We had no idea where the missing employees were, or what had happened to them. At all times there were people with guns watching over us.

"My friend Mr. Umekawa was responsible for Japanese currency and took care of a safe that was located upstairs. The FBI agents watched him very closely and had a gun on him at every moment. I felt sorry for him because he didn't speak much English, so I tried to help him and the other employees who were frightened. Little by little, the FBI picked up all the other Japanese employees, until there were just five employees, those of us who were U. S. citizens, left working at the bank.

"Strangely enough, I was not afraid. After all, I was a citizen, I spoke English, and I had many friends. No one threatened me or said anything, but I heard that the men received threats. Later we learned that the aliens were all taken to a special camp and eventually repatriated to Japan."

TUESDAY, DECEMBER 9, 1941

(Wednesday, December 10, in Japan, the Philippines, and Guam)

HONOLULU. Ensign Sakamaki was interrogated in Hawaii. He burned his face with cigarettes while in prison before having his photograph taken. He was deeply humiliated by the fact that he was captured alive and asked his guards if he could commit suicide. His request was denied. Sakamaki was kept in a camp in Hawaii for several months and then sent to the mainland.[16]

DAVAO. Simon recalled: "Everywhere there was a commotion. No work was being done. Rumors circulated as to what would happen next. No one knew what we should do."

GUAM. Garth recalled: "All the patrolmen spent the night in the jail building—right across the street from the palace. Then, an hour or so before daybreak, we took up our posts. Navy Chief Lane was in charge of the native troops (the Guam Militia). He had them—with some old '03 rifles, which weren't supposed to be fired—positioned in front of the palace in the plaza, a big grassy area with a hexagonal bandstand, called the 'kiosk.' The plaza was bordered by a wrought-iron fence and hedges, where the militia took up their positions. The machine-gun squads were farther away. Patrolman Ballinger and I were assigned to the back door of the palace, which was a concrete building with steps leading down from the door. There was a wrought-iron fence around the palace as well. From our viewpoint we would look east and see the Catholic church, the Dulce Nombre de Maria Cathedral.

"The main Japanese landings took place about fifteen miles away, on the west coast between Merizo and Facpi Point. The invasion force of 5,500 Japanese troops was under the command of Major General Tomitara Hori. It was accompanied by a small naval detachment from Saipan. The Japanese overlooked the fact that there was no road there, so they had to load the troops back on the

Governor's Palace, Agana, Guam, before the War

boats and move them north, where they finally landed near Agat after the fighting was pretty much over.

"The smaller naval force landed in Agana Bay, about two miles north of the palace. They began coming in before sunrise. Some of the sailors took two .30-caliber machine guns to the beach and established a cross-fire field that was effective for a few minutes, but the Japanese quickly overran their position and killed them all—eight guys.

"Then the Japanese troops proceeded cautiously toward our position. I guess they were surprised not to meet greater resistance. Their leaders kept wondering: Where is the main body of the American forces?

"Our orders were to hold our fire until the machine gunners in the forward positions opened up. At first the Insular Guard machine guns inflicted heavy casualties on the Japanese, but the guard was too small to hold back the Japanese for long. When the Japanese got near the plaza, they set up some machine guns, fired some short bursts of tracers, and sprayed them around until the militia fired and revealed their position. Then the Japanese just shot through the hedges. It didn't last long. Behind the kiosk and the plaza, stood the cathedral, which was also the direction the Japanese were coming from. The militia was firing and hitting the church—we could see that they were shooting too high. Most of them didn't know what the hell they were doing. We only had .45s and a handful of ammunition, so we just watched.

"We could see the Japanese firing tracers back. The tracers were coming across the plaza chest high and hitting the palace. We ducked down and waited. It quickly became clear that we were vastly outnumbered and outgunned. Pretty soon we heard a car horn honk three times, the signal to fall back to the palace. Firing stopped as people moved back from the forward positions.

"As everything got quiet, the Japanese quit shooting as well. One of the Japanese officers stood up and yelled in English, "Captain McMillin, come forward." Instead of the captain, who served as governor of the island, Lieutenant Commander D. T. Giles came out and met with the Japanese to make arrangements for the surrender. He went off somewhere and then came back with the Japanese commanding officer, Captain Hayashi, who met with Captain George J. McMillin to dictate the surrender terms.[17] All men would disable their weapons, and enlisted men were to strip to their shorts, while officers could retain their uniforms.

"There was a lot of confusion. At the back of the palace we didn't get the word about the surrender until later, so I couldn't get out in front of the palace until the Japanese were practically on their way in. We were all told to strip down, dismantle our .45s, and wait with our hands up for the Japanese to come in. Because it was so late, I didn't get my khakis off, although I did dismantle a navy yeoman's .45. He was having trouble, having got a round caught in the chamber. I grabbed the .45 automatic away from him, broke it down real fast, and threw it into a fish pond just about the time the Japanese arrived. They came running across the plaza with fixed bayonets glinting in the morning sun. However, I was still in my khakis, with no time to strip to my shorts, so they mistook me for an officer.

"As for the rest of the marines at Sumay, and the sailors at Piti, the governor surrendered before the main body of Japanese troops reached them. They got word of the surrender and were spared further fighting, which undoubtedly saved many lives.

"Two things saved my life that day. The first was being called to Agana that week. My replacement at Inarajan was killed trying to get back to Agana to join our force there. I'd probably met with a similar fate if I'd stayed at the outstation. The second thing was the fact that I didn't have time to get out of my khakis, and the Japanese moved me over with the officers. At first, they didn't notice that I wasn't an officer. We stood out in the plaza in the sun for a couple of hours when I saw two guys going through the ranks of the enlisted men. Holy Christ—it was those two infiltrators we'd captured and whom I had threatened in jail. I think they were trying to point out the guy who had threatened them, but fortunately

I was over with the officers. I even had my sun helmet on since there hadn't even been time to take it off. I suspect that if they'd fingered me in the plaza, there would have been a quick beheading right then and there.

"As I watched them going through the enlisted men's ranks, another Japanese soldier came running at me with his bayonet. My first thought was this is it; the two guys had pointed me out. But the bayonet went right by my face, nicked my ear, and flicked my helmet off, all in one smooth motion. Then the soldier walked away without even looking at me. They were Japanese marines, bigger than the other troops, and they wore hobnailed boots, which you really felt when they kicked you. We presumed they were seasoned troops, maybe from the fighting in China.

"Others weren't so fortunate. A marine private named John Kauffman was bayoneted for no reason by the Japanese after the surrender.[18] He died on the spot. Two other marines, Privates Burt and Bomar, were made to kneel and were beheaded. In all, thirteen marines and navy personnel were killed, along with one American civilian, four Guam Militia, and several dozen Guam civilians shot or bayoneted, most for no reason. Marines were bayoneted in the butt for not moving fast enough when ordered. More than thirty military and civilian personnel were injured by bombs, shooting, or bayonets.

"Once the Japanese got organized, they marched us all over to the cathedral. There we began to get the first impression of what life was to be like. First, they reduced our rations, in part due to all the chaos and in part because of their opinion of prisoners. We got two meals a day, usually a boiled potato and a slice of lunch meat.

"The first night we fell asleep on the hard teakwood floor of the church—hungry, a little afraid, and totally exhausted. Japan had just taken over its first piece of American territory in a battle that lasted two hours. Although we did not know it, for us the war was over. They say the marines never retreat. Well, we couldn't anyway. There was nowhere to go on Guam."

WEDNESDAY, DECEMBER 10, 1941

(Thursday, December 11, in Japan, the Philippines, and Guam)

DAVAO. Simon recalled: "Word came to us of the terrible bombings on Luzon, and at Cavite and Clark Field. Of course, we did not know that most of the U.S. aircraft had been destroyed on the ground, leaving the Philippines vulnerable to the Japanese. We also heard of Japanese landings on Luzon. But there were so many rumors flying around, no one knew what to believe.

"At first we thought if the Japanese came, we would flee into the mountains. So we made some preparations, dug some caves and tunnels, took some provisions and hid them, so we had a place to go, and some supplies. We also buried the last of the gold that the mine produced so the Japanese would not be able to get it.

"You see, the mill was down on the beach, about twenty miles away. We had a tram line that ran down to the mill, and of course, we had a telephone connection with the mill. After a while we disabled the tram so no one could come up to the mine from the coast. The only way in to reach us was through the mountains, which meant they had to pass by the mill. Whenever the people at the mill would see the Japanese going in the direction of the mine, they would call us, and we would go off into the mountains. Finally, after many false alarms, we stopped running into the mountains. Then most of the Americans decided to leave. They planned to go to Malaybalay, in central Mindanao, thinking that they could join up with the American forces there and be rescued."

GUAM. Garth recalled: "We spent the next thirty days in the cathedral. Pretty soon one day merged into the next, and we lost all track of time, except we knew that we were getting hungrier and hungrier. Most of us lost a lot of weight that first month in the Catholic church.

"Some of the Chamorros tried to bring us food, which helped, but it was risky for them. They could be beaten up or bayoneted for bringing food to the Americans. There was a fellow named Ben Butler, the son of an American sailor who had married a Chamorro woman. Their family owned the drugstore, soda fountain, a general store, and a tobacco shop in Agana. At one point before the war he attended Loyola University in California and came to our home for dinner. While I was in the cathedral, he arranged to get some pipes and tobacco brought to me as well as some food. I later learned that the Japanese had also imprisoned his father.

"After a day or so, the Japanese began calling out certain people for interrogation. Many of the officers were called in an effort to obtain information about the U.S. forces and defenses. One day they came in and got me. I guess they thought that the Insular Patrol had knowledge of special weapons. They took me over to the Governor's Palace building they'd taken over as part of their headquarters. There was a stairway up, then a landing, then a stairway up to the next landing with carpets. When I got to the foot of the stairs, the interpreter told me to walk up the stairs slowly and to keep my hands stiffly at my sides. I went up the stairs two at a time. At the landing, the guard stopped me, didn't say anything, but hit me with the butt of his rifle, and I rolled down again.

"The interpreter said, 'You didn't understand me,' and then he repeated his instructions. This time I went slowly, but I guess my hands weren't at my sides. The guard knocked me down to the landing again. The interpreter hollered up to me, 'Next time they shoot you.'

"They took me in a dark room, shined a light in my face, and started firing questions at me: 'Where are the Garand rifles, where are the airplanes, etc.' They did it for three days, then they stopped. They couldn't believe how poorly equipped we were.

"This was the classic 'sit under the bright light and tell the truth or I'll beat the shit out of you' stuff. Hell, there weren't any Garand rifles, and that was what I told them, plus some other stuff they didn't want to hear. They did their part—they beat the shit out of me, with sticks and with the backs of their swords. Then they hauled me back to the Catholic church and tossed me in on the floor.

"The one thing I did know—and never told them—was that I knew where some money was buried. I'd taken money out of the bank to buy Christmas presents to send home. When the bombing started, some guys were formed into a detail to go hide money from the commissary. I went along and added my little bit to the cache.

"After that, time passed slowly in the church. Most of the time we'd sit around, they'd count us, come through and slap us around, give us a few kicks.

"The Chamorros tried to bring us food, but it was dangerous because the Japanese were unpredictable. They allowed it for a while, but then stopped it altogether. Everything was improvised—toilets, water, beds. Bathroom facilities were outside on the ground. We slept on the floor or the ground. It was at this time that I met Luther D. Orr.

"I had two sheets laid out on the floor for sleeping. One time I came back and found another marine laying there in my bed. 'Hey buddy, move' I said. 'That bed is mine.'

"He rolled over real slowly, looked up at me and said back to me, 'Who the hell are you?'

"'Hey, come on, move out of my sack.'

"This time, when he didn't budge, I reached down and grabbed him and smacked him. Then I told him to get off my bed. After that, he moved over, introduced himself, and from that day on we were close friends. Everyone called him 'L. D.' We were together through three camps, and he was an exceptionally fine person.

"We remained in the church until they took us off the island on January 10, 1942. With nothing to do, we played cards, talked about when the war would end, and what we would do once it was over. Since we didn't get enough to eat, we were always hungry, so we talked about food constantly.

"Already you could see people's attitudes changing. Of course, at that time everyone believed the war would be over in a few weeks or months at most. No one knew the full extent of the Japanese success at Pearl Harbor, nor the magnitude of the Japanese attacks in the Philippines, Wake Island, and elsewhere.

"Since we had lots of time to think, we tried to figure out what had happened, what caused our world to come apart so suddenly. How had the United States gotten itself in such a position of weakness? Where was the power of the much-vaunted Asiatic Fleet? Where were the forces we thought must surely be on the way to rescue us?

"Some people started resisting right away—in small ways, since no one wanted to get killed. Others tried to maneuver into special positions, where they could curry favor with the Japanese. It was a pattern repeated throughout our long imprisonment."

CHAPTER 2

꿰 꿰 꿰

ORIGINS

I was intrigued with these individuals swept up in World War II, who had lived when so many others died. What were their backgrounds, I wondered. Was there something about them that made them uniquely able to survive their many ordeals? During my conversations with them, I asked them to tell me a little about their childhood, what experiences they had growing up. I found it interesting that they had known adversity.

SIMON: My ancestors had a long tradition as seafarers and warriors. The story of one of them—a story I learned as a boy—stuck with me all these years. He was a Ukrainian named Peter Solomaniuck, a tall blond fellow with whiskers, so strong that he could bend horseshoes with his bare hands. Because of his exploits he received the nickname "Silach," which means "strong man."

There was a time when it seemed the Russians were constantly at war with Poland, fighting the Hussars. During this period the soldiers' best friends were their horses because their lives depended on them. They lived and frequently even slept with their horses as battles raged around the small Ukrainian villages.

During an attack by a superior force of Polish Hussars, Peter was taken prisoner. Impressed with his tremendous strength, the Poles tied him up with a thick rope and put him on the back of a horse. It was their intention to take him back to Warsaw to exhibit. However, he wanted no part of being a prisoner in a Polish sideshow. When the Poles were resting that night, he gnawed through the rope, hung underneath a horse so he could slip away undetected, and made his way back to Kiev.

In 1853, French, Turkish, and British armies attacked Crimea. Once again the young men of the Ukraine were called to arms. In one of the battles, the French overran the Russian artillery position. They continued to pursue the retreating

Russian soldiers. In the midst of the smoke and fire, the Russian commander, badly wounded in the eye, called for "that bastard Solomaniuck, the Silach." My ancestor hastened to his commander's side.

"Here I am, sir," responded Peter Solomaniuck. "Let me bandage your bleeding eye."

"To hell with my eye, you bum, get the cannons turned around."

Even though the cannons were hot from the previous firing, Peter grabbed them, badly burning his hands and shoulders, but nonetheless swung the massive barrels around so they could be brought to bear on the oncoming French. They were immediately loaded and fired at the approaching enemy troops until the French soldiers were driven back.

My ancestor was awarded a golden cross hanging from a tricolored ribbon. The inscription on the cross read:

> For bravery in the Crimean War
> 1853–1856
> For your descendants to admire and emulate
> CZAR NIKOLAI I

This medal was among my cherished possessions until I lost it somewhere in the Philippine jungles while running from Japanese marines in 1942.

A number of my Ukrainian ancestors stayed in Crimea after the war. Their reputation as tender and passionate lovers made them popular among the southern girls—who were mostly brunettes of Greek, Georgian, and even gypsy origins. In addition to the local girls, these Ukrainians liked the climate, the smell of tar, the salty breezes from the sea. Most of the Solomaniucks found work aboard oceangoing merchant marine vessels, with their allure of foreign lands, and exotic, kaleidoscoping changes of scenery.

Both my father and uncle followed careers in the merchant marine. During the First World War, my father was aboard a ship in Pacific waters. Turkey closed the Straits of Bosporus, cutting his ship off from its homeport of Odessa. Eventually the ship made its way to the port of Vladivostok. At home in Odessa, my mother decided to end the lengthy separation. She packed a few things, we closed up our wonderful house, and took the long train ride clear across Russia to be with my father in Vladivostok. As it was, we never went back to Odessa, so this marked the first time our family lost all its possessions.

After the war, the Russian Revolution that had been boiling under the surface finally took place. In 1923, the USSR was created. After a while things got bad in Vladivostok. By then my father had a teaching job at a merchant marine academy. But the Marxists were suspicious of anyone associated with the intelligentsia or in any way connected with the czar's regime. They encouraged people to act as informers. Some of my father's students, who did not like the marks they received in his classes, falsely accused my father, causing him to be dismissed from his position. With this dismissal—and since we feared something worse might happen—the whole family fled to Shanghai in 1925. I was fifteen years old at the time. We left at night with a small handbag. This was the second time my family lost its home and all its possessions.

Some Russians eventually tracked us down in China and tried to talk my father into returning. But my father wanted no part of this plan and emphasized the point by taking me to the harbor one day. There, looking out into the East China Sea, a few white clouds scudding across the sky, the breeze westerly, he tore up our Russian passports and scattered the fragments into the murky waters of the harbor. "So much for returning to Russia," he said, as we walked back to the place where we were staying.

My father joined the Chinese merchant marine. In 1929, he was serving as chief engineer on a Chinese boat that struck a submerged rock outside of Hong Kong and sank. There was a great loss of life, and my father died in this tragedy.

Later, I had an opportunity to talk to the chief officer, who was one of the survivors. He told me that when last seen, my father was checking the passengers' life jackets to be sure they were tied correctly. He left on the last lifeboat, in accordance with maritime tradition. Apparently, the overloaded lifeboat capsized. The next morning, when the Hong Kong harbor tug arrived at the scene of the tragedy, many people were found floating face down, drowned.

My family was one of hundreds of other "stateless" people who lived in the international community in Shanghai. Eventually we were able to obtain League of Nations passports, which were issued at that time to displaced persons.

In spite of these difficulties, I managed to get an education. With encouragement and assistance from the Belgian Consulate in Shanghai, I received a scholarship to study engineering at the Royal University of Ghent in Belgium. My twin brother George was sent there first, and I followed. At the university I met a beautiful young Latvian girl named Lydia, who was studying chemical engineering.

In 1934, I graduated with honors. At that time, the world was still recovering from the effects of the Great Depression. But friends told me of new developments in the mining industry in the Philippines—a gold rush was going on—so I decided to seek my fortune there.

‖‖ ‖‖ ‖‖

Shanghai lies just above the 30th parallel, while Vladivostok is above the 40th, at about 43 degrees. If you spin the globe, you encounter the California coast across the Pacific in this same zone. South of this band, centered on the Tropic of Cancer, lies Midway and the Hawaiian Islands, while still farther south, one encounters the Philippines and Guam. These imaginary arcs line up in such a way that Southern California is a degree or two north of Shanghai, while northern Iowa is about in line with Vladivostok.

In April 1921, at the time Simon Solomaniuck's family was reestablishing itself in Vladivostok, an American family celebrated the birth of their first son, Garth, at their home in Burlington, Iowa, on the banks of the Mississippi River. The Dunns were staunch midwestern Americans, of Scotch/Irish/English descent. Garth's grandfather was a prosperous farmer in the area. In addition to a 350-acre farm at Earlville, he owned a drugstore and a creamery in Manchester. Garth's father studied to be a mathematics teacher, but at the time Garth was born, he was an advertising manager for a department store. His mother was a local girl from Burlington. Her father was a railroad engineer.

When Garth was two years old, and his brother, James, barely one year old, their grandfather lost the creamery and things were not going well on the farm. The family decided to move west. In 1923 they boarded a train for the long trip across the Midwest to California, where they settled near Los Angeles.

GARTH: When we arrived in California, our first house was in Maywood. We must have had some money then, because the house was pretty nice. Dad had a job at first in advertising, until things started getting rough as the Depression came on. Then he bounced from one job to another, but finally landed a position with the Los Angeles County court system. He was sent to El Centro, California, to work. While he was there, we kids remained with Mom. He mailed his checks back and saw us every few weeks.

Eventually, he obtained a position in the county clerk's office in Los Angeles, we all got back together, and the family had some degree of security during the Depression. We bought a home and settled in Glendale, and that was where I attended school.

I suppose you could say I was a little unruly. When it came time to graduate from elementary school, I didn't graduate with my class. We were lined up in the auditorium. I was messing around talking to some kids, when one of the old-maid teachers came up to me on my blind side and grabbed my arm. Her fingernails cut right through my skin. I was so startled that I jerked around in her direction, trying to pull my arm free. I didn't intend to hit her, but my hand caught her in the face, and I was in a lot of trouble. They called my mother down to the school for a long discussion, and I got held back for an extra semester.

〢〢 〢〢 〢〢

At about the same time that the Dunn family boarded the train in Iowa to come to California, the Takahashi family made a momentous decision. They decided to move from Westwood to Malibu, where Mr. Takahashi had an opportunity to lease land on a ranch. There they would have a farm of their own and raise produce for the rapidly expanding Los Angeles market.

Just before the outbreak of World War I, when he was in his early thirties, Kitaro Takahashi came to Los Angeles from his home in Hiratsuka, Japan, near Tokyo. Japan's surprising defeat of the Russians in 1905 led to an opening up of Japan. After that time, many Japanese came to Western countries to start new lives. There were obstacles to immigration to the United States, however, such as the Gentlemen's Agreement of 1907, by which the Japanese government no longer issued passports to workers coming to the U.S. Next, the U. S. Immigration Act of 1917 required literacy tests for immigrants over age sixteen and established an Asiatic Barred Zone, which barred most immigrants from Asia. As a result, no Japanese could immigrate, become a citizen, or own land legally, until the McCarran-Walter Act was passed in 1952. In spite of these obstacles, some people from Kitaro's prefecture came to Los Angeles, where they found work as domestics. From a friend who returned to visit Japan, he learned of the opportunities in California and decided that he would try this avenue to a new life.

In Westwood, Kitaro was hired to work in the home of a bank executive. This man, an important figure in the California Bank company, treated him kindly. Kitaro saw opportunities in California and decided to stay.

He needed a wife, however. Several letters went back and forth from Los Angeles to Hiratsuka, until finally a young woman arrived in California. When Kitaro met his future bride after her long trip by sea, he was stunned by her beauty. Her name was Yoshie Hosaka. She had a beautiful face, shining dark hair, and was eleven years younger than him. This was, after the custom of those times in Japan, an arranged marriage, negotiated by the families of the bride and groom. Kitaro was happy that his parents had made such an excellent choice and considered himself an extremely fortunate man. Following their marriage, Yoshie joined her husband in domestic service in Westwood. Soon they had a son. A year or so later, in January 1918, she gave birth to twin daughters. The twin girls were born a month short of eight years after Simon and his twin brother George were born in faraway Odessa.

The girls were named Mitsuye and Fumiye. After entering school, they adopted Americanized versions of their names and called themselves Mitzi and Dorothy.

MITZI: My family continued their life in Westwood, adding another brother and sister and eventually moving to a house on Veteran Avenue, just north of Wilshire, in present-day Westwood Village. Then, in 1922, my parents reached a decision to leave domestic service and start a farm on the Rindge family's ranch in Malibu. This was not without precedent; there were a dozen other Japanese families farming on the ranch, which occupied a large area in Malibu Canyon, behind the present site of Pepperdine University. Malibu Creek wound through much of the property, there was a dam constructed on the creek for the water supply, and the Rindge family made their home in a large house—"the castle"—that dominated the surrounding area from its hilltop location.

The Rindges liked my father, and our family prospered in Malibu. As we children reached school age, we attended public schools in Santa Monica. When not in school, we all helped on the ranch, each with his or her chores to do. There were some hard times during the Depression, but as father said, "People always have to eat," so our family managed to earn enough income for necessities, and food was never a problem.

We rode the bus from Malibu to Santa Monica to go to school. There were only a handful of Oriental kids at Santa Monica High, but we felt like we were part of everything. We were not aware of any prejudices at that time. Dorothy and I were close. The family teased us, because we always stood up for each other. I was the happy-go-lucky one as a child; she was more serious, a better student.

We participated in as many school activities as we could, but had the constraint of having to ride the bus back to Malibu after school every day. One of our favorite activities was the Girl's Athletic Association. Dorothy and I were guards on the basketball team—two peanut-size guards, you could say—but we loved it. I liked all sports, though I didn't enjoy algebra and geometry!

After school, we rode the bus home to Malibu, and then did our chores on the ranch. Japanese families were strict about boys and dating and dancing, and we were not allowed to participate in these things to the same extent as our Caucasian classmates. However, there was another family living on the ranch, with eight children, and I liked one of the boys. I got teased a lot about this as we rode

Mitzi and Dorothy Takahashi, Santa Monica, 1936

the bus back and forth from Malibu to Santa Monica. I remember that those were happy times, the bus windows open, our hair blowing in the breeze, the smell of the ocean and the sound of surf, as the old bus rattled along Pacific Coast Highway.

I was five feet tall, perfect oval face, delicate features, short dark hair, smooth clear complexion. Quiet, self-effacing, modest, I was a model daughter in most respects. Somehow I managed to achieve an acceptable balance between the various forces that pulled at me.

On the one side, there were my parents, with their first-generation Issei concerns for Japanese tradition and culture. They clung to some elements of the old ways, while recognizing that they had, by seeking a new life in California, forever forsaken other aspects of their deep-rooted cultural traditions. On the other side, I saw myself as an ordinary American girl, growing up with all the usual concerns: What kind of job would I find? What kind of husband awaited me? Would I someday have a house of my own? What would my children be like? I worried about myself: I was too chubby; no one would find me attractive enough to marry; I wished I was more outgoing, or had the easy charm of some of my girlfriends.

I graduated from Santa Monica High School in 1936. After graduation, I returned to the ranch in Malibu to live and work with the family. For the next three years, my twin sister and I, and our older brother, assisted our parents, while my two younger sisters and younger brother went to school.

There were a thousand, never-ending chores to do on the ranch. First, there was the livestock, taking care of the chickens, milking the cow. Then there was planting, weeding, watering, picking—time stretched out forever, or so it seemed, before the seeds sown on the farm became the beautiful produce taken to the Central Market in Los Angeles and sold.

卌 卌 卌

On the opposite side of the Pacific Ocean from Malibu, another Japanese family worked a small farm in Japan. The son, Masashi Itoh, and I had a remarkable adventure years after the war's end.

ITOH: I was born on March 1, 1921, in Shimobe, a small farming village near Kofu, in Yamanashi Prefecture, located 150 miles west of Tokyo. I was the eldest son of Tanuki Itoh. I was born at home in the house where we lived and grew up on the farm with my mother, father, and sister, Kimiko. Japan was hit hard by the Great Depression when markets for Japanese products collapsed and unemployment became widespread. This situation was aggravated by several years of bad harvests, leading to food shortages and near starvation conditions in some rural areas. During this time I attended the Primary Department of Furuseki Normal School from 1927 until graduation in 1935, and then attended Kofu Middle School until 1936.[19]

In 1941, with Japan's invasion of China in full swing, I was summoned by my local draft board. I was a farm boy, strong, and at five feet ten inches, taller than most Japanese. I passed the conscription tests with merit and was found fit for service in the Japanese army. When I got home after the tests, the whole village turned out to congratulate me on the results.[20]

I joined the Japanese army on January 10, 1942, with a friend named Fumiya Aihara. After three months of training, Aihara and I were sent to Manchuria. In April 1943, we were transferred to Bei'an, in northern Manchuria.

卌 卌 卌

Prior to Itoh joining the Japanese army, another young Japanese from Shikoku Island decided to forgo a career as a schoolteacher and join the Japanese navy. I knew Shikoku Island because of the POW camp for Allied soldiers there. The island's most famous POW was not an American, however. It turned out to be this young naval officer.

SAKAMAKI: I was born on November 18, 1918, just after the end of World War I, so I was named Kazuo, which in Japanese means "peace boy." I grew up in a small village on Shikoku Island, where I spent a happy childhood in the peaceful surroundings of this rural area. My father was a schoolteacher, and I originally intended to follow in his footsteps, but in 1937 while still in high school, I watched soldiers departing for the battlefields of China, and changed my mind.

I decided that I wanted to enter the Naval Academy. My parents were surprised at this decision and initially opposed it. In part they were concerned about my ability to succeed in the rigorous training program.

Six thousand boys from all over Japan applied for admission to the Naval Academy. Ninety-five percent of them were rejected after competitive examinations based on intellectual and physical qualifications. I could not believe it when I discovered that I was among the fortunate 300 who passed through the narrow gate. On April 1, 1937, I became a full-fledged student at the Naval Academy, located on Eta Jima, a small island in the Inland Sea.[21]

The Naval Academy was Japan's equivalent of Annapolis. There I underwent rigorous physical training along with academic studies. I learned that for a naval officer, duty, responsibility, and absolute obedience to superior officers were

Ensign Kazuo Sakamaki, Imperial Japanese Navy

mandatory. Cadets were taught "that in war the most important thing was to die manfully on the battlefield; that in war there is only victory and no retreat."[22]

I graduated in August 1940 and was commissioned a midshipman. By this time I knew there was a high probability of war with the United States and Great Britain, and it would be necessary to defeat their navies in a sudden attack. Initially I was assigned to a light cruiser and saw duty in Formosa and Saigon.

In April 1941, I was promoted to ensign and ordered to report to the *Chiyoda*—a seaplane tender undergoing strange modifications. There I learned that I'd been assigned to take part in a highly secret mission—to guide a midget submarine with two torpedoes into an enemy harbor. I understood that this was likely to be a one-way trip.

JHT JHT JHT

In 1936, the world was more or less at peace. True, there were a few ominous signs—Japan had invaded Manchuria, Italy had invaded Ethiopia, and Germany had announced that it was building an air force and reinstating compulsory national military service. Throughout the United States, there was a strong isolationist movement, which argued against permitting the country to become involved in another European war. These feelings eventually led Congress to pass the Neutrality Act of 1935, which instituted arms embargoes and restrictions on travel to warring countries. In addition, the decline in military preparedness since the end of World War I left the United States few alternatives other than neutrality.

In varying degrees, Simon, Garth, Mitzi, Itoh, Sakamaki, and their families had experienced difficult times and had overcome them. They survived the Great Depression, moved to new lands, started new lives. If you asked them, they would say that their lives to that point were no different than other people's lives. If any single aspect stood out, it was their determination to succeed in whatever it was that they decided to do.

CHAPTER 3

JHT JHT JHT

DAVAO GOLD MINE

SIMON: I sailed from Hong Kong to the Philippines in 1935. I'd been fortunate enough to find a job with the Elizalde Company, which was involved in rope fabrication, import/export trade, and mining. After traveling by boat to Manila, I went by train to Legaspi, in southern Luzon. There I began working at a gold lode mine located near the tiny village of Paracalle. We were dredging in a wide expanse of river that cut through the jungle.

A year went by, and the novelty of this new job and home wore off. I began to spend more and more time thinking of my faraway family and friends. At night, I lay awake in my bed and listened to the mosquitoes buzzing angrily outside the mosquito net. I thought about Lydia—the beautiful, mischievous Latvian girl I'd met at the university. She was in the same year at the university as me, but studying chemistry. Here, far away in the Philippine jungles, I could imagine her face, the sparkle in her eyes, how she used to make little jokes at me. Now, there was a woman!

In 1937, as I approached the end of my second year in Paracalle, on a warm night when the buzzing of the mosquitoes seemed particularly intense, I reached a decision of great importance to my future: I decided to get married. The next day after work I went into the town, where I knew Enrique, the postmaster and telegraph operator. I said that I wanted to send a telegram.

"It shall be my pleasure, Señor Simon. This telegram, she is for the mining company?"

"No, Enrique, it is for my wife."

"But Señor Simon, I do not know you have the wife."

"I don't. That's why I want to send a telegram. Now if you . . ."

"But if you no have the wife . . ."

"Enrique, my dear amigo. I don't have a wife. That's why I'm going to send the telegram—to get one!"

"You are going to send a telegram to Manila and ask for a wife?"

"No, I'm going to send a telegram to Europe and tell a woman to come here and marry me."

"But Señor Simon—forgive me—what woman would want to leave Europe to come here? And to get married by a telegram?"

"This one will, Enrique, this one will. Just send the telegram, and exactly as I've written it, please."

The next day the whole village knew that the crazy "Russo," as I was called, had sent a telegram to Europe for a wife. Rumors circulated like wildfire, and the whole town speculated: Would the Latvian beauty come to Luzon to live in the jungle with the crazy Russian?

A month went by, then two. Still no response. People whispered in the village. "Ha! That Latvian, she's got good sense. She doesn't want to leave Europe and come here to live in the jungle with the loco Russo."

Enrique suffered for me, his friend, when he heard this gossip. In the bar at night, he defended me. "The Russo is a big man," he said. "He knows about women. If he says this Latvian will come, then she will come. I know he's got balls, that Russo."

Other villagers were less optimistic, according to Enrique, who would recount these stories in great detail to me. "Ha! If he were such a man," they would argue, "why does he not even notice Maria Elena, the daughter of the pharmacist, who looks after him with longing in her eyes?"

"Why should he?" Enrique would reply. "A man who can choose from the most beautiful women in Europe, what does he want with a pharmacist's daughter in Paracalle?"

After three months, Enrique began to lose hope. He dreaded seeing me in the village, because I always looked at him, as if to ask, "Where is my telegram?" Then, one morning, Enrique saw me on my way to the mine and blurted out, "Simon, Simon, no telegram today." I was deep in thought and did not register the comment at first. Then I paused in the middle of the plaza, as I recognized my meddlesome friend. Oh shit, I thought, go stick your telegrams. I was tired of the questions by then, but I said nothing of this to Enrique. "It takes awhile," was all I said. "Latvia is a long ways away."

"*Si, pero tantos dias . . .* " came Enrique's reply. " . . . so many days? But Simon," he persisted, "I have the idea for you." Wearily I resigned myself to hearing his scheme, since I knew I'd hear it sooner or later, one way or another. Poor Enrique—the issue of my wife had become a matter of personal honor to him.

"Okay, Russo, here is the idea. She does not answer the telegram, yes? And you, being the man you are, you cannot be one to beg a woman to marry you, yes? So you need an intermediary, a marriage ambassador, yes? Someone to intercede on your behalf, preserve your honor, yes?" His eyes were bright with excitement. I could not imagine what was coming next, but was certain it would be some harebrained idea. Yet I said nothing. Enrique continued to outline his plan.

"Now, you cannot send another telegram, but I—the postmaster and chief telegraph operator, and your humble emissary—I can send the telegram, no? I can send the telegram to ask, 'Where is the prepaid reply to our message?' Then it is a matter of procedure, regulations, orderly conduct of business, and so on. That way we make sure the Latvian got your telegram, no? And, maybe we give her a little push, so she gets the reply to you, huh?"

I thought about it for a minute. Maybe it wasn't such a bad idea. Knowing Lydia, I didn't want to hurry her. Still, it was possible that the first telegram had gone astray. Why not try it? "Okay," I said. "You are the emissary of love. But do just what you said—nothing else!"

"Of course, Señor Simon. I shall handle this urgent matter immediately and with great care. You should not worry yourself with such small things. Leave it in my hands, go work in the mine, and find some more gold so we'll all be rich."

I went to the mine, consoling myself, as I had for the past three months, with the thought that she would come, once her family agreed to the marriage, once she made up her mind. After all, it was not easy to go halfway around the world, to marry someone you had not seen in two years, someone last viewed as a university senior in a distant land. I knew it was hard, and frankly I wondered myself if she would really come. But wondering was no good. So I shook my head as if to clear out those thoughts. No, I insisted to myself, she'll come. I'm not sure of many things, but I'm sure of this. Those damn Latvians are all crazy, and she's just wild enough to get on the boat and do it. She'll come. I'll just keep waiting until it happens.

Several days later, I sat in a hammock on the veranda of my house and listened to the forest sounds while sipping a beer. It was early evening, and I thought of her, of her blue eyes, white skin, blond hair, her smile . . . It was a little routine I went through every night. On that night I heard the faint sound of a bicycle from the direction of the village. I got up, walked to the edge of the porch. Down the road, I could see the flickering of a dim light. I watched with amusement as the dying glow approached. It was somebody on a bicycle, and whoever it was, they were tired, pedaling slowly.

"Simon, Simon," I heard shouted in the semidarkness, "a telegram *para usted.* She's coming, she's actually coming! You are a man after all," screamed Enrique, as he pedaled up to the porch, out of breath, and dropped the bicycle in front of my house. "A thousand pardons, but for your sake, I opened the telegram, and she really is coming, all the way from Latvia. What a man you are!"

Through this outburst I said nothing. Finally Enrique stopped talking, the tattered telegram still clutched in his hand. "Can I see it?" I asked.

"Yeah, sure," said Enrique. "You're not mad at me, are you?"

"No, my friend, of course not. Go on in the house and get a beer. You've had a long ride."

"Gracias."

I opened the telegram. It said: *Arriving April 9 Manila on British steamship. Wither thou go, I will go. Love me. Lydia.*

I folded the telegram carefully, and put it in my shirt pocket. I turned and stood with my hands on the porch rail, staring off into the blackness of the night. In the distance, I could hear the sounds of crickets and other night insects, while behind me, Enrique was banging around inside the house. Then he came out, smiling, eyes full of joy, beer half gone. "Simon, I can hardly wait to see this *mujer* of yours. *Que mujer, que hombre!* What a man, that a woman would leave the capitals of Europe and come to a shit place like this." He spat over the porch rail.

I laughed at him. It was starting to sink in to my dulled brain. She was coming! At last! But to Enrique, I said nothing of this. "Where is my beer, you *cabron? Anda-le,* and get me one too. All this talk of yours about women. We Russians take a different approach. I'll look this one over, see what I think. If she's no good, I'll send her back and get another one!"

░░░ ░░░ ░░░

LYDIA: I'd been thinking about Simon's telegram, but truthfully, I wasn't anxious to get married. I was working, had a good job, and had a couple of boyfriends who were courting me. I wondered about going so far to meet up with Simon. As I searched my memories of him, I recalled that he was a serious fellow, with an underlying sense of humor that always delighted me.

But, as it was, the man from the telegraph company came by my house one blustery cold evening when I'd had a hard day at work, and asked about the prepaid reply. The reminder forced me to admit I had to make a decision. At the time, the thought of going somewhere warmer appealed to me. I decided a nice ocean voyage wouldn't be so bad. If it didn't work out, I could always come back, since I had some suitors there in Libau to return to. Once I'd decided, I made the arrangements and sent the telegram to Simon. In spite of the fact that the reply was prepaid, he didn't pay enough, so it cost me to send my answer. That should have been a warning!

I went by train to Belgium to spend a few days with Simon's mother, who happened to be there at that time. There I met a tall, handsome Russian I'd known from my university days, and almost changed my mind again about getting on the boat!

Eventually the sailing date came, so I took my suitcases and my steamer trunk and boarded the ship in France, at the port of Le Havre. From there we went via the Suez Canal and the Red Sea, south around India to Ceylon, through the straits of Malacca to Singapore, then to Manila. All in all, it was a twenty-five–day trip. Each day it got a little warmer, making me happy to have put the cold Latvian winter behind me.

⧍⧍⧍ ⧍⧍⧍ ⧍⧍⧍

SIMON: By 1938, I was back in Manila. I'd quit my job at the mine in Paracalle and had gone to Manila to wait for Lydia. I found a part-time job teaching mining engineering at a private university, Adamson University. Lydia had been working in a Latvian sugar factory as a chemist. She was shocked when she got my telegram since she had a good job and had two or three fellows courting her. It took her awhile to decide what to do. Surprisingly enough, her parents didn't try to persuade her one way or the other; I suppose since she'd been away from home five years at Ghent, they felt she was mature enough to make up her own mind.

Finally, the magic day arrived. On April 9, 1938, I went to the docks to pick her up. What do I see? There on the promenade deck is Lydia with a big husky sailor, or maybe an officer—and she's kissing him passionately! My bride to be! To this day she maintains that he was the husband of a German couple who had befriended her on the long voyage, and that his wife was standing nearby as they said farewell.

I'd sent her money for the boat, but she's never forgotten—nor allowed me to forget—that it wasn't enough, and she had to pay the difference herself! First the telegram, then the boat.

The first day or two in Manila was a shock to Lydia. The heat cooked her fair complexion, the humidity sapped her strength. She caught a rash, broke out, and had to have some horrible medicine for her face.

She was staying with some Russian friends of mine. At least I thought they were friends. Later I learned that this scoundrel, when he saw how beautiful she was, got her off to one side and had a talk with her. "Lydia, why do you want to marry Simon? There aren't many European women here. You can find someone rich to marry, better wait awhile. Look around, girls are in demand."

Fortunately for me, she didn't listen to this "friend." To top it off, it was Lent, which meant we couldn't get married right away. You had to go for instructions, confess; the whole process took weeks. Finally we found a Unitarian church, and we were married on May 17, 1938. Then I started looking for a job in earnest. About that time I ran into a friend, a man who was a geologist for the Elizalde Company. He got me a job in an iron mine in northern Luzon, near the town of Aparri. We made the journey there by ship. For us, it was like a honeymoon, even though we'd been married a few months.

Once in Aparri, we settled into a new life as I began my work at the iron mine. The village was small, and soon we knew everyone. There were few Europeans or Americans there—just a handful—and we quickly made friends with all of them. We especially liked an American woman who was married to a Filipino doctor. Before we came, she had been lonely and had few friends in the village. We became good friends with this couple. He had a little office in the village with a sign over the door: Dr. O. Camero.

Malaria was a terrible problem at Aparri. To help keep the workforce healthy, we gave them atabrine, which they hated to take because it tasted bad and turned the skin yellow. Each day as the workers left the mine, they had to stop at the gate, where they were given two pills. The guard watched to make sure they put the pills in their mouths and swallowed them. The workers didn't really swallow the atabrine; they were clever at faking it. Once they'd gone a short way beyond the gate, they'd spit out the pills. Over time, the edges of the road were stained yellow with all the discarded medicine.

Our house was a native type, called a nipa hut, with palm-thatched walls and roof. We slept with mosquito netting. At night, when we went to bed, we could see all the mosquitoes—hundreds of them—coming in and congregating on the net. All night long they crawled around, trying to find a way to get in and feast on us. Eventually, two or three would find a hole they could squeeze through, because in the morning we'd find them trapped inside the net, so gorged with blood they couldn't escape. After a few nights of this arrangement, we got worried because we thought that for sure we'd get malaria. So one day I went to the foreman at the mine and asked his advice. "No problem," he told me. "Don't worry. For a few pesos, I'll fix you up."

The next day he showed up at our house with a huge carabao, a water buffalo, which he tied up in the front yard. That solved the problem—the carabao attracted all the mosquitoes, and they left us alone.

Aparri was our first experience with really living in the jungle. We were some miles outside the town. To visit us, our friends had to come by boat, cross a river to our island, and hike through the jungle until they reached our house. Camero and his wife were our most welcome visitors. Besides being good friends, he brought medicine that helped Lydia's skin problems.

We stayed there less than a year because it soon became apparent that the ore body was not rich enough to mine economically. In 1939, the company transferred me to the Davao gold mine, so Lydia and I got our second honeymoon by boat. On the 16th of September, we sailed aboard the SS *Bisayas* for Davao.

We went from one extreme to another: Aparri was on the northern tip of Luzon; Davao was far to the south—on the south side of the island of Mindanao. The mine was up in the mountains, at about 3,000 feet elevation, about twenty miles from the coast and connected by an overhead railway or tram. There was a landing strip where small planes could fly in and out. We called it Maraut airport.

The company built houses near the mine for the employees. Our house was beautifully finished, painted white on the outside, with Philippine hardwoods inside and furnished with rattan furniture. It sat on stilts, with an open porch and railings, a comfortable home—much better than the nipa hut we'd had at Aparri. Lydia kept a garden, and we raised chickens and ducks. It was really a wonderful life—almost "colonial," I suppose you could say, but we were happy there with our small group of friends, mostly Americans.

Our photo album of those days showed a group of us sitting around playing poker on a Saturday night. There were several snapshots of Lydia pushing a wheelbarrow, working in her garden. Another showed Blackie, our myna bird, sitting on my desk trying to decide whether to steal a pencil or a draftsman's ruler. There are pictures of us and our friends the Willses on a fishing expedition. One photograph shows Jane Wills sitting on the grass, as beautiful as a fashion model, wearing a spotted dress with a lace collar, and holding ten-month-old Trudy in diapers.

Our group included the general superintendent and his wife, Mr. and Mrs. Sundeen; another couple, the Livingstones; Tom Garley and his wife and daughter; Jack Boyd; Mr. McKenzie, our one-eyed master mechanic; Mr. Garcia, our storekeeper; Hugh and Jane Wills and their baby, Trudy; and a man named Wellguch. Besides these people and a few others, we had several hundred Filipino and Japanese workers, both at the mine and down below at the mill, which was located on the coast near the town of Pantukan. The workers had their own village built near the mine.

Lydia Peters and the House at the Gold Mine

Simon Peters (right) and Tram Car

The mine was nestled in a little valley. Steep mountains rose on all sides. At one end of the site, the tram came down to a building where ore could be loaded into the cars. Nearby were the powerhouse and some shop buildings. A road ran through the site, past offices and the commissary. In the distance stood our house and the houses of the superintendent and other managers.

We were isolated. At night, we'd read, listen to the radio, or perhaps play poker. Once a week, one of our group would have a dinner or a little party for everyone else. We would go on weekend picnics or take fishing trips to the beautifully clear streams that tumbled down through narrow canyons in the mountains.

We had a little spotted dog called Rijic, and the myna bird that had adopted us. It would fly with Lydia everywhere, and loved to steal things and carry them back to our house. We also had several cats and a parrot. The main excitement was the occasional snake that would find its way into our garden. Once we caught a large python that had gotten in and eaten one of our ducks. We killed it and had beautiful shoes made from its skin for all the ladies.

Cockroaches were a nuisance—the big black or brown ones that liked to hide in dark places. Once a week or so, Lydia would put a suitcase (opened just a crack) under our bed. At night all the cockroaches would crawl into it. In the morning she'd take the suitcase outside to the chicken pen. The chickens would

The Davao Gold Mine

gather, and when she opened it, they'd rush around and eat all the cockroaches. Usually none escaped.

All in all, our life at the mine was pleasant in spite of the isolation. The surrounding area was a dense tropical forest—beautiful with orchids and flowers, but also foreboding in a dark, ominous way. The mine itself had a good safety record, and we had no major problems with the work, but every now and again there were minor disasters.

For example, once I was underground in the mine. Usually it was quiet there, but I kept hearing snapping sounds in one section. I went to the superintendent, because it appeared that we had not put in enough supports to hold up the roof, and the noise I heard was the cracking of reinforcing timbers. I told him the roof of the mine was not stable. But he didn't want to spend more money on that section, so we did nothing. Then one Sunday, around twelve o'clock, the whole section collapsed. There was a big crater aboveground, and in that area the trees were all sloping inward. Fortunately, no one was in the mine when it happened.

Another time, we ran out of ore. We were mining gold from an ore body. We followed it up to a certain point, and then it just stopped. We had to stop shipping the ore down to the mill on the coast. We expected a shift in the position of the ore body, but when we looked to the left, and then to the right, we couldn't find it. We drilled exploratory holes everywhere but still we couldn't find the ore body. Days passed, until one day we were sitting around, sort of in a state of apathy, and it started to rain hard, a heavy tropical storm. I went under one of the houses nearby—they were all up on stilts—to get out of the rain. While I sat there, I picked around with my geologist's hammer and heard the characteristic sound of quartz. I knocked off some samples and took them in to be assayed. They looked pretty good, so I went to the superintendent to tell him that this might be the continuation of the ore body. At first, he laughed at me. Finally I talked him into taking a few minutes to go with me to look at it. When he saw it, he couldn't believe it. There was the ore body, right under the workers' village! The next day we took down all the houses and reassembled them across the river. From then on, we mined there with an open-pit mine and just bulldozed the ore. Of course, after that discovery, my stock went up. They recognized me and gave me a raise. That occurred just before the war began.

CHAPTER 4

卌 卌 卌

INSULAR PATROL

GARTH: While we were stuck there in the church, I had a lot of time to think. At first we all speculated about how soon it would be before the navy came back in there with guns blazing to rescue us. Most of us thought it would take three months at most. As the days dragged by and the Japanese kept bragging about their victories, we began to wonder. I remember a couple of nights when I laid on my back on my bed on the floor, stared at the roof of the church, and thought back over all the things that had led me to come to Guam in the first place.

Despite being held back one semester for my problems in elementary school, I'd made it through junior high and into high school. I guess you could say I was a rowdy. Being the oldest, I was the biggest of the brothers, but later they outgrew me. All the boys in our family were real close, so we stuck together and looked out for each other. Once someone picked on our youngest brother, Donovan, when the three of us were at Roosevelt Junior High. James, my middle brother, went to the bottom gate at the school and I stayed at the top gate, waiting for this guy to show up in the morning. After a while, I saw a bunch of guys at the lower gate, but by the time I got there, James had found the guy and knocked him cold.

When I was in high school, I mowed lawns, or delivered or sold papers to earn spending money. I always had money sitting around, which I kept in a jar in my room. One day one of the neighborhood kids was at the house—he just lived a block away—and he stole the money. I'd saved it all year so I could go to Balboa at Easter Week with my buddies. We asked around the neighborhood, and someone finally told us that he'd stolen it. I went looking for him, finally caught up with him, and we had a little battle right out on the street. He was bigger than me, but a year younger. Anyway, I got thrown in the clink.

You see, everybody knew me. When Dad came home he had to go downtown and get me out of jail. All he had to do was vouch for me. They wouldn't let me out on my own because when the cop asked me if I'd leave the kid alone, I told them, "Hell no, I'm not going to leave him alone. I'm going to beat the shit out of him until I get my money back!" So they held me until my old man got there. It's fair to say that I was an ornery little bastard.

I was also pretty resourceful. During my last year in junior high school, ninth grade, I had a paper route. A neighbor had an old Model-T Ford coupe with a flat tire, parked in front of his house. I asked him how much he wanted for it and he said $3. I got the money from my Dad and promised him to pay it off by mowing lawns at 10 and 15 cents and selling newspapers, where I made maybe $2.50 on a Saturday night and $2 on a Sunday morning. I went to a junkyard, got a tube for 50 cents, put it in the tire, and that was my first car. I had to have a special permit to drive since I was only fifteen. I got it on the basis that I had to have the car for my paper route.

I enjoyed playing football in high school—even though I was third or fourth string quarterback and too small to be really good. But I liked to get in and mix it up, knock heads a little. During the summers of '38 and '39, the football coach wanted us to get a manual labor job. My brother and I worked up on the desert at Little Rock, California, either in the packing sheds or out in the fields picking pears or peaches at a place called Wheelock Orchards. Pay was 4 cents a field box. Our goal was a hundred boxes a day—that is, if we were lucky enough to get "choicy" trees. These were small ones, loaded with fruit, short enough that you didn't have to use a ladder to pick them. We slept out alongside an irrigation ditch on a canvas cot, took baths in the ditch, and earned some extra money. Times must have been tough for my old man. I had to mail the money back to him, and he used it for the family.

Overall, we were good kids, although we got out and raised a little hell now and then. My brothers and I liked the outdoors. We'd go fishing once in a while with the old man, and other times we had groups that would go out to the desert—say over Christmas vacation—and we'd camp out. We'd hike around, shoot jackrabbits, and then roll out our sleeping bags on the ground and sleep out under the stars. If we were lucky, somebody would have snitched some bourbon from their old man's supply. We'd sit around a campfire and have a belt or two.

As it turned out, because of my problem in elementary school, I didn't gradu-ate from high school in the summer of 1939 as I should have, but got out in the winter of 1940 instead. After graduating, I got a job and started saving my money to go to college. My brother James had a full scholarship to play college football in the fall of 1940; he was a half year behind me in school and graduated in the summer of 1940. I had a partial scholarship and intended to go along. There was no way I was headed for the military—I knew I wasn't cut out for it.

Dad had joined the army near the end of World War I, when he was finally old enough to enlist. But he never went overseas because the war ended. Still, he was in favor of the service. He used to tell us that he thought war was coming, but he preferred that my brother and I get into officer training somewhere, so we'd be better prepared. I never followed up on that idea.

Anyway, one warm day in June 1940, when we were sitting around the house in the evening drinking ice tea, James came home and to everybody's surprise announced that he wanted to join the marines. One of his buddies had talked him into enlisting.

Naturally, we had a big family discussion about this, the kind that any family would have, and then it died for a while. A few more weeks passed, and he brought it up again, and then later, again. One night we had the usual family argument, except this time it had an air of finality. James said he was going to enlist the next morning and he hoped my parents would understand. We all sat around quietly for a while, and then my mom offered the opinion that if James was going to join, then I should also. She'd rather see both of us go than one go alone, so we could look after each other. I never forgot that—it surprised the hell out of me to hear her say that.

I said, "Heck no, I'm not going. I don't want to be a marine"—and I went to bed.

The next morning James woke me up to say good-bye. When he came into the bedroom, like a fool I jumped out of bed. "Oh hell," I said, "wait a minute. I might as well go with you."

So three of us—my brother and I and another friend of ours—all joined at once. The friend's father drove us down to Los Angeles to sign up. When we got to boot camp in San Diego and walked through that gate, I looked around, then turned to them and said, "Hey man, we're in jail!"

In retrospect, in spite of the hard times we had, we were lucky as hell. My brother was in every major battle that the marines had, except Okinawa and Iwo Jima—and he didn't mind missing out on those two. He got shot twice and still carries one bullet in his chest. As for me, I was only in one battle—the first battle for Guam, if you could call that a battle. Of the original squad that left boot camp in 1940, only nine, including my brother, made it back. Unfortunately, the other guy who enlisted with us didn't return. He was killed by a grenade on Okinawa.

We did our basic training in San Diego in July and August of 1940, and joined the Fleet Marine Force. We were put in the Eighth Marines, as riflemen and scouts with Browning automatic rifles. This group later became part of the Second Marine Division.

We kept volunteering for every overseas opening. Finally, I got the word that I was on the list to go to Guam, along with two other guys I knew, Al Legato and Hollis Smalling, but my brother wasn't selected, so there went our mother's plan that we'd look out for each other.

In February 1941, we boarded the USS *Henderson* for the thirty-one–day trip to Guam. Ostensibly, we were relieving another group that had taken a beating from a typhoon that had hit the island. We stopped over in Hawaii for five days, and then had another stopover at Wake Island, where we unloaded some of the guys. Oh, it was fun—cruising the Pacific, not a worry in the world! We reached Guam in March 1941, where Hollis and I eventually were assigned duties to the Insular Patrol.

Before the war, Guam was known as the "Gem of the Pacific." Life there was delightful. The island was nearly self-sustaining: there was fresh water; fruits, vegetables, and meat were raised locally. The native population, the Chamorros, were a friendly, happy people, many of whom had married Americans. Some of the Americans who'd intermarried stayed on the island; others took their wives to the States.

The island had spectacular bays, lagoons sheltered by the reef, white sandy beaches almost devoid of people except for an occasional fisherman throwing his net. There were bright-hued tropical flowers—poinciana, hibiscus, bougainvillea, croton, shower trees, coral trees—blooming in a blaze of reds, oranges, and yellows. Elsewhere, there were the palms, Norfolk Island pines, bananas, tall dark mango trees, and in the center of the island, the dense tropical jungle.

Guam had no malaria, no dengue fever, no venereal disease—none of the diseases that soldiers experienced in the Philippines. The only thing the natives had was yaws—a disease resembling syphilis. Sometimes you'd see them with ulcers all over their bodies.

Actually, it's not correct to say there was no venereal disease at all on Guam. Occasional cases would crop up, transported to Guam by the navy. Sailors would bring it from the Philippines on the supply ship *Goldstar*. The prostitutes were jokingly called "Monday Ladies" since they had to have an examination every Monday. If an infection showed up, right away the woman was "jailed" until she was cured. Actually, the women were treated in the naval hospital daily and returned to their cell. As patrolmen, we'd see them there, and when we were checking out to go on patrol we'd talk to them. Once they knew they were cured and were due to be released they'd hang around in the doorway and talk to us.

"Hi honey, you working hard? Say, I'm getting out in a couple of days. How'd you like to make a date to try my Guam cherry?"

In those prewar days, Agana was a small sleepy town, not too different from a small village in, say, Mexico or maybe the Philippines. The center of the city was the plaza—Plaza de Espana, which was six or eight blocks inland from the sea. On the east side of the plaza was the main Catholic church on the island, the Dulce Nombre de Maria Cathedral. The Governor's Palace and the post office were on the south side, while the Insular Patrol's headquarters was a block or so away on the west side. The jail was across the plaza from the Governor's Palace, on the north side. Not far from the jail was the Service Club, while east of the plaza were the stores, soda fountain, and the bars—in a barrio known as San Nicolas. This area, with the plaza, constituted "Beat One" for the patrol, while the western half of Agana was called "Beat Two."

The patrolmen worked shifts—6 a.m. to 12 noon, 12 noon to 6 p.m., then 6 p.m. to midnight, and so on. So if you had an afternoon or late shift, after you got off work, you'd sleep till about noon, have some lunch, and go to the Service Club or to one of the bars in town. They were just junk bars, like you could imagine in a tropical island where there wasn't much going on. There was one that had a cocktail waitress, heavy set, ugly as hell, whom we called "Chong." I don't know what her real name was. We'd meet there after work, or before work, to have a couple of drinks. There was hardly any ice on the island, but the local bars had some. You drank your drinks warm. If you were nice, you could ask Chong for ice, and she'd bring it to you. If you weren't nice, she was deadly with an ice pick. She could throw it clear across the room, and stick it right in your table. Guys would swear at her and run out the door, and she'd throw that ice pick from across the room so it would stick in the wall two inches from their heads as they dashed out the door.

Normally things were pretty quiet for us patrolmen. One little bit of excitement occurred when a merchant ship anchored out in the harbor. It had one of its crew in the brig, a guy who'd killed another crew member while the ship was at sea. Somehow he got loose, got off the ship, came ashore, and was running around Agana. We'd been alerted that he was on the island. I was walking my beat one night when I saw someone standing back in the shadows on a dark street after curfew. "What are you doing there?" I asked.

At that point he hesitated for a moment and then started to come for me. I reacted instinctively, just whammed it to him. I got my .45 out of the holster, out in front of me, and aimed at his face—I was quick with that pistol. Once he saw it, he backed off, didn't argue, but went along quietly back to the jail with me.

It turned out he was the escaped killer. I got a commendation from Captain Charles S. Todd, head of the Insular Patrol, for doing my duty that time.

There was another time when I almost shot a guy, although I'm ashamed to say so. For a while, I wanted to get off of that goddam island. If you shot someone, they court-martialed you and fined you a dollar for the bullet. That way, you couldn't be tried again. Then you got your choice of staying on Guam, or hopefully, going back to the United States.

I was down by the canal one night and ran into one of the natives who was a Peeping Tom. We were always on the lookout for "serious crimes" like that. Anyway, I caught this guy peeping into a window. At first I thought he was trying to break in, so I put the pistol on him. "Come on," I said, "I'm taking you to jail!" At that moment he ran like hell.

I didn't have a shell in the chamber, so I tried to slide one in as I was running after him, yelling at him to stop. I damn near took my little finger off on those serrations on the .45. It was greasy and my hand slipped as I was running. I finally caught up with him, and for a moment I almost shot him, just so I'd get sent home. That's how bad I wanted off the island.

At one point I was assigned to be the Insular Patrol orderly in the Governor's Palace, which was a long, two-story, white building that had an upstairs balcony. The palace looked out on the plaza where there was a gazebo, or small bandstand, called the kiosk.

In the palace you had to wear military khaki, and I mean with military pressed creases, shined shoes, everything spit and polish. There was a fan right in front of you and a podium by the wall where you stood. I was an orderly for the navy officer—Captain McMillin—who served as governor of the island.

When the governor came downstairs, the orderly was supposed to have his car brought up for him, open the door, and help him get in. When he returned, the orderly would do the same thing. The orderly was there to keep anybody from going upstairs and also to do anything else the governor needed.

Well, part of the Marine Corps rules stipulate that you don't read on watch. One day I lifted up the top of the podium and there was a copy of *Our Navy* magazine. I pulled it out, looked around, and figured there was nobody around because the governor had just gone upstairs. I started reading a couple of articles. I guess I was concentrating, because suddenly behind me I heard a voice. "Are you reading on watch, sentry?" I turned around and there was the governor.

I said, "Yes sir, I'm reading *Our Navy* magazine."

"I don't care what you are reading. Call up your captain and tell him you are reading on watch and relieve yourself immediately."

So I swallowed hard and called the assistant chief. The assistant called Captain Todd, and they had me relieved immediately. I knew I was in big trouble. Before long they put me up for summary court-martial. But because of the commendation I'd received earlier for capturing the escaped killer, the captain got me out of it. Then they sent me to Barrigada, the outstation close to town—the assistant chief's old station where he had married one of the native girls. This was his second tour on Guam. I think the assistant chief had it in for me because of an earlier incident where I'd accidentally bucked one of his buddies. This story went back to how I got on the Insular Patrol in the first place.

I'd scored "expert" with the rifle in boot camp, and then on the transport ship coming over I'd passed the Pfc. test No.1, so Lieutenant M. A. Marks told me I had my choice of duties once we got to Guam. I told him I was interested in joining the Insular Patrol.

The problem arose when Gus, an old Greek gunnery sergeant, favored a young Greek private named J. D. Mucciacciaro, whom he wanted to send to the Insular Patrol rather than me. When he did that, there were no more vacancies. So I went to the lieutenant with my seabag and told him that it looked like the patrol was out for me. "Absolutely not," he said. "If you want the patrol, you got it."

"But lieutenant, somebody else is already on the truck."

"Come with me," he said.

The lieutenant told the sergeant to pull the other guy off the truck. Off he went, and on I went, but the sergeant let it be known that he wasn't happy with the decision. I'd gotten myself in a situation where a recruit was going against a thirty-year Marine Corps gunnery sergeant. I didn't mean to cause trouble, but you can imagine what happened. I'm sure he called the assistant chief in Agana, who'd been a patrolman at Barrigada years ago, and told him, "Fix this smartass." That was probably the beginning of my problems.

This assistant chief had a Chamorro assistant chief, who was his buddy there at Barrigada. The system was that a native cop would go around with an American in each area. Several nights a week this assistant chief would come out there at midnight to visit with his pal. They'd get into my kitchen and cook up some food for themselves. After eating, they'd take off and leave all the dirty dishes behind for me to clean up. In the process, they also woke me up when they had one of their little dinner parties. One night, after he'd done this a few times, I waited up for him. I told him, "Sarge, I'm not your goddam houseboy. If you keep coming out here in the middle of the night, you might startle me sometime, and when I wake up I might accidentally shoot you."

It wasn't long after that—a couple of nights or so—that he decided to come again. This time when the noise of them banging around outside woke me up, I pulled out my .45 and shot a couple of holes in the roof. They left real quick and I went back to sleep. Of course, the next morning he was there with the paddy wagon. He said, "Come on, I'm taking you in to jail."

I said, "What the hell for?"

"Destroying government property."

I had to go in and they had me up for another summary court-martial. Fortunately, Captain Todd saved my ass again and got me out of that problem. He sent me out to Inarajan, to one of the patrol stations all the way at the other end of the island, about as far away from Agana as you could get. He told me, "This is your last chance. Don't get in trouble again."

Inarajan was a small village with a few dozen houses, a slaughterhouse, a couple of small stores and bars, and St. Joseph's church. My house was at the outskirts of town, on the north side, the opposite side from the church. We were a few hundred yards from Inarajan Bay and the mouth of the river. At the out-station I was judge and jury, the law for the local people. There were two of us— myself and a navy corpsman (Pharmacist's Mate R. D. Harrod) who was supposed to be the local doctor and provide medical assistance to the villagers. We patrolled all the backcountry. Usually it was pretty quiet, not much going on, and people were nice.

In the fall of 1941, we were told to be aware of any aircraft in the vicinity. We knew Japan had a big military base on Saipan, which was about 120 miles from Guam. Rota was another nearby island—about 30 miles away—which was Japanese. On a clear day you could see Rota from Guam with the naked eye. We knew there was tension, but none of us dreamed that Japan would attack the United States. That was beyond imagining, or so we thought!

CHAPTER 5

卌 卌 卌

YOKOHAMA BANK

MITZI: As it turned out, the war gave me lots of time to think about things, since I joined more than 100,000 other Japanese Americans who were imprisoned by their government. Just a few years before the war, it would have seemed unimaginable to me that such a thing could happen.

My life changed one night, after work on the ranch was done and the dinner dishes were cleared away. Mother sat with Dorothy and me in the living room. "I've been thinking," she said. "There's no future for you girls here on the ranch. I think you should each make plans to go back to school and learn something about business, so you can get a job and make a future for yourselves. That will also make it possible for you to help us here, but in other ways."

At first, we didn't know what to say. At that time, it was not the custom for Japanese girls to leave their families and start careers. Was this really our mother speaking? "But mother, how can we go to school—where will we get the money? And how will you and father manage here at the ranch?"

"Mitzi—this is the United States and you are twenty-one years old. You are a citizen here, and you can vote. Of course, it is the proper thing for you to do. You have some money, you can get a job with a family and work for room and board, so you can live near school. As for your father and me, we'll be perfectly fine. Your sisters are getting old enough now. They can do more of the chores."

So, in the fall of 1939 I enrolled at the Willis Business College in Santa Monica, where I took classes in stenography, bookkeeping, typing, shorthand, and use of office equipment. Dorothy went to a business school in Westwood. Through a mutual friend in Westwood, my mother had became friends with a lady named Phyllis Jones in Malibu. I had worked part-time for Mrs. Jones, helping take care of her mother. They had a big two-story house. I clearly remember her son, a nice boy, a regular boy—his room always a mess, radio blasting away, the bathroom dripping water everywhere after he took a shower. They were wonderful people, and Mrs. Jones was one of the two or three people besides my mother who had the greatest influence on my life. It was through her help that Dorothy found a family to live with in Westwood and I got a job with a family in Santa Monica, so I could live there while I went to school.

In Santa Monica I took care of an eight-year-old girl in exchange for room and board. This kid was dynamite, a real bundle of energy. Her parents were older—her mother had a twenty-five-year-old son by a previous marriage, and perhaps the daughter felt neglected. She was mischievous to get attention and kept me busy when I wasn't studying. One of her tricks was to soil her panties and then toss them in the closet for me to find and clean up later. At one point she got sick with tonsillitis and cried and cried, poor thing.

In spite of the other demands on my time, I enjoyed school. I worked hard, but it was fun and I felt that I was accomplishing something for myself. Almost a year flashed by. In eleven months, I completed the course of study prescribed by the college, received my diploma, and began to search for a job. I mailed out twenty letters with my resume. Unfortunately, no one seemed interested in my qualifications, and my efforts to get a job led to refusal after refusal. For the first time, I experienced personally the effects of racial prejudice. Maybe the whole idea was wrong: I'd be better off staying on the farm! Of course, I would never admit that, but there were times when I wondered.

Then one day, I received a telephone call from a woman at the Yokohama Bank. They had received my letter; and could I come in for an interview? I was nervous as I filled out an application and some other papers required by the bank. I was to have an interview with Mr. Hatori, the bank manager. He asked me a few questions after looking once again at my resume. He seemed to like me immediately and spent most of the interview asking me about my family and what they did in California. Then he told me that I would hear from them in a few days. Outside the bank, my mother and brother waited in the car. "Well, how was it?" mother asked. "Did you get the job?"

"I don't know," I replied. "I hope so. They're nice people, and I think they liked me, but we'll have to wait and see."

One day dragged by, and then another. Everyone in the family waited to hear the outcome. In the meantime, another rejection arrived from one of my earlier letters. At this point I'd nearly given up hope that anyone would hire me. What if my new education, so hard earned and costly, should prove to be of no use? How could I go back to the farm at this point?

Then, on the third day, I received a letter from the bank. My mother and sister stood by as I ripped open the envelope. "Oh mother," I shouted. "They want me! I got the job!"

Mother was overjoyed. At last a job, and a job that was different from farming! "Mitzi, this is wonderful news for you, and an honor for our family. The Yokohama Bank is an old, long-established institution with a good reputation. You're fortunate to get such a fine position. Now, the whole world will open up to you. You are no longer just a farm girl!"

Everybody was excited, and mother gave me a big hug. Mother had a tremendous impact on my life. She encouraged me to try new things, and without her support, I would have never dared to continue my education. She gave me dreams. Phyllis Jones was my advisor and confidant. She helped make the dreams come true.

At the bank, I had a ninety-day probationary period before I was accepted as a regular employee. During that time I worked hard, trying to master all the new tasks. One day, one of Mr. Hatori's assistants took me aside. "Miss Takahashi, the Americans tell me that you speak perfect English. But your Japanese, well, if I may be blunt, you speak the Japanese of a farm girl, not a banker. There is an excellent Japanese language teacher here in Los Angeles whom I highly recommend. Since many of the bank's dealings are with Japanese businessmen, it would be useful if you would take some classes to improve your Japanese."

At first, I was shocked. I didn't speak good Japanese—what could they be saying? But I said nothing about this to anyone at the bank. Instead, I bowed and said, "Thank you so much for the advice. I am grateful for the opportunity to work here and want to do anything necessary to make myself more useful. I would be most happy to take classes and improve my Japanese; this is something I have always wanted to do, but have not had time for yet. With this job, I will now be able to do it."

Other arrangements had to be made. The long commute to Malibu made living at home impractical. An acquaintance of my mother operated a hotel on Wall Street in downtown Los Angeles. This friend allowed me to work at the hotel in exchange for my room. So, before many weeks had passed at the bank, I found myself with two jobs and language classes at night. Each night after work I would rush back to my room for a quick dinner. Then I'd take the bus across town to the Zenshuji Buddhist Church where Reverend Yamashita taught Japanese. I attended classes every night, six days a week, from 6 p.m. to 9:30 p.m.

The hotel was an old, dilapidated, dirty place, three stories high. The owner was a short, fat man who lived there with his mistress. I had a little two-by-two room with a bed in one corner and a sink in the other. Each morning before I went to the bank, I worked in the kitchen, and then came home at night after my class and did other chores.

The first few months at the bank were extremely hectic—trying to learn new procedures, terminology, details of the banking business. Besides serving as secretary to the manager, I also spent time as receptionist and switchboard operator and assisted the woman who operated the teletype. The teletype was a busy job, since many of the instructions for the bank's transactions were handled by teletype. Also, business was booming in spite of the tension with Japan.

I made friends with a number of people: there was Mr. Yamaguma, a teller who worked in the cage; Miss Yamamato, one of the clerks; the Caucasian lady who operated the teletype; and Rosie Ishi, whom I worked with part of the time. We would meet upstairs in the lunchroom and chat over lunch or sometimes go to the movies together.

I also developed friendships with two other men at the bank. Of course, my social life was limited, because according to our upbringing we could not go on dates or go dancing without a chaperone. This was further complicated because the bank had policies against any dating between employees. Our get-togethers were therefore limited to company dinners or other events where the entire staff was present. One of the men liked me, but I was not really too interested in him. The second one—Mr. Kiyoshi Umekawa—was more interesting. He had a responsible position, was well educated with a degree from Tokyo University, and was a real lady's man. He was eleven years older, but came from the same prefecture in Japan as my parents. My mother liked him—she thought he'd be a good catch for me, if she could just make the arrangements!

By the summer, we were aware of an increase in activity at the bank. Before long, the women in the bank were working twelve hours, from 8 a.m. to 8 p.m., the men as late as 2 or 3 a.m. On July 26, 1941, President Roosevelt issued the order for an embargo on oil and rubber to Japan (iron and steel had been embargoed previously). In addition, another executive order froze all Japanese and Chinese assets in the United States. Even more activity now occurred, as the bank issued affidavits and other legal documents in connection with the frozen assets. In spite of the ominous signs, business was still brisk.

That summer my mother planned to return to Japan for a visit, her first in several years. At the last minute, the voyage was canceled. From that date on, no more ships would leave for Japan until after the war, unless they carried guns or soldiers.

CHAPTER 6

卌 卌 卌

ARGENTINA MARU

GARTH: We spent New Year's in the Catholic church, wondering what would happen to us, trying to figure out what was happening in the war, trying to sift the truth from the rumors that flew about. We knew that the Japanese had rounded up all the Americans, including priests, and were holding them in another building. Some sailors had fled to the center of the island and were still at large, but their prospects for remaining at liberty were not great since the Japanese announced severe penalties for any Chamorros harboring the fugitives.[23]

Shortly after New Year's, we were lined up outside the church and made to watch a Japanese military parade and inspection—as much to impress the civilian population as us, I suppose. The Japanese unlimbered some World War I–style field pieces and proceeded to blast away at a wooden barge anchored in the bay. They destroyed the target and it sank. Then they marched us back into the church and locked us up.

Another week passed, and then early one morning, before sunup, we were rousted out of the church, lined up, and made to march eight or ten miles down to the wharf at the Piti Navy Yard. The smell of sea and salt blew over our crowded column, momentarily cleansing the air of the rank odor of the filthy captives. The harbor was chock-full of ships, both gray warships as well as nondescript rust buckets. I had the impression that the Japanese had commandeered every boat in the Inland Sea to put together this invasion fleet, and now it was all here, anchored in or off of Apra Harbor. I couldn't help thinking grimly to myself: thousands of Japanese to take on a few hundred marines and sailors.

The marines around me spoke in quiet tones, wondering where we were being taken, what kind of ship it would be. At the moment, anything was better than being cooped up in that goddam church for days on end, staring down the ever-present Japanese bayonets. The column stopped abruptly, and I pitched into the man in front of me, a burly sailor who had swum ashore when the *Penguin* went down in December. "Jesus, you stink," I said.

"You ain't no rose yourself."

"Where in the hell do you think they're taking us?"

"Shit if I know. They're probably going to load us on one of those rust buckets, tow us out to sea, and use it for gunnery practice."

"Hell, they don't need no practice. They won't waste the ammo. They'll just scuttle the sonofabitch."

"Naw, seriously, we're gonna get an all-expense-paid vacation to the Empire of the Rising Sun. I just hope we ain't got no submarines between here and wherever we're going."

As we approached the wharf, I suddenly caught sight of a different ship. Contrasting starkly to the nondescript merchant ships and naval vessels, this one had the appearance of a cruise ship. I turned again to the sailor next to me: "They must know we're marines. They wouldn't have brought that baby for a bunch of sailors, now, would they?"

"Hell, they ain't putting us on that."

Our column edged up to a loading ramp extending from the side of the ship. From my position in the line I couldn't see what was happening, but I could sense some reduction in the pressure of humanity around me. I heard shouted commands in Japanese. Then I could see the prisoners filing on board the ship. Slowly the line of prisoners walked up to the top deck. The presence of grim-faced soldiers, with fixed bayonets, seemed strangely incongruous with the polished teak walls and the shiny brass rails. A lifeboat revealed the ship's name: *Argentina Maru*. Obviously, it had recently been involved in a very different type of service!

We were marched to the top deck, around one side, through the first-class cabin area, then down another set of stairs, through the second class, then farther down, to the third level. I heard subdued laughter, some jokes, and chatter from the prisoners behind me in the line. "Not bad," someone said.

"Hell, those guys are crazy," I said to the sailor behind me. "This isn't going to be any luxury cruise. We're going to end up in the bilge on this tub, you wait and see."

True to my prediction, we descended lower and lower into the bowels of the ship. Finally, we couldn't go any lower. The hold was dark, dank, and warm. The heat settled over the crowded men like an oppressive blanket. Above us, we could hear hatches closing and doors locking. The men, crowded together in the hold, shifted slightly, trying to make room in the semidarkness, trying to find a dry spot out of the dank bilge water. I leaned against the bulkhead, still next to the sailor I'd talked to on the march. "So much for the luxury cruise. Here we are, stuffed in like a bunch of rats. I suppose the first-class cabins will be used to bring the next contingent of troops over to Guam. I hope to shit they travel in comfort, because it will be their last ride."

"Hey man, you better hope this bucket gets wherever it's going in one piece. If one of our subs is waiting out there and puts a tin fish into the middle of this tub, we'll all be shark bait."

Little by little, silence descended over the hold. The ship rocked at anchor. There was subdued grumbling, punctuated by crashes and thumps overhead as the ship made ready to go. In one corner of the hold, someone got sick and started retching. Men scrambled around, trying to find something, anything, to serve as toilet facilities. Eventually a couple of buckets were produced. In the still air of the hold, the heat and smell increased in intensity. I maintained my position against the bulkhead, but settled to the floor and waited. It was January 10, 1942, exactly one month to the day since our capture, and three months short of my twenty-first birthday.

After a couple of days at sea, the *Argentina Maru* lost all resemblance to a cruise ship for the prisoners. Many were sick, all of us were hungry and hated the putrid smell of the bilge, now contaminated with our own excreta from the overflowing slop cans. In spite of the hardships, a certain ragged discipline prevailed. Mostly, individual groups hung together, marines with marines, sailors with sailors.

The Japanese had rigged some improvised wooden shelves in the hold for bunks. Some men slept on these, others on the metal decking. L. D., my friend from the Catholic cathedral, and I found a spot on the metal deck, and put our bedding there. We passed the time talking about home—L. D. described his boyhood in Alabama, and I told him stories about growing up in California. Invariably the discussion swung around to one topic: what we planned to do when the war was over. Our plans centered around the girls we planned to take out and the food we would eat—hamburgers, malted milks, big thick steaks, and any good old American food. After a while, these conversations were discontinued. The thoughts were too painful to endure, laying there awake on the rough steel deck, the continual rocking of the ship, the endless churning emptiness of our shrunken stomachs.

Once a day we were marched on deck for exercising. Rumors circulated about trying to take over the ship. I discounted these stories. One look at the armed Japanese told me that an attempt would be suicidal and those who participated would be bayoneted and dumped over the side.

Each day it got a little colder in the hold. Most of the men were wearing their light tropical khakis. One afternoon the Japanese opened the hatch and dumped winter clothing down into the hold for the prisoners. In the ensuing scramble, I grabbed a wool overcoat and a navy pullover shirt. Obviously, the ship was moving north. But to where?

The daily routine was unchanging. At dawn the restless prisoners would begin to stir, try to stretch to relieve their cramped muscles. At noon the guards would appear with buckets of rice to feed us. Some of us had mess kits; others had only their hands. At first, the more squeamish recoiled at eating the rice when someone detected weevils or some type of worms among the grains. These qualms quickly passed, however, as hunger set in. We ate it—worms and all, scrambling like animals for any remnants. At night, silence crept through the hold as the grumbling of the prisoners gave way to muted conversations, snoring, an occasional argument or scuffle.

The third night out, I was awakened by a rumbling noise. The entire ship trembled. The engines quieted momentarily, and we realized that the huge vessel had come to a dead stop. "Hey, L. D., wake up," I said, shaking the inert body next to me. "Wake up, man, something's happening."

He turned over, sat up, looked around sleepily. At that moment the engines roared to life. We could feel the ship reversing. A moment later, it stopped again, and then surged forward. In the darkness, we could see that other prisoners were also sitting up. A sailor got to his feet, hands on the bulkhead. "Shit oh dear," he said. "Sounds like evasive maneuvers trying to duck a submarine. Maybe they saw a torpedo."

"Hell man, the navy wouldn't sink a ship with American prisoners on it, would they? Surely they know we're on this tub."

He stopped speaking midsentence, as the ship turned violently to the port side, causing everyone to grab for support to keep from falling down. Silence descended over the hold, as the ship shook to the sound of the throbbing engines. Another two or three minutes dragged by, and then there was another violent maneuver, this time to the starboard side. Then there was more rumbling and vibration as the engines reversed again.

These maneuvers were repeated several times as the minutes crept by. Then the ship steadied on a forward course and the sounds and movements became routine once again. The prisoners slowly settled down and waited for morning. We knew that if the ship was torpedoed, the torpedo would most likely explode among us, below the waterline. We also knew that none of us would escape from the locked hold if the ship sank.

After five days, the motion of the ship stopped, and the banging and clanking sounds associated with anchoring could be heard. Several hours passed before sentries threw open the doors to the hold. With shouts and arm movements, they told us to leave the hold. We had no idea what awaited us above. As we filed out into the early evening, we were marched to the side of the ship and instructed to scramble down nets into a waiting barge. As we descended onto the barge, it began to tilt dangerously in one direction. Finally one of the officers gave a command to divide ranks, and half of the prisoners moved to the other side, righting the flat-bottomed boat.

Once on shore, we were lined up under bright lights at the dock. Guards pushed or prodded with rifle butts to form up in lines. We were tired, hungry, and cold. Many were shivering, in spite of wearing an extra shirt or sweater. In the darkness we were marched to a railroad station, and loaded onto a train. Along the way, civilians screamed insults at us, spit in our direction, or hurled rocks and trash at our heads.

After a brief train ride, we were again lined up, counted, and told to march forward. We proceeded a short distance through narrow, dark streets, finally passing through a gate into a fenced area. Sentries stood at attention as we filed in and were directed to several dark, wooden buildings. As we entered, I looked around trying to decide where we were. The building resembled a barn. The fact that we'd walked in on a ramp, rather than stairs, seemed to confirm that it was a stable. Once inside, no one spoke. I saw and heard silent gray shadows—rats, whose quiet home we'd abruptly disturbed—as they scurried into hiding places. A bitter cold breeze made rasping noises through cracks in the thin wood siding. Once inside, the men sat down, laid down, or collapsed on the cold wooden floor. There was a single light bulb in the drafty wooden building, and no heat. There were no beds and no blankets. We'd had no rations in at least twelve hours, although I no longer knew what time it was. After the last man entered, the door was slammed shut and bolted. The chill night air settled in on the exhausted prisoners.

We huddled together on the hard floor, trying to extract heat from each other and the overcoats and jackets a lucky few possessed. Most of us were so cold we scarcely noticed the fleas and lice that quickly invaded our clothes.

It was January 15, 1942, and this was Zentsuji, the island of Shikoku, Japan. For many of us, this was the beginning of nearly four years of deprivation and hard labor as "Guests of the Emperor." For some—nearly one-third of those taken prisoner by the Japanese—this was the end of the line. They'd remain in Japan, unless their ashes happened to make the return trip home.[24]

JHT JHT JHT

In April 1986, I decided to stop off in Guam on my way back from Japan and see what I could learn about the island and the places Garth had told me about. I knew the island had been heavily damaged when it was retaken by the Americans, so I wasn't sure what I might find. Shortly after I checked into the Agana Hilton hotel, a bellboy approached me and asked, "Are you going to the ceremony?" Not knowing what he was talking about, I said no. Then I learned that there was a ceremony planned in the Talofofo area that would be attended by Shoichi Yokoi, a former Japanese straggler who had been captured in 1972— twenty-seven years after the end of the war. Suddenly my interest was piqued. Could Yokoi have known Masashi Itoh, the straggler whose diary I had found just a month before in the National Archives? I went to the hotel desk and asked how I could go to the "ceremony."

"Sorry, sir, you are too late," the clerk replied. "The bus has already left." Too bad, I thought, but on an impulse I asked for directions. I found a taxi driver willing to take me there—it was half-way around the island—for $50. I figured that I could hitch a ride back on the bus, and anyway, I'd come to Guam to see the island, and this was a good place to start.

The ceremony was to dedicate a new park by the waterfall on the Talofofo River. Yokoi was the guest of honor at the dedication. It was here that he'd hidden in a hole concealed in a dense grove of bamboo. The entrance was covered with a camouflaged trapdoor made of bamboo. A replica of Yokoi's hideout had been constructed in the park by the two men who had caught him. After looking at the hideout, I spoke with Yokoi and asked him if he'd known the straggler Masashi Itoh. He said the name sounded familiar, but didn't offer any details. I sensed that either he did not know him or was reluctant to talk about him.

After returning from Talofofo, I had dinner with Don Farrell, at that time the public relations officer for the Guam legislature. I'd sought out Don because he'd written a book about the American liberation of Guam. I'd told Don about my interest in prisoners of war and he graciously agreed to help me find answers to some of my questions. We had a pleasant dinner together—Don, his lovely wife Carmen, and I—during which he gave me dozens of names and phone numbers.

Don told me that Jim Butler was still alive and involved in the Butler family business. His brother Ben Butler had brought food and supplies to Garth when he was imprisoned in the cathedral. He provided introductions to Tony Palomo, who was a young boy during the Japanese occupation, and also to Pedro Sanchez, a local historian. Don also knew of the Shimizu family, mentioned in Itoh's diary. After finding Itoh's diary and meeting Yokoi, I was also interested in information about other stragglers and details of the Japanese invasion and American return to the island. Don also suggested a friend who could drive me to the historic spots I wanted to visit.

The next day Vincent "Ben" M. DeLaCruz took me around Guam to visit the Guam museum and the Plaza de Espana. In the museum there were a number of historical photographs, including one of a Japanese sentry. A display told the story of Father Jesus Baza Dueñas, a Catholic priest who stuck up for the population during the occupation. On July 2, 1944 he was ordered to appear before the Japanese authorities to answer questions about George Tweed, the American radioman who had escaped the Japanese occupation and was suspected of being sheltered by Chamorro families. Dueñas and his nephew were interrogated and tortured, and before dawn on July 3, 1944, beheaded.

I made a sketch of the Plaza de Espana, which borders the museum. Some of the original walls were built in 1736. The Governor's Palace and the cathedral were destroyed during the war but have been rebuilt. The old photos showed the location of the palace; the Azotea, a covered veranda attached to one end of the palace; and another structure called the "Chocolate House." Standing in the plaza, I tried to imagine early December 1941 and the marines taking up defensive positions and their anxiety as they awaited the approaching Japanese troops.

We drove in a counterclockwise direction around the island, first to the naval station at Sumay, where I saw the site of the old marine barracks (now navy housing) marked by a monument. Then we headed to Fort Santiago (viewpoint on Orote Point), and down to the old Orote airfield, and the new marine barracks, the naval yard, and wharves. At Orote Point I stopped to look at the rocky shore and a pretty little cove with clear water. Beyond it was Pacific Ocean, where once the American armada had dropped anchor.

We then drove south along Agat Bay to see remains of the Japanese fortifications and field guns and visit a war memorial and pillboxes. Numerous caves lined the shoreline facing the beach, hiding spots for the Japanese waiting for the Americans to land. Here the roles were reversed: I tried to imagine the feelings of the Japanese defenders who sat hidden in these shelters, staring out to sea at the immense flotilla of American naval vessels, awaiting the onslaught they knew was about to happen.

Next, we drove to the village of Inarajan, passing first through Merizo and then Agfayan Bay with a beautiful beach. Inarajan was still a small, sleepy village and hadn't changed much since Garth was there. The road wound along the coast, with rocky beaches and a rugged shoreline on one side, and inland, the green of the jungle, broken by clearings here and there for small farms. Continuing on, we drove north, past Talofofo Bay, Ylig Bay, Yona, and up to Pago Bay—another beautiful spot—then northwest through Sinajana. Pago Bay looked to be the perfect spot for snorkeling, its turquoise waters sparkling in the sunlight. At Sinajana we stopped at Butler's Store and learned that Jim Butler was in the hospital, badly crippled by arthritis, so I arranged to go to the hospital the next day to see him.

At Guam Memorial Hospital, I introduced myself and told Mr. Butler about Garth Dunn. I said, among other things, I was there in Guam to express Garth's thanks for assistance he received in 1942. Jim remembered the prisoners in the cathedral. He said that his brother Ben had passed away in 1952. He told me that his father was also taken prisoner, as were the American Catholic priests. He recalled that they were kept in a different place—the old Knights of Columbus building.

The Butler family was well off prior to the war. They had a drugstore, a dry goods store with general merchandise, and a soda fountain (these were mentioned in Garth's account). During the war, the Butlers lost everything, their stores destroyed by bombing. Like others, they had to start all over again.

CHAPTER 7

〱〱〱 〱〱〱 〱〱〱

THE DENTIST'S HOUSE

SIMON: The Japanese bombed Davao, but the city did not suffer much damage. Japanese aircraft destroyed the mine's single-engine airplane on the ground at our small dirt landing field, and then bombed our powerhouse. Fortunately, Mr. McKenzie, our mechanic, was able to repair the damage quickly and restore electrical power. We expected the Japanese to land in Davao any day. Gradually most of the Americans left. Mr. Sundeen, our superintendent, sent Hugh Wills to Davao to assist the American forces with demolition. They blew up some of the harbor facilities and the Generosa Bridge over the Davao River to make things harder for the Japanese.

Jane Wills and her ten-month-old daughter, Trudy, left with the Sundeens for Davao. They were going to join a convoy going north to Malaybalay, where they hoped to join the American forces, and from there find transportation out of the Philippines.

We sent a telegram to General MacArthur, telling him about the Americans and giving him a report about the bombing. After we did this, the Japanese sent a plane over and bombed the telegraph lines. Of course, there was nothing MacArthur could do for us anyway.

In Davao the convoy for Malaybalay finally left. Jane and the baby got on it at the last minute, along with other foreigners and some Filipinos. In the confusion of the departure, Jane's trunk with all the baby's food was tossed off the truck to make room for suitcases of fancy dresses that belonged to some wealthy Filipinas attempting to escape.

Hugh did not go with the convoy, since he was still placing explosives. A few days later—the last possible moment before the Japanese landed on December 20, 1941, he set out on foot with a small group of Americans to walk through the jungle to Malaybalay—a distance of over a hundred miles. They passed through remote areas, bartering for food with some of the primitive tribes. In one place he traded his electric razor for some chickens and fruit from natives who lived near a natural seepage of petroleum. They used crude oil for fuel and for lamps.

As the American stragglers trickled into Malaybalay, Jane rushed down to meet each new group. Days passed—still no sign of Hugh. Finally, she couldn't bear to meet the incoming groups anymore—couldn't stand to face the disappointment.

Word had come through of the Japanese landings in Davao. Everyone was giving up hope, knowing it was only a matter of time before the Japanese came to Malaybalay. Fewer and fewer planes were coming from Australia to land at the Del Monte Field, and they were only taking out key military personnel, not civilians.[25]

Then one day another group of stragglers arrived. One of the women in the camp rushed to tell Jane that Hugh had finally come. At last, the Wills family was reunited! Hugh was thin and weak from dysentery, and worn out by the long march from Davao, but just the sight of Jane and Trudy improved his spirits measurably.

At the moment, food was not a problem for the refugees. Enough food was available locally. Also, thanks to the kindness of some of the Del Monte workers, Jane obtained several cases of "Klim"—powdered milk—which she resolved to save at all costs for the baby.

At the mine we were in communication with the coast through our telephone line. The tram was still disabled, which meant that any Japanese troops coming after us would face a stiff one- to two-day uphill hike through rugged mountainous terrain to reach the mine. The Filipinos at the mill were in a position to give us advance warning when the Japanese troops headed our way. So, we sat there and waited.

Meanwhile things were quiet at the mine. Lydia and I remained, along with Mr. McKenzie and a few others, waiting for the Japanese. I knew that eventually they would come, in spite of the disabled tram. But I decided that once you start running, there is no alternative but to keep running, and I didn't see how we could survive.

Then one afternoon, about 3 p.m., they arrived.

We first saw them coming down the mountain, sun glinting off of their bayonets. They wore camouflaged uniforms, with leaves and grass sticking all over their helmets. Once they got close to the mine, they shot a few times in the air, and spread out to surround the buildings.

McKenzie was playing cribbage when we first caught sight of them. At first, he was okay. But when they started shooting, he panicked and fell to the ground,

The Tram at the Gold Mine

screaming he'd been shot. He laid there for the longest time, and we couldn't convince him that he was not injured.

One of our neighbors, Mr. Hughes was also with us at the mine. He was an American married to a Filipina and lived on a plantation nearby. Even though he was eighty-two years old, he'd walked all the way to the mine to see how we were. Before the Japanese arrived, he told me that Lydia and I should go to his plantation if we had any trouble. His wife would try to help us.

The Japanese took over the mine. They said we could stay, but all the buildings and equipment were now confiscated, and we must cooperate and not make problems. They let us stay in our house, but right away they put a soldier there to watch us. He sat in the living room, all the time with his rifle and bayonet, so we stayed mostly in the bedroom and kitchen. After several days of this situation, we couldn't stand the tension of living with the soldiers all around us. They were arrogant. We worried that one slip of the tongue—even the wrong expression on our faces—and they would shoot us.

We had some canned food and other supplies hidden in the attic. At night Lydia would station herself so she could watch the guard in living room, while I crept into the attic to get some provisions for the next day. This sneaking around was dangerous, because if the Japanese had any suspicion we were spying on them, or had weapons hidden away, they would have shot us immediately.

Mr. Hughes had quietly slipped away one day, walking out of the mine back through the jungle to his plantation. We didn't know what would happen to us next. Meanwhile the Japanese got some Filipino laborers and repaired the tram. Other than that, they did little besides making an inventory of the equipment, inspecting the tunnels and works, and looking everywhere for gold. Then one day our situation changed abruptly.

"Simon, come here quickly, please." It was Lydia. She stood near the front window, looking out of our house. I got up from the bed where I'd been reading and went to the front door. Outside there were two soldiers, with an interpreter. I stepped out to meet them. Lydia was watching anxiously, keeping an eye on the guard in our living room, and on the two soldiers and interpreter outside with me. A moment later I returned to the house. "Lydia, pack a few things. The Japanese say we must go with them to Davao to get a pass. In one day we can return—on the boat tomorrow. But they say we must come with them right now."

"But Simon, do you think we will be all right?"

"I think so. Anyway, we have no choice. They say we have to go immediately with these fellows. You grab your things and put in my blue shirt while I talk to this man a little more and see what he knows."

The two soldiers and interpreter rode with us on the newly repaired tram down to the mill and then accompanied us to the waterfront, where we all boarded a ferry for Davao. Lydia kept eyeing the soldiers who had been sent to escort us. "Simon," she said, "what will they do? Why do they want us? Look at them: they seem lazy—they're not like the regular soldiers, those who were at the mine."

"I don't know, Lydia. We'll just go with them and see what they want, and then we'll get our passes and come back. I'm sure they have no interest in us. Who would care about an unemployed Russian civil engineer and a Latvian housewife with only one dress?"

Lydia took my hand, moved closer to me at the rail of the ship. "Simon, don't make jokes with me. I don't like these soldiers. They go everywhere with rifles and bayonets, and they are so demanding, all this bowing and ordering people here and there. It frightens me, Simon."

I tried to calm her, but I was not convincing. There was little I could say. No one could predict what was going to happen. As we crossed the bay, everything seemed so peaceful. Beneath us through the sparkling clear water, we could see coral, small fish darting to and fro. Once the boat edged out into deeper water, it passed occasional coconut husks floating on the water and flowers washed down into the gulf and borne by the morning tide in the direction of Davao. In the presence of so much beauty, it was hard to accept the fact that overnight our world had changed.

In Davao, we disembarked at Santa Ana wharf, and then walked through the city streets, one soldier in front of us, one behind. The interpreter faded away into the city, leaving us alone with the soldiers. After walking for half a mile or so down Magsaysay Avenue, the soldiers stopped in front of Davao Central Elementary School, which had been taken over as the headquarters of the Imperial Japanese Army. Outside a sentry spoke briefly with one of the soldiers, then motioned us inside. We were told to take a seat.

The town was unchanged. The principal difference, as far as I could tell, was the presence of Japanese soldiers on every street corner. Otherwise, most of the shops were open and it seemed to be business as usual.

After a wait of half an hour or so, a guard appeared and motioned to me to follow him. Lydia got up, but the guard stepped between her and me. His intent was clear. "Wait Lydia," I said. "I'll be right back. Don't worry." Reluctantly, she sat down again.

I was escorted through one office into another. There an officer asked my name and place of employment. I gave him my name and started to say that I worked at the mine. The officer looked down, shuffling through some papers, otherwise ignoring me. After a moment he seemed satisfied and glanced sideways at the guard, ignoring me altogether. The guard pushed me toward the rear door, where I stepped out into the bright sunlight. There I found myself in a small courtyard, surrounded by a wall. Not long ago, children had probably played there. Now several sentries stood at the corner of the courtyard, which had a gate opening onto a side street.

There was a small group of foreigners in the courtyard, mostly Americans from other American businesses in Davao. No women were present. I was surprised to see my friend Mr. Hughes seated in one corner of the yard. He hadn't shaved in several days. I went over to his side and sat down next to him, keeping an eye on the guards. "Mr. Hughes, what you doing here? Do you know what's going on?"

"No idea, Simon. Two days ago some Japanese came to the house and then brought me to Davao. Last night, they kept me in another building, and this morning they brought me here. No one knows, and they won't talk to you. And they don't want you to talk to the soldiers. Hell, they don't speak no English, so it wouldn't do no good anyways."

Hughes spat. Even though he was eighty-two years old, he looked sixty, and he had lived in Mindanao for decades. All the Filipinos admired him, because he had twelve kids; the youngest—just two years old—had been born shortly after his eightieth birthday. "I think they're rounding up all the Americans," he muttered beneath his breath, looking around the compound. "Look, they got no Filipinos here. I suspect they're going to lock us up, just like we did to the Japanese when we heard about Pearl Harbor."

I shuddered, thinking that Lydia was somewhere there inside the building. "But Lydia's in there." I said. "What will they do with her?"

"Don't worry, Simon, she'll be okay. She'll probably be along shortly."

We leaned against the wall, watching as other foreigners were ushered into the courtyard. Soon the group included American missionaries and some French-Canadian priests. No women appeared. After an hour or so, a Japanese army truck drove up. The gate opened, and we were herded out of the courtyard into the back of the truck. Armed soldiers followed the truck through the city streets to the outskirts of Davao. Outside the city the truck lurched to a stop, causing me to slide into the man next to me. We staggered out of the truck and found ourselves in front of a large private home with an enclosed courtyard.

As we were marched inside, I realized the Japanese were using it as a temporary prison camp. Sentries stood outside. Inside, some prisoners stood in small groups talking quietly, while others sat against the walls, looking dejected. All I could think about was Lydia. She would be worried. Where was she? And for god's sake, was she all right? I kept walking to the door, watching other men arrive, hoping to see her step off one of the trucks. But she never appeared.

Once I realized that only men were being detained here, I felt a little better. I tried to convince myself that there must be a similar camp for women. After the first hectic night, when we slept anywhere we happened to find space—those who slept at all, that is—the camp took on some semblance of organization. In the morning we were awakened by a bugle blast. We stumbled into the courtyard to line up for roll call. There we filed by to receive a meager breakfast, usually some fruit, tea, and rice. Mats had been brought in so we could sleep on the floor Filipino style. Toilet facilities, although not completely adequate for the number of men in the camp, provided some degree of sanitation. Water from a pipe was rigged up outside to provide a crude shower. A few of the prisoners were organized into a cooking detail. The Japanese brought some supplies to the camp. In addition, the cooking detail occasionally was marched to town to buy provisions.

After the first few days, the prisoners with Filipino relatives or friends were allowed some contact with the outside world. Some received eggs or other packages of food from their friends. During the day there was little to do. We talked, played cards, walked around the compound. It was a dreary and monotonous existence.

As word concerning the camp spread through Davao, I hoped that Lydia would learn where I was and would know that I was alive. I was frantic to learn something about her, but no one knew anything, neither the new arrivals to the camp, nor the Filipinos who visited. I asked everyone, promised them money if they could find her, tried everything I could think of. Most important, I tried to convince myself that she was all right—I could not allow myself to believe anything else.

卌 卌 卌

LYDIA: I sat in the Japanese army building, watching as soldiers entered and left, and additional Americans entered and passed through the same door that had swallowed Simon. I expected him to return at any minute with our "passes." After I'd been waiting for nearly two hours, an officer appeared with a soldier. In broken English, he told me to go with the soldier. I started to protest, "But Simon, my husband . . ."

The officer turned abruptly on his heel and left. The soldier took my elbow and pushed me in the direction of the door. Mutely I followed him into the bright sunlight, hoping they would soon bring Simon along as well. The soldier led me through the streets of Davao, in a state that I can best describe as half fear, half shock. I tried to get my mind working. What could they have done with Simon? Where were they taking me? Could I possibly run away from this small man with the big rifle who trod along in front of me?

Before I could reach any decision, the soldier stopped. He pointed to a house and signed for me to enter. I was so happy—I knew the house. It was the home of the only dentist in Davao—an elderly Filipino who lived there with his wife. Simon and I knew him since we'd been to see him on several occasions. The dentist's wife told me that I was to stay in the house. They would try to find out about Simon. No one knew what was going on. That afternoon the dentist came home and greeted me. "I'm so sorry for you to worry, Señora Solomaniuck," he said. "You are to stay with us as our guest. The Japanese commander says that you must not leave the house. We are responsible for you. Please do not go from our house, or I fear we will be punished."

"But, doctor, I have no clothes, I don't know where Simon is, no money, nothing! How can I stay with you like this? What will happen to us?"

"I will see what can be learned. In the meantime you have a room here, and my wife will give you some clothes and a robe. Please eat something, take a bath, try to rest, and don't worry. You'll be all right here with us."

Endless days passed. I never left the house. I helped, did a few small things in the kitchen, talked to the gentle dentist and his wife, and sat outside in a small courtyard behind their house. There I watched insects humming around the shrubs, listened to the occasional songbird that appeared, and prayed daily for some word concerning Simon. The terrible uncertainty, the absolute lack of knowledge, was the worst thing I experienced.

‖‖ ‖‖ ‖‖

SIMON: The number of people in the men's compound kept increasing. It was apparent that the Japanese were systematically rounding up all the Americans and other foreign nationals and putting them in internment camps.[26] Time passed slowly for me. More than three months passed, and I still had no word of Lydia. I couldn't believe that she wouldn't make an attempt to contact me. Her silence would mean only two things: she was imprisoned herself or, god forbid, she was dead.

I never allowed myself to consider the second alternative, but concentrated on the first. Each time there was a new arrival in camp, I asked: "Do you know where the women are? You know of any woman's camp?" But no one could help me. Finally, one day a soldier came for me. He took me to the camp commander, who informed me that, as a Russian, I was not at war with Japan and therefore was free to go. I rushed back to the courtyard. "Hughes, they say I can go. I'm going to get out of here and find Lydia. Then I'll go to your plantation and tell your wife about you. Maybe now they'll start letting everyone go!"

In my excitement, I rushed to the gate. I was so anxious to leave that I forgot the cardinal rule, the one that was strictly enforced by the Japanese: I forgot to bow three times to the sentry as I left. The sentry screamed at me in a maniacal, high-pitched voice. I turned, took three steps back toward him, as he kept shouting at me in Japanese. Before I knew what was happening, he hit me viciously in the face with the butt of his rifle, and then in the side. I collapsed on the ground, where he kicked me repeatedly in the head and sides as I lay there, stunned, blood gushing from my face. I passed out.

Several of the prisoners dragged me back into the compound. I was unconscious, bleeding from the mouth, nose, and ears. The prisoners cared for me for the next several days, nursing me back to health. It was a week before I felt able to walk from the camp once again. This time, I bowed ten times to the sentry at the gate.

I went on the back streets through the town, seeking someone who knew Lydia's whereabouts. Finally a Filipino lady told me about the dentist's house. I rushed there, knocked loudly on the door. Suddenly there was Lydia. She burst into tears upon finding me at the front door. "Oh god, Simon, I was so worried."

"Never mind," I said, "now it is time to leave this place, to return across the bay. It won't be safe here in Davao."

"But what can we do?" Lydia asked

"I don't know, but we won't stay here. They could change their minds tomorrow. I know where there is a carpenter from the mine married to a Filipina. We'll go to his house and see if he will help us."

"But Simon, he is Japanese."

"Yes, Lydia, but he is also a kind man, and I think that he will help us."

We spent two days at the carpenter's home, never leaving the house for fear of encountering Japanese troops. Then one night we left quietly after dark following him to the harbor. There we got on a small fishing boat, which he had arranged to carry us across the bay to the other side. As we boarded the boat, I took his hand: "Thank you, my friend. Thank you very much for all this kindness." Then the boat slipped away into the darkness of the night and we were on our way away from the terror of Davao. Most important, we were once again together, and we promised each other that no matter what happened, we would always stay together in the future.

CHAPTER 8

卌 卌 卌

ZENTSUJI

GARTH: I was like a man who wakes up and finds himself deep in a hidden cave. I imagined struggling to my feet and lighting a match, not knowing what beauty or terror the faint light will reveal.

Zentsuji—that was the way it was. One day we were living ordinary lives, joking around, drinking beer at Chong's when we didn't have the duty. The next day, it was as if we were in a dark cave, not knowing what to expect, and the world as we knew it had gone off somewhere to wait out the end of the war.

Zentsuji is not just my story, but a story that belongs to hundreds of prisoners. I shall endeavor to be a faceless speaker, a conduit by which prison thoughts and words, mumbled in the dark corners of the cave, are brought forth. Are we not all prisoners at one time or another? We're trapped by race, by religion, by birthplace, by judicial system, by economic status, or by limits imposed by our own narrow mentalities. At Zentsuji, the subtleties were lost on us. We were just victims. But why then? And why us?

From my perspective, the worse part was to be ripped from all that was familiar, carried off to a strange land to be beaten, starved, and threatened with death, and then to suddenly emerge from this hardship with four years of my life gone—disappeared like dirty water down the bathtub drain. In an instant, it was gone. Years later I wondered: Where did it go? Did it happen? But I know it happened because I remember the water swirling down. I recall the dirty ring it left behind in my mind.

For years we pictured that swirling water, felt the outrage. We carried hate with us, bitter, burning, blind ferocious hate. Hate was how we survived. When all the other reasons for living were gone, we lived to hate.

There was a picture taken of me at Zentsuji. Years after the war, I saw it. I no longer remember when it was taken. Beneath the photograph it says, Garth G. Dunn, Jr., Pfc., U.S.M.C., California. I am drawn to my eyes in the photograph.

They burn out of the paper, out of my young face; they stare fiercely at me across the years. They say: Remember this!

Actually, of the three camps I was in, Zentsuji wasn't so bad. I was there from January to June 1942. During that first year we had a couple of advantages. First, the Japanese were winning everywhere. They could afford to be magnanimous to prisoners even though, in their culture, they looked down on anyone who would surrender. That was part of the underlying philosophy behind our treatment—it stemmed from contempt. They expressed their contempt in many ways: humiliating us, forcing us to do coolie labor, beating us, and starving us.

Secondly, they still had enough food. Even though our rations were limited and much less than we were used to, they were more than we had during 1944 and 1945, when Japanese shipping was pretty well bottled up or was sunk by our navy.

We came to Zentsuji at night. It was dark when we got to the camp, still rattled by our march through the streets with the populace screaming at us, throwing stones, or spitting on us. We knew we were being brought for propaganda purposes, so the Japanese people and news media could see how the Imperial troops had overcome the Americans. They wanted the public to believe that Americans were not fighters like the Japanese. To heighten this impression, we were made to look as bedraggled as possible. The government wanted the Japanese people to see us for another reason. They wanted them to understand that Japan was really in the war now, no backing out, not with American prisoners in Japan. Hopefully these impressions would help rally the public to even greater support for the war.

It was in this spirit that they ushered us into what they called the "barracks" and then told us it was a most delightful place. Actually, it was a stable. We were moved to the barracks a few days later, once they got it ready for us.

Later on in the war, when we learned more about the Japanese mentality, we understood more clearly the reasons behind our treatment. It was a deeply ingrained Japanese trait that the highest form of dedication and loyalty was to die in battle. Japanese propaganda claimed that the war would be continued for a hundred years if necessary, or until every soldier and citizen "ate stones"—their expression for lying facedown on the battlefield. To the Japanese soldier, capture by the enemy was not only the ultimate failure, but it also brought disgrace to his family and relatives.

We were the first American prisoners to arrive in Japan. The Japanese were not really organized for POWs at that time. The Zentsuji installation had originally been used as a prisoner-of-war camp during the Russo-Japanese War in

1904, and then was used as a Japanese army barracks. It became the first camp prepared to receive Allied prisoners. Nearby, and surrounding the prison camp for all practical purposes, was one of the Japanese army's largest training camps.

On a typical day we were rousted at daybreak by one of the guards blowing a bugle—they called it *tenko,* which was Japanese for "reveille." We had to step out and line up for roll call. Then they made us count off. I could still say my POW number in Japanese forty years later: *hachiju,* or 80. After roll call we had our bowl of rice, maybe some warm water that they called soup, and some tea. That was breakfast. After we ate they would march us out to work.

Once we were settled in, we were assigned to a work detail on Oasa Yama, a nearby mountain. They would take us out of the barracks, march us a couple of miles, and then we'd work on a hillside. They gave us mattocks, and we were supposed to construct terraces where they planned to plant rice and other crops. Our job was to dig out the big rocks and stones and use them to build the walls to make terraces.

It wasn't all bad. There were some humorous things. For example, the word for "eggs" in Japanese is *tamagos.* To get to the mountainside, they made us march in rows of three, which was the old-fashioned way of marching along a road, like three rows of corn, as it was called. Someone asked about the area we passed through, and one of the Japanese pointed out a chicken ranch as we marched and told us that was where they got their eggs for the camp. Of course, we *horyo*—prisoners—never got eggs. So from then on, every time we walked by that spot, the head of the column—Navy Chief Podries—would holler out "Attention!" We'd start doing the goose step, and as we approached the chicken farm, the chief would holler "Eyes right!" and we would all shout, "Tamagos, tamagos, tamagos!" It was one of those small forms of resistance that kept us alive.

While we worked, there were Japanese guards around us, always trying to make us work harder and faster. "Speedo, speedo!" they would yell at us. There was one guy who was a tiny soldier, smaller than the rest. He was an older man, and he would run up behind us and kick or slap us and yell, "Dig deeper, dig deeper!" so we called him "Dig Deeper." He would come after us whenever we were leaning on a shovel taking a break. Someone would spot him coming and would shout "Here comes Dig Deeper," so then we'd start moving and would keep working until his attention was drawn elsewhere.

In retrospect, they were easier on American POWs at the beginning of the war, in part because they'd had a long string of victories, and in part because we were a novelty. Most of them had never seen an American before. Also, we were all bigger than they were and they were a little afraid of us. They weren't so pushy with us every time we set a mattock down or leaned on a shovel—they didn't jump right on top of us. Later on it got tougher.

The guards were veterans from fighting in China—in some cases guys who had been injured. They were definitely military people, you could tell that. I think they probably resented having to guard us, rather than joining the real fighting, so they took their frustrations out on us.

At midday they let us sit down for a while and eat the lunch, or *bento*. Of course, we only got a little bit of rice. When you had to take a piss, you'd just wave at the guard and tell him *benjo*. Then you'd go over and go on the ground somewhere. In about a half hour, after we ate that little rice ball, we'd have to go back to work.

We worked until almost dark, and then they'd march us back through town to the camp. Sometimes a couple of the guys would try to reach in the little stores we passed, hoping to steal cigarettes or candy. They rarely got away with it. Shop owners beat their hands, or the soldiers would see them and kick the hell out of them. At first we didn't have any really bad beatings. Later, when we were starving and got caught stealing food, the beatings were a lot tougher. At Zentsuji, as long as you followed orders, you could stay out of trouble most of the time.

There wasn't any opportunity for major sabotage in Zentsuji. Later on, at Osaka and Hirohata, we had chances to damage the Japanese war effort, but not at Zentsuji. We did try though. We were supposed to be removing rocks to make nice rice paddies. When we could get away with it, instead of removing the big rocks, we would cover them up or roll them down the hill, hoping that one would mess up the terraces or possibly roll over a guard. That was about it for our sabotage efforts.

After work, back at camp, we got dinner, which was another bowl of rice. Usually the rice ration was about a teacup full of cooked rice in the morning, half that for lunch, and then a teacup full at night. They gave you hot tea in the morning along with the rice; at noon it was hot water. If you had any tea left from the morning, you could make some tea at noon with the hot water they gave you. At night we usually got a cup of soup. The soup was better in Zentsuji than it was later on in the war. It did have something in it—maybe some kind of leaves, or some daikon, a Japanese radish, and maybe a slice of carrot. Later on, at the other camps it was nothing but green water.

That was it for the day. They let us stay up for a little while, but at dark we went to bed. They would blow the bugle, come in and count us, and then it was into bed. They'd turn off the lights.

They had a guard shack at the gate. In winter there was a deep pit filled with charcoal there, and the guards would stand by it to keep warm. Also, a couple of guards were always wandering around, watching us, and making rounds through camp. They didn't worry too much about us escaping, because there was no place we could go, and no way could we blend in with the local population. They would've found us immediately. In addition, there was a tall wooden fence surrounding the camp, and on the top of the fence there were sharpened bamboo staves.

During those first weeks, I'd say the nights were the worst. During the day, we'd either be looking forward to eating, or working, or marching back to camp, and our minds were occupied. At night, it was different. We'd lie there shivering on those hard wooden platforms, feeling the fleas searching out a fresh place to bite, thinking of our families, the war, our future, how long we were going to be stuck there.

Late at night, when everything was quiet, those who couldn't sleep would hear the faint scratching sounds of the rats as they crept around looking for something to eat. They didn't really bother us, but we resented their boldness. A couple of us decided to see if we could discourage further rat forays. There was one particularly adventuresome rat that came into our room near a corner. We decided to bait this spot with a few grains of rice and scraps of rotten vegetables from the garbage. The marine who slept nearest to that spot found a piece of wood about fifteen inches long while we were working, smuggled it into camp, and hid it in his blankets. Both of us stayed awake that night, our ears tuned to the slightest sound, watching for the faintest sign of movement in the darkened room. One moment there was nothing, and then a moment later it was there.

The rat had bright, beady black eyes. It stood frozen, watching the marine lying still on the sleeping mat. The smell of life was there, but no movement, no sound. In the dark, the rat's eyes were enlarged, focused, attentive. The rat wanted to eat. But more than that, it wanted to live. So it waited, unmoving. The marine on the sleeping mat waited, unmoving, scarcely breathing, watching the rat with half-opened eyes. His field of view ranged from the rat at the wall to the scraps of food in the corner. An imaginary arc, drawn in a perfect half circle from the bait to the other side of his mat would intersect his tensed right arm holding the heavy piece of wood.

After a long pause, the rat shuffled over to the bait, eyes moving rapidly about the room, nose sniffing nervously. At the first grains of rice, it stopped, stood motionless, once again scanning the room. The figure on the sleeping mat did not move. More long seconds went by, until finally the rat seized a scrap of vegetable, moved its eyes for a second, and began gnawing on it. At that instant the man's clenched hand, holding the heavy piece of wood, followed a semicircular arc toward the opposite side of the sleeping mat, developing a murderous momentum as it picked up speed. The rat heard, rather than saw the movement. As it leaped backward, it heard and felt a violent movement of air.

The wooden club whistled through air and with an ear-rattling crash, met the wooden floor a good ten inches behind the spot where the rat had crouched a second before. But the rat's frantic backward leap brought the animal to this precise spot at the same instant the club arrived. The man felt the shock ripple up his wrist and into his shoulder. "Uh-oh," he exclaimed, at the same time rubbing a jet of warm rat blood from his forehead. He rolled the club to one corner of the room. The shattered rat gave one or two feeble kicks and was still. "Got you, you bastard," the marine rasped, as we both sat up in bed.

"Meat for breakfast," he chuckled, pulling a string out from under his sleeping mat and hanging the rat up on the wall. "That'll keep the roaches off," he said, then fell back to sleep. I slept soundly that night, knowing it would take several days for a new rat to learn that the territory was vacant and move in.

In the morning, when everyone awoke, there was our visitor hanging from the wall. Someone threw the body outside in disgust. A few years later, I remembered the incident, thinking how much I regretted the waste of some perfectly good meat.

When we first arrived, the camp wasn't much, but gradually the Japanese got it organized. My description only applies to the first six months of its existence, because after that I was moved to another camp. Zentsuji was roughly rectangular in shape, with a sentry post at the front gate and behind that a guardhouse. There were two barracks buildings and behind them the benjos—open-pit latrines—and wash facilities. Behind the two barracks, and more or less on the camp center line, was the galley and storeroom. Nearby there was another building used as an office by the camp commander, Lieutenant Yuhei Hosotani. Near this building there was a tall pole with a bright light on it.

Enlisted men were separated from officers. We slept on a wooden platform, about two feet off the floor, and about six or seven feet deep, which went the length of the room. At first we slept on bare wood, but later they brought in some straw mattresses. Six or seven people could fit on one of these shelves and there were two in each room, so we had twelve or so men per room. We were on the second story of the barracks. A bunch of navy nurses—and the wife of one of the navy chiefs—had been captured along with us on Guam. They were on the ground floor beneath us in the barracks.

After we'd been there for a while, the Japanese made us establish a chain of command. The "camp officer" became Chief Boatswain Mate R. B. Lane. He was the channel through which the Japanese relayed communications to the prisoners. In keeping with their basic philosophy of humiliating us, they picked him rather than one of the officers. He appointed other navy personnel to various chores, including keeping records, cooking, and other duties. A lot of the men felt that he was a little too accommodating—maybe got a few special favors—by going along with the Japanese.

For example, after the food and cooking were organized, we still didn't get enough to eat. Chief Lane had appointed his buddies to serve the rice. Naturally the marines were suspicious of the sailors, so we started watching the galley when they brought out the rice. We saw that when the navy chiefs brought the rice out of the galley, the wooden buckets they brought to the sailors were heaped up, whereas the ones they brought to the marines were level or less than level. L. D. and I decided we were going to sneak into the galley one night to see what was going on.

At night there was only one guard who walked around the courtyard, where there was the one big light. Since the courtyard was pretty long, once the guard passed, you had time to slip out of the barracks. We did this a few times, although it was dangerous if the guards ever caught you out of your bunk at night.

The first time we sneaked into the galley, just to look around, we found the chiefs were stashing rice scrapings, the burnt part of the rice left over from cooking it in a big iron pot. We stole the scrapings and brought them up to our room, where we ate all we wanted. Actually, we ate, and ate, and ate—stuffed ourselves, we were so hungry. After we were done, we passed the rest out to our buddies, the other guys in our room. Everybody in our room got some of the rice scrapings. I don't want to give the idea we were generous, because we weren't. After all, we were taking the risk. We gave them what we didn't want or couldn't eat. That was the moral code.

Afterward, as we lay in bed that night, our stomachs swelled up and bloated with a nauseous sour gas from the surfeit of food, until we could no longer sleep. We stumbled out of bed and staggered around, belching and gasping at the rotten egg odor that permeated the room. Naturally, the next day we had a bad case of the shits.

We went back several times after that. In the evening, we'd wait until everything got quiet, then we'd sneak downstairs, hiding in the shadows, and wait until the guard went by. Then we'd run across the courtyard and into the galley, where they kept the rice scrapings and get a little extra rice for our room. But

Chief Lane and his cronies—no surprise that they missed their rice scrapings—they figured out real quick that someone was helping themselves. So the chiefs got together and set a little trap for us.

When we snuck into the galley, we noticed things weren't quite right. The rice scrapings weren't in their usual hiding place. They'd been moved to a spot that looked suspicious to us. We didn't say anything to each other, we just pointed to different pots and pans. L. D. grabbed a pot and I grabbed a big pan. When we made a move to grab some of the rice scrapings, three guys came out of the darkness and jumped us. At the time, we couldn't tell who they were—later we knew it was the navy chiefs. Anyway, there was a brief struggle, but we banged them with the pots and pans and got the hell out of there, while they flailed around on the floor and fought with each other. The next morning, we saw them walking around with black eyes and beat-up faces. We got away with it because they didn't catch us, but they had their suspicions. When it came time to break up the camp and send some prisoners to Osaka, L. D. and I were on the list. In other words, the troublemakers were shanghaied the hell out of there!

We had Sundays off at Zentsuji. We'd sit around the camp, wash our clothes, talk, play cards. L. D. was pretty good when it came to shooting craps; I rolled the dice. I was a long roller. After a while, we had most of the yen in the camp. The yen wasn't worth much though, because there was nothing to buy. There was a little store that only had junk, almost never any food. Eventually the Japanese outlawed gambling.

There was one civilian woman on the first floor of the barracks with all the nurses who had been captured on Guam. She was the wife of one of the navy chiefs, a woman named Mrs. Parker. She was pregnant at the time the USS *Henderson* sailed in November 1941, taking all the dependents from Guam back to the United States, so she had stayed behind. As it turned out, she had her baby—a little girl—in the camp. The Japanese treated her fairly well, got her milk and other things she needed.

Some of the Japanese guards liked to sneak in and look at the nurses. There was one guard in particular who got his jollies by sneaking up and watching them undress, or by marching in to pull an inspection when they were undressing. One old nurse was in charge. She had quite a vocabulary—even the marines learned new words listening to her swear. Also, she had a voice that could carry for miles. Whenever the Japanese came in and bothered the nurses, she'd start swearing, and that was the signal for all of the marines to pile downstairs and mill around outside the nurses' quarters. Having us around prevented the Japanese from doing anything serious.

Later on, all of the nurses, including Mrs. Parker and her baby, were sent home on the *Gripsholm*, a neutral ship that exchanged Japanese diplomatic personnel and aliens in the United States for the nurses, priests, and other noncombatants in Japan.

Early in the war the Japanese brought in copies of an English-language newspaper—the *Osaka Mainichi*. We read it, even though we knew it was mostly propaganda. I actually quit reading that paper and so did a lot of the other prisoners, because the propaganda was somewhat believable and it was better if you didn't even think about how the war was going. Some guys kept reading it, and Jesus, they became depressed about the war, worrying because the Japanese were winning victory after victory. The rest of us found other things to do to keep our minds off the war.

But it was through this newspaper that we found out about General Doolittle's raid on April 18, 1942.[27] I remember it, because it was the day after my twenty-first birthday. Of course, the Japanese claimed that no damage had been done, that all the planes had been shot down, and that they had killed all the aircrews. None of us foot sloggers could figure out how the planes got there. We never imagined land-based bombers taking off from a carrier! We took heart from the fact that the United States had shown the Japanese that their homeland was not invincible.

The Doolittle raid really had an impact. It changed a lot of things for us, bolstering our morale, but as far as the Japanese treatment was concerned, the raid made it worse. People in the nearby villages threw rocks at the POWs as they marched to the mountain.[28] The Japanese were strange. You would think that as the war progressed—as they could see the handwriting on the wall—that they might ease up on the prisoners a little bit. But they didn't; in fact, as the war progressed, they got worse, and worse, and worse.

In the spring of 1942, they let us broadcast a message home. The authorities told us that we would be allowed to tape-record a message, but that it would be censored. I had Mr. Tajima, our interpreter, look at mine to make sure it was acceptable. In the end it was short and sweet. I stated my name and hometown, and then said: *I am safe and unharmed. Do not worry. I hope to see you soon. Love to all. We are in Japan.*

After the war I learned that this broadcast was heard by a number of people. Several family friends telephoned my parents to let them know. May 1942 was the date that my parents received the first news about me since Guam was taken. My mother wrote to me immediately to let me know they'd received the news, but her letter was returned by the Japanese. Afterward, my folks sent me innumerable letters, but I only received a couple of them. Most were returned, but they saved them all and gave them to me when I finally returned after being away from home for four years.

Under the circumstances of a prison camp, people react differently. Some go crazy, some resist, some give up, some look out only for themselves. For example, Captain Todd, who had been the head of the Insular Patrol, was a good friend—or at least so I thought. I'd had that problem when I got in trouble for reading on watch, but he steered me in the right direction. But when we were in Zentsuji, he asked me if I would be his orderly. He said that maybe we could help each other get along. So I asked what was involved.

He said, "What I'm telling you isn't what I want, but what the Japanese want. You have to bring my meals every day. And, you'll have to make my bunk for me every day, and you'll have to empty my slop can, or clean it up every day." You see, the officers were allowed to have a slop can in their room so they didn't have to go outside to go to the toilet at night. I thought about it for a while. Somehow it didn't seem right. After all, we were all in the shit together, and no one was waiting on me. So I said, "No, Captain, I'm not built that way. Thanks, but no thanks." He eventually got someone else to do it.

In a way, life in prison camp was harder on the officers, since they weren't allowed to work. All they could do was sit around and think and worry. The camp was especially hard on the POWs who were married and had families. Chief Parker—whose wife and baby girl had gone back on the *Gripsholm*—damn near went nuts worrying about what happened to her and his kid.[29]

As time passed, when things got rough with the beatings and people starving, you really only thought of yourself. A person's responses change when life boils down to just one person—yourself. I don't care who you are, you're not going to worry about the other guy when you're starving to death. That's why we stole stuff—to stay alive. You only had time for one friend. If you had one good friend, you were lucky.

Why did you need a friend? Because if you had a lot of that rich food—maybe some canned fish or something stolen from the docks or a ship—you couldn't eat too much at once. You tried to eat as much as you could, because it was hard to hide it and some things would just spoil. But eating too much in our condition would invariably give you the shits so bad that the food didn't do any good. You would rather share the food with someone else so you could get some benefit from what you ate. Sharing wasn't the humanitarian thing to do; it was just a way to preserve yourself. With one other guy you could trust, you hoped that he would reciprocate, that you would share in some of his surpluses. Plus you could be sure that he wouldn't give you away to the guards. And if you got sick, maybe he could help you, cover for you at work, get you some extra food. The more people involved, the less you got, and the greater the risk that someone would give you away if he were beaten. You placed your life in the other guy's hands when you shared stolen food.

When some prisoners began trading a bowl of rice for cigarettes, I quit smoking. I needed that bowl of rice. And the poor bastard who craved a cigarette, he could have it. I was willing to hide my cigarettes and pass them on to someone who wanted a smoke worse than they wanted to eat a bowl of rice. I quickly became a nonsmoker, and my ten cigarettes that we got every three days went for extra bowls of rice.

In June 1942, I learned that my sojourn in Zentsuji was coming to an end. Chief Lane announced that 160 of us—80 marines and 80 sailors—were going to move to another camp at Osaka. It came as no surprise that L. D. and I were on that list.

We were marched down to the harbor and loaded on an inter-island steamer. There were a lot of Japanese civilians on the ship who looked at us with curiosity. We arrived at the new camp—if you could call it that—in July 1942. We were temporarily billeted under a stadium of some kind in Osaka. Our quarters—something resembling bleachers—were used until the camp was ready. At Osaka we all became stevedores—coolies in the eyes of the Japanese—who loaded and unloaded ships. It was hard, backbreaking work, with brutal guards and overseers. In spite of the difficulties, Osaka had one definite advantage over Zentsuji. On the docks at Osaka, we could steal food!

CHAPTER 9

卌 卌 卌

RELOCATION

MITZI: We were relocated in April 1942, along with 100,000 other West Coast Japanese. We had almost no advance warning. Suddenly we learned that we had to leave our home. We were allowed to take two suitcases per person. The instructions said to bring bedding and linens, toilet articles, clothing, knives, forks, spoons, plates, and bowls for each family member, and "essential personal effects." Can you imagine? Everything else had to be left behind or sold, although the government offered to store our furniture for us at "our risk."[30]

A few weeks after we arrived in camp, I was lying down on an iron bed in the barracks. It was May 1942, during one of those rare moments when everyone else had gone somewhere, and for the moment the building was empty. I watched little puffs of dust swirling through cracks in the rough wooden floor—it seemed that the sand and dust were forever blowing at Manzanar—and then traced patterns in the dust on the floor with my finger. After a while, I turned over on my back, stared at the wooden rafters overhead. My thoughts were the same every day. What was this place, why were we here, when could we leave, and why had this happened to me?

I felt like a traveler who'd begun a long journey—a trip to a faraway place, dark and dangerous. It was a journey with no end in sight, and I could not accept the fact that fate had selected me for such a trip. I had done nothing to deserve such a blow. All my life I'd learned that in America people are rewarded for doing the right things—so why me?

I never thought of Manzanar as the end of the journey—it was an outpost along the way. My life had taken an unexpected turn, and I didn't know what would happen to me. I could hardly believe that what we'd been through was real. I remembered vividly those terrifying nights, early in 1942—the air-raid warnings, blackouts, sitting huddled together in the kitchen with only candlelight to see by, feeling the fear everywhere.

WESTERN DEFENSE COMMAND AND FOURTH ARMY
WARTIME CIVIL CONTROL ADMINISTRATION

Presidio of San Francisco, California

May 3, 1942

INSTRUCTIONS
TO ALL PERSONS OF
JAPANESE
ANCESTRY
Living in the Following Area:

All of that portion of the County of Alameda, State of California, within the boundary beginning at the point where the southerly limits of the City of Oakland meet San Francisco Bay; thence easterly and following the southerly limits of said city to U. S. Highway No. 50; thence southerly and easterly on said Highway No. 50 to its intersection with California State Highway No. 21; thence southerly on said Highway No. 21 to its intersection, at or near Warm Springs, with California State Highway No. 17; thence southerly on said Highway No. 17 to the Alameda-Santa Clara County line; thence westerly and following said county line to San Francisco Bay; thence northerly, and following the shoreline of San Francisco Bay to the point of beginning.

Pursuant to the provisions of Civilian Exclusion Order No. 34, this Headquarters, dated May 3, 1942, all persons of Japanese ancestry, both alien and non-alien, will be evacuated from the above area by 12 o'clock noon, P. W. T., Saturday, May 9, 1942.

No Japanese person living in the above area will be permitted to change residence after 12 o'clock noon, P. W. T., Sunday, May 3, 1942, without obtaining special permission from the representative of the Commanding General, Northern California Sector, at the Civil Control Station located at:

920 - "C" Street,
Hayward, California.

Such permits will only be granted for the purpose of uniting members of a family, or in cases of grave emergency. The Civil Control Station is equipped to assist the Japanese population affected by this evacuation in the following ways:

1. Give advice and instructions on the evacuation.

2. Provide services with respect to the management, leasing, sale, storage or other disposition of most kinds of property, such as real estate, business and professional equipment, household goods, boats, automobiles and livestock.

3. Provide temporary residence elsewhere for all Japanese in family groups.

4. Transport persons and a limited amount of clothing and equipment to their new residence.

The Following Instructions Must Be Observed:

1. A responsible member of each family, preferably the head of the family, or the person in whose name most of the property is held, and each individual living alone, will report to the Civil Control Station to receive further instructions. This must be done between 8:00 A. M. and 5:00 P. M. on Monday, May 4, 1942, or between 8:00 A. M. and 5:00 P. M. on Tuesday, May 5, 1942.

2. Evacuees must carry with them on departure for the Assembly Center, the following property:

(a) Bedding and linens (no mattress) for each member of the family;
(b) Toilet articles for each member of the family;
(c) Extra clothing for each member of the family;
(d) Sufficient knives, forks, spoons, plates, bowls and cups for each member of the family;
(e) Essential personal effects for each member of the family.

All items carried will be securely packaged, tied and plainly marked with the name of the owner and numbered in accordance with instructions obtained at the Civil Control Station. The size and number of packages is limited to that which can be carried by the individual or family group.

3. No pets of any kind will be permitted.

4. No personal items and no household goods will be shipped to the Assembly Center.

5. The United States Government through its agencies will provide for the storage, at the sole risk of the owner, of the more substantial household items, such as iceboxes, washing machines, pianos and other heavy furniture. Cooking utensils and other small items will be accepted for storage if crated, packed and plainly marked with the name and address of the owner. Only one name and address will be used by a given family.

6. Each family, and individual living alone, will be furnished transportation to the Assembly Center or will be authorized to travel by private automobile in a supervised group. All instructions pertaining to the movement will be obtained at the Civil Control Station.

Go to the Civil Control Station between the hours of 8:00 A. M. and 5:00 P. M., Monday, May 4, 1942, or between the hours of 8:00 A. M. and 5:00 P. M., Tuesday, May 5, 1942, to receive further instructions.

J. L. DeWITT
Lieutenant General, U. S. Army
Commanding

SEE CIVILIAN EXCLUSION ORDER NO. 34.

Notice for Japanese Americans to Relocate

Slowly I had come to recognize—although it was hard to understand or accept—that we were feared. We heard it in hushed tones—the "Japs." Even our good friends changed. Of course, the war changed everyone and everything, but still I asked, shocked by the unfairness of it all, ripped by the dull pain in my soul. Why us? Why *me?*

Our journey began at the ranch in Malibu. After we received the notice about relocation, we had only a few days to make arrangements. On April 28, we went to Culver City—I think it was near Lincoln and Washington Place. There our entire family got on a train, and the next thing we knew we were several hundred miles away in the Owens Valley, disembarking at Lone Pine, then traveling the last few miles by bus to Manzanar. The camp was located ten miles north of Lone Pine and six miles south of Independence on Highway 395.

In Manzanar we joined hundreds of other frightened and confused people who were herded here and there by the military police. My memory of that first traumatic day records the chaos, the total confusion, as people began piling into the camp. We had to register—give the army authorities our names, the number of people in each family, receive barracks assignments, then go to another table where we were directed somewhere else to receive inoculations. There was so much confusion, people were milling around, resentment was boiling beneath the surface, tension was rising. Eventually the authorities asked for volunteers to help staff the tables so everyone could be processed more quickly. I was one of the first volunteers—glad to have something to do rather than stand around.

Once the "evacuees"—for that was what they called us—received their barracks assignment, they had to get in other lines to be issued army blankets for their cots. There were still other lines where warm clothes—baggy army jackets, and pants—were issued to those who either had none or who had been unable to bring them along. At another place in the camp, evacuees received mattress ticking; nearby were bales of straw to be used for stuffing mattresses.

In the coming weeks, our new home revealed itself to us: a vast expanse of raw desert land, blowing sand, wood-and-tarpaper shacks—"barracks," as the authorities called them—families crowded together, in many cases three generations dumped together in an open room with no furniture other than army cots. We suffered the indignity of communal bathing; the coarse food of the mess hall; sharing living quarters with other families, complete strangers, with virtually no privacy—a situation unheard of in our culture, shocking to the old-timers. Then, the dry, barren landscape of the desert, hot during the day, cold at night, the snowcapped beauty of the Sierras, dominated by Mount Williamson, mocking us

Manzanar Barrracks, 1942

in the distance, just beyond the barbed-wire fence. And then, the guard towers, the MPs with their .45s and their M-1 rifles.

I wondered: Was this all a horrible dream? Had America suddenly become Germany, and were we the Jews? Then I told myself: This is an enormous outrage. You, Mitsuye Takahashi, a U.S. citizen, denied your rights and due process of law, you have been horribly wronged, you and your brothers and sisters, your patient, hardworking parents, you and all your loyal American friends who are here and share your fate. After saying this once to myself, I put it out of my mind, knowing it was a burden we had to bear because of the war. No good would come from allowing such bitterness to poison my soul.

Still, I could not stop thinking about myself. I was 24 years old, unmarried, now unemployed, confined to a crude tarpaper barracks with my family and the Tanaka family, stuck there for god knew how long.

We were lucky. We heard so many terrible stories of suffering. There were many people in the camp from San Pedro and Terminal Island—fishermen. They received twenty-four hours' notice. Many of their menfolk were arrested and imprisoned, only because they owned a fishing boat. Their families did not know where they were, or what had become of them. All of their boats were confiscated. They were treated as if they were spies. Meanwhile, at home their families tried to sell furniture and belongings; no one would buy them. If they did, they offered such low prices that some families piled items in the streets and burned them rather than give them up. Those with stores lost them, unless they were able to sell them or find a non-Japanese friend who would take care of the store for them. Usually, there was no time to make proper business arrangements.

We heard about other people who had to go to the Santa Anita racetrack. They were put in stables or in tents. It didn't matter who you were, if you were Japanese: old, young, men, women, even expectant mothers. They all went. One lady—Mrs. Nakashima—was pregnant and she had her baby at Santa Anita. Undoubtedly, there are dozens of other families with similar stories.

We left most of our possessions at the ranch. The people there promised to keep them for us, and to find someone to take care of the crops, to work the ranch. Because of this, we could say that we were fortunate.

The relocation and internment of persons of Japanese ancestry was authorized by Executive Order No. 9066, issued on February 19, 1942. On February 23, 1942, a Japanese submarine surfaced and shelled the Elwood oil field near Santa Barbara. It didn't do much damage, but the attack added to the general hysteria and led many people to think that there were spies and saboteurs everywhere.

A few days later, there was the great Los Angeles air raid. Sirens went off, the antiaircraft batteries opened fire, and a thousand acts of heroism were reported by air-raid wardens, police, and patriotic citizens. Hundreds of Japanese gardeners and nurserymen were rounded up as suspects, accused of "signaling" the planes. A few days later, the secretary of war stated that it was all a mistake—a case of the jitters—there had been no enemy planes at all!

Against this backdrop of panic and fear, it was no surprise that on March 2, all Japanese—including U.S. citizens—were barred from Pacific coastal areas, and in this same month, the Army Corps of Engineers began constructing Manzanar. On April 1, the army began forced evacuations of Japanese Americans from the Pacific states. On April 19, we heard about the Doolittle raid on Japan. Then it was our turn: on April 28, we were relocated.

Manzanar was originally a farming community—the name comes from the Spanish word for "apple orchard"—abandoned when Los Angeles diverted the water into its aqueduct and desiccated the land. The camp was stark when we arrived. Eventually it consisted of thirty-six blocks, each with fifteen barracks. We were in Block 23, Barracks number 1. Each barracks was further divided into "apartments." In each block the number 1 barracks had a small office, so there

were only three apartments in ours, for three families: ours, my twin sister Dorothy and her husband, and the Tanaka family.

Not counting my married sister, we were seven people: my parents, my
brothers and two unmarried sisters, and me. The Tanakas also had a large family.
The whole barracks was open, with the exception of some partitions or dividers
that gave a little privacy. The floor was constructed of rough wooden floorboards,
no carpets or floor coverings. The walls were also rough wooden siding covered
with tarpaper outside, with walls and ceilings uncovered inside. An oil-fired furnace provided heat. Some people dismantled the oil furnace packing crates and
used them to make crude screens or partitions to provide some measure of privacy in the barracks. For furniture, we had army cots for beds, army blankets,
and practically nothing else. Elsewhere, a mess hall, washroom, and bathroom
facilities were associated with each group of barracks. These were located in
separate buildings.

A typical block was laid out in rectangular fashion, with the long axis point-
ing east–west, toward the Sierra Nevada mountains. On one side of the rectangle
were eight barracks buildings—smaller rectangles, with their long axis north–
south. On the other side, there were seven barracks and the mess hall. In the
center, between the two rows of barracks, there were four other buildings. These
included our laundry, another building for ironing, a bath and latrine for women,
and a bath and latrine for men.

People volunteered for different jobs. At first, food for the camp came from
local farms and ranches. Later, a 400-acre farm was established, where more than
twenty varieties of vegetables and fruit were grown, and pigs and chickens were
raised. There was even an experimental production of guayule plants, used to
produce a rubber substitute for the war effort.

Some people became chefs, others worked on maintenance, others worked
in administration. My father became a chef in Block 24. I got a job working in the
hospital, then later I worked for administration. We worked eight hours per day,
and got paid $12, $14, $16, or $19 per month, depending on our classification.
Later on, there were other facilities in the camp, including a school.

First we had a canteen, which became a small store. There was the hospital
and a nurse's training school. Manzanar had its own police force and fire department. Besides the school, there was an auditorium; eventually high school graduation ceremonies were held there. There were baseball fields, picnic areas, shops,
warehouses, Christian and Buddhist churches, even a cemetery. Babies were
born, and people died. Since there were 10,000 of us there, this is not surprising. There were also barbed wire fences, eight guard towers with searchlights,

military police and soldiers with rifles and bayonets. We were not allowed to leave the camp.

As the camp got organized, things became more comfortable. Some of the gardeners planted trees, flowers, and shrubs. Block 12 had a beautiful garden with a pond and a small waterfall. Block 34 had a park—called Pleasure Park—with a pond, stones, a small wooden bridge, and beautiful landscaping. With time, various hand-made articles of furniture and household necessities appeared. People fixed up the barracks so they began to resemble homes. Rock paths and flower gardens began to adorn each block.

Various kinds of sports were taught—judo, baseball. One of our championship baseball teams was the Manzaknights. A woman's team was known as the Roughnecks. Musical groups and entertainers emerged: a hillbilly band called the Sierra Stars; a girl's singing group, the Forget-Me-Nots; the Songbird of Manzanar (Miss Mary Kageyama Nomura); a male vocalist, Yas Tatsuma. The entertainers were sought after for block parties. Beginning with its first issue on April 11, 1942, we had a newspaper, the *Manzanar Free Press*— first mimeographed in camp, later printed outside. It was published twice a week and distributed to all the barracks.

Our lives took on a certain kind of normalcy. We got up in the morning, got dressed, and then went to the mess hall for breakfast. We went as a family and had breakfast together. It was mostly American-style food—toast, cereal, scrambled eggs—whatever the camp administration could provide. At first, there was almost no Japanese-style food, but later on we had some, once gardens were planted. It depended on the chefs. You were supposed to eat in your block, but sometimes we'd go to another block and eat with our friends. Near the end of the war, I learned that the cost of feeding the internees at Manzanar was 25 to 40 cents per day per person.

After breakfast, we'd go to work while the kids would go to school. I worked in the hospital taking care of records and helping with the administration. We had good medical assistance available in the camp. People would come in for inoculations, medicine, or to see the doctor if they were sick. I enjoyed working for public health and made many new friends. Even years later, as I walked down a street in Los Angeles, people would bow to me when I passed. Many times I would not recognize them, but they knew me from my work in public health.

Overall, health conditions were fair. There was a lot of sickness, and at the beginning there were minor illnesses—people sick with diarrhea and other things. Eventually the camp had its own water supply and treatment plant, which helped. Many people were sick from the cold and from the continual winds and dust. There were some cases of venereal disease. Part of the difficulty was our own, because Japanese families were close and they were reluctant to seek help outside their own community.

There were some skilled doctors who visited the camp from the orthopedic hospital, but it was hard to get people to come see them. We even went around door to door talking to people, trying to find out if they had problems or needed help. On a typical day, we'd go back to the barracks at noon, then to the mess hall for lunch, then back to work until it was time for dinner.

At night, we read, went to school, did crafts, or listened to the radio. Once in a while there were movies. People sewed, played cards, or got together and talked. Some weekends we had block parties in the mess hall. We'd decorate it, have our own entertainment, and everybody would join in. Of course, we'd have to arrange with one of the Caucasian staff members to buy anything we needed in Lone Pine, if it wasn't available in the camp. Kids ran around the camp, played baseball, or participated in other sports. There were picnic areas; on the weekends we might go off somewhere for a picnic—all within the camp, of course, all within a one-square-mile area jammed with 10,000 people.[31]

We were fortunate in many respects. Granted, we were forced to go to Manzanar—and that in itself was a terrible wrong—but we could accept that our situation was not so bad. We were not mistreated, not beaten, not starved. We ceased referring to ourselves as "evacuees"; the term became "internees," which seemed less odious than "prisoners," though indeed that was what we were.

The worse part was the uncertainty—not knowing when or how it would end, and not knowing what would be waiting for us when the war was over, not knowing how we would resume lives that had been interrupted by the war.

It is ironic, because today the eastern side of the Sierra is a favorite vacation spot. Being uprooted, torn from our homes, living there as we did, it was hard to appreciate the beauty. Confined to the camp, we could see the snowcapped mountains rising a few miles away, and we knew about the lakes and streams, the places for trout fishing, the beauty of the mountains, Mount Whitney rising above the others. But this natural bounty was inaccessible to us, except for what we could see on the other side of the barbed wire. Our impressions were shaped by the sand and dust that forever blew across the camp and permeated everything. Mother cleaned the barracks every day, but there was always gritty sand everywhere. It seemed to come out of the walls.

Life went on, with everyone trying to make the best of the situation. Friendships developed, and people made adjustments for the way we had to live, with families thrown together, the lack of privacy, and the absence of all personal belongings and family treasures. Birthdays and holidays were celebrated. Each year, as my birthday came and went, I reflected on the time I'd been in camp. Another year gone from my life. Another year, sans job, sans husband, sans the small liberties that made life worth living. When would it end?

JHT JHT JHT

In all the years I knew Mitzi, I never once heard her speak against the government that had unjustly imprisoned her and her family. Her style was to not look back, but to look forward to new challenges and what it would take to overcome them. Although a great deal has been done to recognize and redress the unjust treatment of the Japanese Americans, this event will forever remain a dark moment in American history. What makes the wartime relocation program particularly odious is the underlying racism behind it and the misinformation and falsehoods used to justify it. The perception that 110,000 West Coast Japanese Americans presented such a security risk that the government had to uproot them and move them inland, without legal recourse or compensation— while 160,000 Japanese Americans in the Hawaiian Islands could remain in their homes and businesses—is incomprehensible.[32] The government forced no internment of German Americans or Italian Americans. In fact, German and Italian POWs were brought to American camps and then furloughed to work on American farms and in factories, in food processing and meatpacking, on railroads and military bases, largely without incident—and they were not citizens.

CHAPTER 10

卌 卌 卌

AMERICAN SOJOURN

After his initial incarceration and interrogation in Hawaii, in February 1942 Ensign Kazuo Sakamaki was transported by ship to the mainland. His first sight of America created a profound impression. He was processed through Angel Island in San Francisco, and then traveled by train across the country to Camp McCoy, Wisconsin. The only other Japanese in the camp were civilian internees. While in camp, Sakamaki read about the fall of Bataan in a newspaper. Then, a few weeks later, he learned about Doolittle's raid on Tokyo. As he noted in his memoirs written after the war, "The news was like a stab in my chest. I was shocked. I was in the United States. America was no longer a country on a map. I saw things that told me there was no easy road ahead for Japan."[33]

During these first months at Camp McCoy, Sakamaki went through a spiritual reawakening. The humanity and kindness of the Americans he came into contact with caused him to gradually shift his outlook from a sense of failure and a wish for suicide to a desire for life.[34] This revelation took time to get used to, but the feeling grew stronger with each day as winter faded into spring.

In May 1942 Sakamaki was moved from Camp McCoy to Camp Forest in Tennessee. It was here that he learned of the disastrous Battle of Midway. In camp, the Japanese internees organized classes in English, geography, religion, and other topics. Sakamaki attended them all, considering it important to learn as much as possible about his captors. Although he did not say it in so many words, he sensed that Japan would lose the war and a new world order would result.

From Tennessee he was moved to Camp Livingston, Louisiana. In November 1942 he was moved to a new section of the camp where for the first time he came in contact with other Japanese POWs, who were captured at the battles of Wake Island and Midway. All told, there were fifty-two Japanese POWs in the camp. In January 1943 sixteen of these POWs were transferred to another camp.

Sakamaki found himself the senior officer among the remaining thirty-six prisoners. He held a meeting to explain the workings of the camp and helped the new POWs make the adjustment to captivity.

While Sakamaki was in Camp Livingston, fifty new Japanese POWs arrived. The senior officer in the group had survived the sinking of the aircraft carrier *Hiryu* during the Battle of Midway. After drifting in a lifeboat for fifteen days, he was rescued by an American warship.

This man sought out Sakamaki's assistance to commit suicide. Once he brought a baseball bat, bared his head, and told Sakamaki to beat him to death. Another time he cut his stomach with a razor blade. He made other attempts, all of which failed. He began to imagine that the Americans were bombarding the POWs with powerful radio waves and they were affecting his brain. When the electrical charge grew too great, he'd take a bath, claiming that water stopped the waves.

Sakamaki related that he did everything possible to reassure and comfort the officer, but to no avail. One day he ran out in the courtyard screaming and ranting like a madman. He was taken to the infirmary but failed to recover and became insane.[35]

The following May, Sakamaki and the rest of the Japanese POW's were moved again, this time back to Camp McCoy in Wisconsin. As the war progressed, the number of Japanese POWs steadily increased. After the fall of Saipan in 1944, there were more than one thousand prisoners. Sakamaki credits the enlightened policies of camp commander Lieutenant Colonel Harold I. Rogers with persuading the new arrivals to abandon their thoughts of suicide and accept life in the camp.[36] As the war progressed and Okinawa fell, the camp officers told the POWs there was no need for shame any longer. America's victory was assured; all Japan would soon be prisoners of the United States, and the prisoners would go home.

In 1945, the prisoners were moved again, this time to Camp Kennedy in Texas. They remained there until December 1945, when they began the long journey back home. Japan had lost the war; now there was nothing to be done except to go home, work hard, and create a new Japan.

CHAPTER 11

☰☰☰

ACROSS THE GULF OF DAVAO

It was September 1985 and I was on my way back to the United States from a trade mission to Taiwan and South Korea. I made my way through the crowds at the International Airport in Manila and got a ride to the airport for domestic flights. I planned to take a few vacation days and fly to Davao, on the southern island of Mindanao, to see if I could learn more about the gold mine where Simon worked, and to see if I could locate the Happy Life Blues Cabaret—the prison camp where Lydia and Simon's friends had been held.

The plane to Davao was only half full. Maybe there was something to the warnings I'd received about not going to Davao because the guerrillas—the New Peoples Army—were killing people. At the Inter-Continental Hotel in Davao I met an engaging desk clerk named Bong Anacio Jr. who seemed knowledgeable and trustworthy. I explained that I was trying to locate some Filipino families who had befriended American friends of mine during the war, and I needed a reliable driver who knew the city. He introduced me to Raphael Mendoza Jr., who went by the name of Jun Mendoza.

Jun drove me on a city tour where I visited the tourist information center, then the library, then a museum. Everywhere the people were friendly. One meeting led to another, as someone would recall someone else who might be helpful. In this manner, I met a local historian, Mr. Ernesto Corcino, who not only knew about the Happy Life Blues Cabaret, but also recalled the gold mine where Simon had worked. He knew of two Americans who had plantations in the area, the Hugheses and Mr. Charles Baker.[37] He invited me to his home, produced old maps, gave me copies of some of his publications. He said that the prison camp had been destroyed at the end of the war, but now there was a fighting-cock pit called La Suerte at the same site. He told me not to go to the mine site: the guerrillas were active and there had been killings and kidnappings in that area and in Pantukan.

After I left Mr. Corcino's home, Jun drove me around Davao to see the school building that had been the Japanese army headquarters, the bridge that Hugh Wills had blown up (now rebuilt), the Santa Ana wharf where Simon and Lydia boarded a *banca* to flee from the Japanese, and finally the La Suerte cockpit. As we drove, Jun kept reassuring me: "See how calm the city is, nothing to worry about—only killing crooked politicians and communists." I didn't tell him that I'd read the morning newspaper—two people found beheaded on the road outside the hotel, four policemen killed 50 miles north of Davao yesterday.

Back at the hotel, the desk clerk, Mr. Anacio, tracked me down in the restaurant. He had remembered that one of his relatives, Mr. Salesiano Tomado, knew something about the mine and might know if any of the Filipinos who had lived and worked there might still be around. The next day Jun drove me out to the Tomados' home.

We drove to the outskirts of the city and soon were driving on a narrow one-way dirt road in a barrio, barely wide enough for the car to pass through the shanties that lined each side. Before long the car was literally surrounded by curious people—thirty or forty, in front, behind, and on both sides. They touched the car, walked alongside it, peered in the windows at me. Jun was now creeping along at about three miles per hour so as to not run over the people walking in front of the car. At this point I was beginning to feel apprehensive, although Jun kept saying, "Don't worry, I used to live here, I know everyone." However, I hadn't noticed anyone saying, "Hey there, Jun, how are you doing, old buddy?"

I simply sat in the car and tried to look unconcerned. There was no escaping; with the press of people I doubt I could have opened the car door. Finally we stopped in front of a small but nice-looking house with a porch. By now the car and our entourage completely filled the street, but people stepped out of the way so we could get out of the car. Mr. Tomado came out of the house to see what all the commotion was about and then he welcomed me to his home. He also remembered the prison camp—told me that he had visited it often to sell bananas and fruit there. He, too, thought he remembered Simon's friend Mr. Hughes, but also did not know the current whereabouts of any of the Hughes children. It was fascinating hearing Mr. Tomado recall what happened when the Japanese invaded—"They came in fast and in twenty-four hours took control. The Philippine and American troops just fled." Life under the Japanese was hard, especially near the end of the war. Then when the Americans returned, there was intense bombing—a dangerous time when he and his family had to hide in caves to escape the bombs.

As we said thanks and started to leave, I asked him why we had attracted so much attention. "Oh," he said, "don't worry about it. People were just curious. The only time we see a car down here, it's either the police or the tax collector after someone."

After returning to the hotel I made arrangements to take a banca part way across the Gulf of Davao, following the route used by Simon and Lydia when they fled to the jungle and tried to return to the mine. Of course, it was impossible to get close due to the guerilla activity in the area. Imagine my surprise when two and a half years later I received a package of photographs from Mr. Anacio. The enterprising desk clerk informed me that he had made his way up to the gold mining area as a passenger on a moped (faster than a jeep, he said), and managed to sneak in and take some pictures for me. The photos showed some of the old mine buildings, as well as new open-pit mines.

Back in Manila I met with Mr. Lee Telesco, who had been a major in army intelligence during the war. Lee described the conditions during the Japanese occupation. Life in Manila was particularly difficult; besides food shortages and lack of medicine, civilians—women and even children—were bayoneted to death, often for no apparent reason.

Lee had grown up in the Philippines, and because of his previous knowledge and connections there, took on the job of providing liaison between General MacArthur and the various Philippine guerrilla factions. He made his first trip into the Philippines by submarine early in the war, on February 27, 1942. After that there were numerous trips to almost every major island, when supplies were brought by submarine to the guerrillas under the leadership of an American, Wendell Fertig, and a Filipino, Salipada Pendatum. Fertig was a lieutenant colonel in the Army Corps of Engineers, who, when the order was given to surrender, ignored it and walked off into the hills to organize a guerrilla fighting force.[38]

Lee told me how they arranged an elaborate system of signals and would bring the submarine in under the noses of the Japanese to deliver weapons, medicine, and equipment, and in some cases, relocate noncombatants from the Philippines to Australia. The primary role of the guerrillas was communications, and to this end Lee delivered shortwave radios that had a hand-cranked power supply. The guerrillas kept MacArthur informed of the status of the Japanese units in the area and ship and aircraft movements.

I asked Lee what the military knew about the POW camps and were they able to communicate with the prisoners? He said that they knew the locations of the camps and sometimes were able to smuggle in food or a message, but it was difficult. The Davao Penal Colony was well known because some prisoners had escaped and been rescued.[39] Near the end of the war, the military prisoners from Davao and other Philippine camps were transferred to Japan. A number lost their lives when the transport ships were sunk by American submarines or aircraft. Prisoners from Davao Penal Colony were moved by ship to Manila beginning in June 1944. The *Shinyo Maru* was sunk by the submarine USS *Paddle* early in September 1944. Hundreds of POWs died but there were 82 survivors who were rescued by friendly Filipinos and then later picked up by another sub, the USS *Narwhal*.

"Sad about the prisoners," he said. "Unfortunately there was little we could do at that time. Later, early in February 1945, the army and airborne troops rescued the civilian prisoners in Los Banos and Santo Tomas from behind the Japanese lines. These surprise operations were spectacular successes and no doubt saved many lives."

I know that Hugh, Jane, and Trudy Wills, who were rescued in those daring maneuvers, would have certainly agreed with Lee's appraisal.

卌 卌 卌

SIMON: The night was quiet except for the sloshing of water against the hull of the boat and the chug-chug of its antiquated engine. Lydia and I were huddled together in the stern of a small motorized banca, a fishing boat with bamboo outriggers. We were exhausted, but too tense to sleep. I still hadn't recovered fully from the effects of the beating I had gotten for failing to bow before the guard. Besides being tired, I had a terrible headache.

We sat still—alone with our own thoughts and worries, listening to the subdued conversation of the Filipino fishermen speaking the Cebuano dialect as they went about their chores. They were Muslims. For them, the coming of the Japanese had made no difference. They kept doing the same thing—each day, out into the gulf in their small boats, just as their fathers had done before them.

Frankly, I had no idea what to do next. At the moment, we had nothing except the clothes on our backs—and of course, each other. At least now we were back together and one terrible uncertainty had been removed. As we sat there, I made one decision. I told Lydia that we had to go back to the mine.

"But Simon, how can we?"

"I don't know. Still, in the morning I think we should go to the mill, see what we can find out. If we can stay at the mine, I think it will be better, now that we know the Japanese don't care about us. If not, we can at least get some of our clothes and things, then try to find a place where it will be safe to stay. Otherwise, what will we do—sleep on the beach? That's what we're going to have to do tonight."

The fishermen put us ashore at a secluded spot and we collapsed on the sand for a few hours' sleep. At daybreak we began a long tiring walk to the mill. There we found that some of the Japanese employees of the mine had returned and were working as caretakers. The mill was not operating. Not much was happening.

My meeting with the foreman was short and caustic. He told me it was not possible—we could not take the tram to the mine. He said it was forbidden. His name was Hideo—I knew him from before. So I tried pleading with him, called on our former friendship, told him we were destitute. I said, look at Lydia—that dress; that is all she has. All of our belongings are at the mine. And the Japanese commander has released us—we are free. We are not at war with Japan—only the Americans.

He was adamant that we were not permitted to ride the tram. He said, "I have my orders from the Japanese." However, I kept persisting. Finally he showed a little pity, and then he said, "If you want to go to your house, go ahead. But you'll have to walk there."

With that, he left us. He turned and walked away. We were sad when he left, because we had always treated this man kindly. But the war had changed him, changed everything. At this point we had no choice but to go to the village nearby. There I thought I could ask the head man to find a boy to guide us to the mine. I told Lydia, "To hell with this sonofabitch Japanese—we'll hike there. We can make it!"

ǁǁ ǁǁ ǁǁ

LYDIA: I knew there was no point in arguing with Simon now. But I was afraid of the trip through the mountains, and worried about what the Japanese would do. It was sad to see this man, our old friend, act this way. I knew that in his heart he had not changed, and so he must have been unhappy to have so dishonored himself. But, as Simon said to me over and over again, the war had changed everyone overnight. Even us, for hadn't we locked up the Japanese ourselves when the war started?

We spent the night in the village. Then, with the help of one of the Filipino mill workers, Simon arranged for a young man to serve as our guide, promising to find some way to pay him once we got to the mine.

In the morning we set out. The "trail" was little more than a narrow track. The distance was more than twenty miles; the terrain was tropical forests that rose from sea level to over 3,000 feet, dipped, then climbed again until finally the trail reached the mine, high in the mountains. We had no provisions, other than a bottle of water and some bananas. Simon fortunately had a small compass, which he'd taken when we'd left the mine, and which, for some reason, the Japanese had never taken from him.

It seemed as though the trail went on endlessly, up one mountain and down another, no sight of people, only the insects, birds flitting silently away as we passed. Everywhere I heard the strange sounds of the jungle. As we walked along, I watched my husband leading the way. Simon was five feet eleven inches tall, about 160 pounds, wiry, his wavy hair a little longer than usual. He hadn't lost much weight at that time and gave no indication that the beating he'd received in the camp was slowing him down. He moved ahead confidently, just as if this was one of our normal weekend hikes in the forest. All we were lacking were our fishing poles!

As we ascended the first range of mountains, I became more and more frightened. Simon kept urging me on, but my feet hurt. I was tired, hungry, thirsty, and the trail was hardly passable. It was a native track, barely distinguishable to the untrained eye. As it wound up the mountain, it diminished to nearly nothing—a stone placed here or there, in some places a small indentation, big enough for one foot, carved in the soil, or maybe a piece of bamboo placed in the soil to make a step. The path wound around the side of mountain gorges so steep that I became dizzy looking down. But I couldn't help noticing the raw beauty of the jungle, the vast green stillness stretching out in every direction. There were steep cliffs, ravines. We came to one place where I had to shimmy across a deep canyon on a tree trunk, holding on with both arms. Simon encouraged me, trying to comfort me, and then suddenly it became too much for me. I got across to the other side, then sat down on the trail in tears. I cried to Simon, "What will we do? I'll never make it. You shouldn't have brought me, Simon. I should have stayed behind." But, he was patient with me.

He said, "No, Lydia. No more separations. We'll rest for a while here, then we'll go on. You'll make it." So we rested, until finally I felt able to go on. After all, it was either continue or go back to the village, and that alternative didn't offer us much hope.

By late afternoon we appeared to be lost. The boy argued for one direction while Simon's compass told him it had to be another way. The only solution was to move ahead, climb another mountain to locate certain landmarks so we could establish where we were. Simon and the boy decided to go ahead and find out the best way. He said it would mean less walking for me. The problem was that it meant that I had to stay alone on the trail, and I knew it would be dark in a few hours. I tried to argue with him, but of course it was no use. "Don't worry, Lydia," he assured me. "Even at night we will be able to see the mountain behind the mine. And I know where you are. You will be safe. Just stay here, rest, and don't let yourself worry."

So I sat there and waited and worried anyway. Slowly the shadows lengthened and suddenly I realized it was almost dark and still no sign of Simon and the boy. Two hours stretched into three, then four, then six. Still they did not return. After many hours had passed I dozed off for a few moments, then woke with a start at the sound of a night bird on the other side of the ravine. Insects swarmed about my face. By then I was too tired to brush them away.

"Oh my god," I murmured out loud to nobody. Why did I agree to stay alone in this ravine? I was sure that something had happened to Simon or the boy, or they didn't remember where they'd left me. A sick feeling of dread rose in my stomach, a feeling much worse than the feeling I'd had in Davao when I was detained in the dentist's house. I wasn't sure—could I find my way back to the coast on my own if I had to? I was so tired that I fell asleep again in spite of these worries.

Just before dawn, I awoke suddenly at the sound of a branch cracking farther up the ravine. Something—possibly an animal—was moving stealthily down the ravine toward me. I debated whether I should remain perfectly still, or try to scramble up a nearby tree, or run on down the trail. Then I heard Simon's voice, speaking in low tones to the boy.

I called out to him. "Simon, Simon, thank heaven it's you." I was on my feet in an instant. First I was relieved, and then mad at him. "All night you leave me here, you crazy man, wandering in the jungle in the dark, anything could happen."

The poor guy was really tired. He slumped against a tree, didn't pay much attention to my ravings. We decided to rest awhile, then go on. They had found the way, and assured me it was not too bad. Of course, I didn't believe them for a minute.

Before I could argue, or say anything else, he was asleep. The boy stretched out on some leaves and fell asleep also. I didn't feel like sleeping anymore, so I just sat there and waited for the sun to come up. Once it got semi-light, I watched Simon sleeping, his chest rising and falling. This was the man I'd come halfway around the world to marry. And now, here we were, in the middle of the jungle in Mindanao. He had two leeches on his right leg. I removed them carefully while he slept, without awakening him. Their bites are slow to heal and I didn't want him to get any infections, especially now. Sitting there, I thought about how far it seemed from Ghent, from my parent's home, from all that was familiar.

Shortly after dawn we were on our way again. By ten o'clock in the morning we could see the mine buildings below us. There was no sign of activity. We paused to refresh ourselves in a small stream that cascaded down the cliff by the side of the trail. Lush green plants grew everywhere. Orchids and tropical flowers hung from trees. Overhead, one of the large Philippine eagles circled lazily, scanning the forest for its favorite food—monkeys. It saddened me to be in such a beautiful spot, burdened by so many worries and not knowing what to expect when we got to the mine. Below I could see places where we'd gone on picnics in happier times and could even make out the place where my garden used to be, saw my chicken coops. At that moment, I wanted to be like the eagle, free to fly to the top of Mount Apo, or even able to fly away from Mindanao altogether.

Simon reached over and took my hand. "Come on Lydia," he urged. "Let's go home." He pulled me to my feet and started down the trail as though we hadn't been gone at all and were returning from a hike.

JHT JHT JHT

SIMON: To our surprise there was a Filipino living in our house. He told us he was the one who'd fixed the tram. The Japanese said that he could have our house as a reward for repairing the tram. All property had been confiscated and was now the property of the Japanese government, so they could give it to anyone who helped them.

I told this Filipino that we had nothing but the clothes we were wearing. I tried to maintain as much dignity as possible, meanwhile watching Lydia who looked like a volcano about to erupt. I gave her a look to tell her to be quiet and not start an argument. I asked the Filipino for his permission to get some of our clothes and some other things we needed in order to live. I could tell he was nervous. He told us to wait while he consulted with the Japanese officer.

As soon as he left, Lydia grabbed my arm and said, "How can you stand by while that 'puppet' kicks us out of our own house?" I had to calm her down, tell her not to be silly. We didn't want to go back to the camp, did we? I said the Filipino doesn't want our clothes—he wouldn't wear them, even if he could. At that moment we had to be careful with the Japanese.

My months of internment had taught me the importance of discipline and authority to the Japanese mind. The Japanese asked no less of the Filipinos than they demanded of their own troops: blind obedience. In the Japanese army, one obeyed because to not obey led to a beating, and perhaps more importantly, to loss of face. On top of this complex and powerful set of deeply ingrained customs, one encountered dedication to the emperor, the most dominant force. So powerful was this loyalty that Japanese soldiers bowed to each other because they wore the emperor's uniform. No wonder they wanted us to bow even to the lowest-ranked private, no wonder ignoring their directives could be swiftly fatal.

In a while, the Filipino returned with one of the Japanese mine workers and a soldier. We bowed our politest and most humble bows. He barely acknowledged us, even though we both knew him from former times. He told us that we were free to take what clothes we could carry, as well as some things for cooking. But the house, furniture, everything else—had to be left alone because it now belonged to the Japanese government, and this man had been ordered to live there and take care of it.

I got some clothes and a few personal things. Lydia packed some of her clothes, some cooking utensils, a few other things. We made three bundles, including some items as payment for our guide. Then we went outside and sat down under a tree. I gazed around the mine. Already the buildings were showing signs of lack of maintenance. I wondered how long it would be before everything was gone. Nobody seemed to be working. The few people who were there just sat around.

While we were resting under the tree, one of the Japanese came and told us we had to leave. I explained to him that we'd walked all night and were too tired to return. I asked for permission to leave tomorrow after we'd rested. The Japanese shrugged, gave no answer and walked away. In a while two Japanese returned with the Filipino who now lived in our house. The Filipino told us that we had to leave now, but that the Japanese had given us permission to ride down on the tram. As the tram started to descend, I took one last look at the mine, and then told Lydia to look too, because we might not see it again. Then I realized something: this was the third time in my life I'd lost my house and all my belongings.

We rode the rest of the way in silence—too tired, too depressed, too concerned about the future to talk. When we came down from the mine, we were so tired from the trip we decided to spend that night at the mill. We'd noticed that the general superintendent's house was empty. We quietly slipped in and stayed out of sight. That night we could hear the Japanese soldiers passing by. Late at night, when we were sleeping, someone discovered us in the house. Some mill workers came with soldiers and told us to get out. They carried our bundles out of the house and dropped them under a tree and told us to sleep there. Meanwhile, soldiers stood around, leaning on their rifles, amused by the scene. Finally, everyone left, and we were alone once again. I moved our things a short distance away to a thick grove of coconut trees.

I told Lydia to try to get some sleep. I was sure she would be safe in this place. Then I went to the village to try to find someone who could take us to Mr. Hughes's plantation. By dawn, I was back with a carabao cart and Harry Hughes, the oldest boy. We moved that day to the Hugheses' plantation. We stayed there for almost two years.

⊬⊬ ⊬⊬ ⊬⊬

LYDIA: It was our good fortune to be accepted by Mrs. Hughes and allowed to live in a little house on their plantation. The Hughes family consisted of Mr. Hughes, who was still in prison camp with the other Americans, his Filipino wife, and their twelve children. Mrs. Hughes was grateful for our company, since she was worried about her husband. We were delighted to be in the company of this patient, gentle woman and her marvelous children.

She spoke little English, but the children spoke English quite well. Harry, the oldest son, became the "man" of the family and oversaw the day-to-day work on the plantation. The oldest girl was Helen; she helped her mother with the work and helped keep the family together. One of our favorites was a younger daughter Lillian, who had a beautiful voice. She entertained us on the long summer nights that first year. A popular song at that time—which she sang quite well— was "Smoke Gets in Your Eyes." There were other daughters; the other son, Bobby, was the youngest child, two years of age.

Of course, we did what we could to help out, but we were basically dependent on the Hugheses and their generosity for our existence. To survive, we picked fruit growing in the jungle. A few times we were able to steal papayas from the Japanese growers. It was difficult to get meat of any kind. Simon tried to trade things for fish. Once he traded a shirt for a few pieces of shark meat. I cooked it and cooked it, but it was almost inedible. After we'd planted our garden, we tried to trade vegetables for fish. We cleared some land and planted *camotes*—sweet potatoes. Simon tried to clear the land to plant more, but it was difficult because the abaca—hemp—plants grew everywhere.

Time passed slowly. At night we listened to the radio—tried to learn what was going on—but all we heard about was the Japanese victories. Of course, we knew that the American forces had been driven out of the Philippines—or at least we knew that the Japanese claimed that they had totally defeated the Americans.

We heard broadcasts from a clandestine Philippine station that called itself the Voice of Juan de la Cruz, which encouraged resistance to the Japanese. This, coupled with the persistent rumors of a guerrilla force in Mindanao, headed by a mysterious American named Colonel Fertig, gave us hope that the tide of Japanese domination would soon turn.

We had heard of the internment of Japanese Americans in the United States in April 1942 and had wondered if that news might have provoked the Japanese actions against our American friends.

The Japanese propaganda drew different conclusions, of course, about the progress of the war. Japanese-controlled radio was full of Japanese victories. We had learned of the fall of Corregidor in May 1942. Then there were other victories reported, many in places we had difficulty locating in our minds. The Japanese made great play of the "East Asiatic Co-Prosperity Sphere," their answer to Western colonialism. Although everyone knew this notion was to justify the Japanese invasion, it had a certain appeal to nationalistic Filipinos. After all, hadn't an Asian nation totally defeated the British, French, Dutch, and American forces? Besides, the Japanese promised a share of greater prosperity and began hinting at independence for the Philippines.

Ultimately two things derailed their chance of success in the Philippines. First, they misjudged the Filipino people, who did not accept the bowing and other humiliations forced on them by the Japanese. More importantly, they failed to deliver the "Co-Prosperity" goods. As time went on, Filipinos were quick to discover that they were worse off under the occupation because the Japanese were diverting everything to the war effort. Once people started starving, the Japanese lost any remaining credibility.

Treatment under the Japanese was unpredictable. In some places they did not intern civilians at all, or only much later in the war. So much depended on the individual commander who ruled the local area, how active the guerrillas were, and how important the region was to the war effort. We stayed away from Davao, where most of the population was, and did our best to remain inconspicuous. There were rare days when we got on a cart pulled by a carabao and made a trip to a neighboring plantation to visit Mrs. Baker. She was another Filipino married to an American, and her husband also had been imprisoned. She had two small children. The Hugheses and the Bakers were the limit of our small circle of friends during the last months of 1942. Things were still not too difficult since food was available and the Japanese had not yet begun to feel pressure from the American military. Even so, Simon and I had two great adventures, as we tried to repay these wonderful Filipinos who had been so kind to us.

Mrs. Hughes made periodic trips to Davao to see her husband. She took produce and eggs from the plantation to him and the other prisoners. They had been moved to a permanent camp in Davao, in what had formerly been a club called the Happy Life Blues Cabaret. With each trip Mrs. Hughes became more frightened by the Japanese, until one day she asked me to go with her. The reason why she thought I could help is now forgotten—not that it mattered—for how could I refuse this kind woman who had helped us so much? Besides, somehow Simon had gotten a bottle of whiskey, and we wanted to smuggle it into the camp for our American friends. We decided to conceal the whiskey by transferring it to a cooking oil bottle—a peculiarly shaped square bottle that was common in Mindanao at that time.

We also had some things for Hugh and Jane Wills and their daughter Trudy, who were also in the camp. They had been captured with the other Americans who fled to Malaybalay. The Japanese forces had rounded up all the Americans and other foreigners who'd fled north. After the American surrender, military personnel were separated from the civilians and then both groups were brought back to Davao. The military personnel were transferred to the old prison, called the Davao Penal Colony, while the civilians first were imprisoned in improvised holding camps, as Simon and I had been. Jane Wills and her daughter Trudy, along with other women and children, were kept for a while in a nunnery. Then they were transferred to the Happy Life Blues Cabaret camp and reunited with Hugh. Besides the Willses, Mr. Hughes was there, along with the Sundeens and the Americans and foreigners whom the Japanese had captured, including some priests.

Simon was opposed to me going to the camp because he worried that the Japanese might do something. Still, he agreed that we could not refuse Mrs. Hughes after all she had done for us. Early one morning, Mrs. Hughes, one of the girls, and I left the plantation and went down to the coast, carrying our "oil" bottle, eggs, and other things for Mr. Hughes and the Willses. We took a boat to Davao—about a two-and-a-half-hour boat ride. Once there, we walked along Quezon Boulevard and then to Rizal Street to get out to the camp. By this route we skirted the Imperial Japanese Army headquarters in the school building in the center of Davao. There were soldiers with rifles and bayonets on every corner, but they did not pay much attention to us. By now they were getting bored with the humdrum life of a small provincial Philippine town.

As we approached the camp, Mrs. Hughes took the lead. The procedure was to go to the guard gate, politely give the guard the prisoner's name, and the guard would call the prisoner out to meet with the visitor. Visitors could not enter the camp. Packages and food were inspected by the guard before the prisoners were allowed to receive them. All conversations took place there at the

Happy Life Blues Cabaret

gate in the presence of the guards. Mrs. Hughes asked for her husband and someone went off to get him. I asked for Mr. Wills.

I could see that the guards thought it was unusual—why was a white woman asking for an American? (Most white women were Americans and were locked up with their families.) But finally they sent someone to fetch him. Jane came out to see me because he was sick. As she came out, there was a little commotion by Mrs. Hughes with the guard pushing her around because he hadn't checked the food before she gave it to her husband. Meanwhile, I had the bottle of whiskey and some eggs for the Willses, and I was nervous about the whiskey. I quickly stuck the "oil" bottle in front of the guard and he waved at me to say okay, so I stepped forward and handed it to Mrs. Wills. At that moment some more guards came over and started pushing us apart, saying, "No talking, no talking!" The guard herded me away by making jabbing motions with his bayonet, so I was unable to say anything more to Jane or anyone else. They also pushed Mrs. Hughes away and made her husband go back inside. After a trip to the prison camp that had taken more than half the day, we were only allowed to stay five or ten minutes, and then had barely said hello to our friends.

At that point we left and began the long walk—nearly four miles—back to the pier, to find another boat to take us back across the gulf. We were both frightened by the incident. That was the thing about the Japanese—one day they would be polite, almost friendly, but the next day they would be cruel, slapping, beating up people for no reason, deriving sadistic pleasure from showing their power over those who could not resist. When we got back to the plantation and told Simon the story, he shook his head and hugged us both. Once again we both resolved: no more separations.

As our first year under Japanese rule approached an end, we continued to think about our American friends in the camp. Although we didn't have much, at least we were free and not living in the daily presence of the Japanese bayonets. Also, we knew from the information that Mrs. Hughes brought back from the camp that life there was getting harder every day. We wanted to do anything we could to help the prisoners, but what could we do?

Then Simon remembered that he had buried some money on a hillside above the mine during those hectic days when we awaited the arrival of the Japanese troops. He decided to make another trip to the mine, see what was happening there, and try to recover the money so we could give it to the prisoners for Christmas. He had buried the money—$200 American dollars—in a Morton's salt bottle. This time it took Simon two days to walk to the mine. He went by himself, careful to avoid the Japanese troops. When he got to the mine, he found our house was just an empty shell; guerillas had robbed everything in it. Since soldiers were patrolling, he decided to wait until nightfall before looking for the money.

Once it was dark, he crawled to the base of the huge tree where he had buried the bottle, roughly six inches deep, as he remembered. The Japanese troops were housed in the mine mess hall in the valley and had sentries posted around the area. One of the sentries heard Simon crawling around on the hillside above the mine, because sound could carry quite a distance in the quietness of the jungle night.

At the noise, the sentry shouted "O bakka mei" ("What are you doing, idiot?") and fired a couple of shots into the side of the mountain. Knowing that the sentry would be afraid to go up into the hills in the darkness, Simon waited for a while and then continued to search quietly around the tree. Finally he found the spot but could not locate the bottle of money. He dug in six inches, then twelve inches, then eighteen inches, and was starting to panic when, at the depth of about twenty inches, he finally found the bottle.

Simon hid the bottle in his shirt and started to crawl quietly away. As he left the spot, he felt something moving on his chest. When he got far enough away from the tree and examined himself, he found termites all over his body. They had somehow gotten into the bottle and eaten up about one-eighth of the rolled-up bills. We were lucky he recovered the money when he did, or there might not have been anything left!

He was anxious to get as far away from the mine as possible before daylight, so he started back along the same trail. At one point he strayed from the path in the dark and suddenly found himself falling into a pit—an old boar trap. Originally there been a sharp stake in the bottom, but fortunately it had rotted away and he landed on a pile of twigs with no serious harm. At this point Simon concluded he had gone far enough and decided to wait until daybreak. Then he continued the trip and made it safely home.

After Simon returned, we found a trusted Filipino and sent the money to the prison camp to be delivered to the mine superintendent, Mr. Sundeen, with the instruction that he distribute it to the prisoners.

We later learned that in addition to robbing our house, the guerrillas had killed the Filipino puppet who occupied it for collaborating with the Japanese. The man paid a heavy price for helping the Japanese. His death made our loss seem small by comparison. Later on, the guerrillas came back and attacked the Japanese again, and this time they burned down our house.

CHAPTER 12

日卄 日卄 日卄

OSAKA

GARTH: The morning after our arrival at Osaka we surveyed our new home. We were billeted underneath the seats of a large stadium. The walls and floor were concrete. The Japanese had built up wooden boxes and put mats on them to serve as our beds. Down the center of the room—if you could call it that—they'd placed tables and benches, with the legs set in the cement floor. That was where we ate.

We stayed at the stadium while they were completing arrangements for Osaka #1, which was to be the official camp.[40] Before Osaka #1 was ready, some of us were moved again. This third and final move was to Hirohata—a camp that proved, of all the places we were imprisoned, to be the most difficult and deadly to some POWs.

While we remained at Osaka, the routine was about the same as Zentsuji. The camp was only two blocks from the docks. In the morning they'd roust us out with a bugle blast. After *tenko*, we stood in front of our bunks while they counted us. Then we were fed. We were informed that our standard rations amounted to 750 calories per day. We were even given a rationale: this amount was what they fed the Korean contract workers.

After breakfast we lined up and marched to the docks, where they split us into work parties. Some days we worked in the harbor on ships, unloading coal, iron ore, bauxite, or bags of rice. If we weren't on ships, we worked on docks or in the warehouse where we performed heavy work. We carried cans of bricks, slings full of other materials, or heavy bags of grain. It was common to carry these things in coolie fashion, with a heavy bamboo pole across the shoulders, a load swinging from each end. We marines called this a "yo-ho" pole.

At that time, there were a lot of ships getting through, which meant there was more food to steal and eat, so long as you didn't get caught. The best thing, of course, was to steal something that you could eat on the spot, because that way you destroyed the evidence. The next best thing was to steal something and hide it where you were working. The risk with that plan was you might be assigned somewhere else the next day, or they might instigate a search if they found something missing. Taking stuff back to camp was the riskiest option, but we all did it.

After work, we'd march back to the camp. Dinner was similar to Zentsuji. They had a big galley where they'd boil the rice, and there was a large cast-iron pot they'd use to make soup.

Once a week or so, they'd let us take a bath. They filled big tubs with hot water. Then we'd be brought in groups. You weren't supposed to wash in the tub; just jump in, get wet all over with hot water, and get out. Then you were supposed to soap up, dip a bucket in, rinse off, and go. But I always tried to stay in the tub as long as possible.

Osaka had the typical Japanese toilets—a slot in the floor, with a cement tank underneath, and an outside door or hatch. There were special workers who came periodically to the camp—we called them "honey dippers"—and it was their job to empty the tanks. They used long wooden ladles to collect the contents for use as fertilizer in the fields. The balance of the camp was about the same as you'd expect: barbed-wire fences, guard posts, and the commander's office. The guards at Osaka were tougher on us; maybe they knew we had more opportunities to steal. Some of them were sadistic and took every opportunity to kick us or slap us around.

Occasionally we'd run into one who would show us some small kindness. One who tried to help me was the interpreter, named Mr. Tajima. He was also in Zentsuji and went to Osaka with us. For a period of time he was fairly friendly—until my big mouth got me in trouble. It turned out he'd been raised on the West Coast (in the Central Valley) and learned that I'd grown up with Japanese kids and had been associated with Japanese people in the United States. When we were in Osaka, he had to go to the dentist a couple of times, and he asked me to take a walk with him. Along the way, he'd let me have some ice cream, some candy, or food—trying to be nice to me, I suppose, because he thought I was different from the other Americans, or maybe because he thought he could line me up to be an informer. Because of his U.S. roots, he spoke nearly perfect American English, without an accent, slang and all. Apparently he'd been visiting Japan when the war started, and had been forced to stay. Because of his knowledge of English, we had to be careful around him; he understood everything we said, including slang expressions we used to confuse the guards.

One day when we were working, some of the prisoners started talking to me about Mr. Tajima, complaining about my friendship with him. They implied that I was brownnosing him. Of course, I denied it and in the heat of the moment I stated (rather loudly) that I was just stringing the dumb shit along, taking him for all I could get. Unfortunately, he was standing nearby and happened to overhear my remarks—and that was the end of my friendship with Mr. Tajima, as well as the end of any special privileges.

Sometimes we worked on the docks for Japanese companies under the supervision of civilian overseers called "honchos." I believe these companies contracted with the army to provide prison laborers. We had a little saying there— "*Sumitomo joto, Mitsubishi joto nai—no damn good.*" In other words, the treatment at Sumitomo wasn't bad, but at Mitsubishi they beat the shit out of us, for no reason, regularly.

In most ways the Japanese were strict and disciplined, and there was little that we could get away with; in other ways they were lax and disorganized. On the docks, once we'd started working at our job for the day, the guards would go somewhere and sleep. I suppose they correctly assumed that we could not escape—we'd be identified immediately by the civilian population. Their laxity gave us countless opportunities to explore lockers, warehouses, storage sheds, crates, railroad cars, whatever was there. If we worked in one area for two or three days, we knew every nook and cranny.

We gave ourselves immense personal satisfaction by a thousand small acts of sabotage: poking little holes in containers or sacks; putting dirt in oil tanks or lubrication systems; cutting wiring or damaging motor parts and then replacing them; breaking or bending things; stacking supplies in the wrong place, or in the wrong order, so the work would have to be done all over again in the afternoon or the next day. Some things were half funny, half symbolic. We'd watch routines. If a particularly obnoxious honcho locked the warehouse at night and unlocked it in the morning, one of us would try to piss on the lock in the afternoon, so he'd have to get our urine on his hands.

We stole anything and everything that we could eat or conceal in our clothes to take back to camp. Food was the prime target, but there were hundreds of other items that made their way into camp in our baggy clothes. Stealing was so rampant it is hard to understand why the Japanese didn't crack down harder. They couldn't have been that stupid!

One day we found a container of naphthalene crystals in a paint locker. A few pounds of this chemical—in the form of granules—went into our pants legs and shirt sleeves, and then back into camp. At night we retrieved it from a hiding place in the barracks wall and sprinkled it on our sleeping mats. The result was dramatic: it either killed the fleas and lice, or drove them away to our neighbor's mats. Suddenly, we were able to sleep reasonably well. Once you had contraband like this, you could trade it for something else—and ultimately, maybe you could end up with something that another person wanted so badly they'd trade food for it.

When we were working in those warehouses on the docks, the Japanese stevedores and storeroom workers often would point out the edible things we could steal. I guess they were not a hell of a lot better off than we were. I remember one great big guy—he must have been six feet four inches and was muscular as hell. I was assigned to work with him, throwing fifty-kilogram (110-pound) sacks of rice with cargo hooks. I tried, but in my weakened state he was doing most of the work. Actually, he could toss those sacks by himself almost effortlessly, so he didn't really need me. This was the one time we were working that I actually had fun.

After an hour or so, he called a halt, and signed that I was to follow him. He spoke no English. He led me over to a warehouse, where we were joined by several other members of his crew. He apparently was the honcho on this crew. They had some grain alcohol stashed away in this warehouse, so we all sat down and passed the bottle around for a few shots. It was cut with something, but I don't remember what—anyway, it was strong stuff and hit awfully hard, especially since I wasn't getting anything to eat. He was careful to make sure I didn't get too much at once. After a couple of pulls on that bottle, we'd all lay there for a few minutes, then sneak out one or two at a time to go back to work, throwing those sacks around again. I worked for him for a week or so, and each day we'd get two or three breaks for a shot of his booze. For a change, work was a pleasure!

Then, one day before I was reassigned—maybe he knew I was going—he let me have a little more than normal, and I got a little boisterous and funny, and started staggering and stumbling as I worked. Unfortunately, I never got on his work detail again. I don't know if he knew I was leaving and gave me extra to be nice, or if it just happened that way. At any rate, that was the only time I got any alcohol during the four years I was imprisoned in Japan.

Women were another story. We had little contact with women except for the occasional Korean or Japanese dockworkers, or the rare civilian woman we'd see as we marched to work. One time L. D. nearly got himself killed trying to mess around with a Japanese girl. We were unloading flour on a barge alongside a ship. They would run a big cargo net from the ship down to the barge. Japanese families lived on the barges and operated them. While we were working, one of the girls who lived on the barge came up and went to the bathroom. There was a split plank over the side of the vessel and whenever someone wanted to go to the toilet, they walked out on the plank and let fly. This girl appeared to be six-teen or eighteen years of age. After watching her, L. D. got the idea that he was going to try and pay her a visit.

While we were waiting for the net to come back down, he watched her go back belowdecks, to her family's quarters. As soon as the net dropped down with another load of flour sacks, he told me to unload it real slowly, because he was going to try to sneak down below and talk to the girl. I guess he was willing to take the risk. He slipped away and went down into their living quarters. He wasn't down there long when all of a sudden he came flying up, just about the time that we'd finished unloading and the net was going back up to the ship.

He leaped up after the net, hung on, and rode it right back up to the ship. And, as he was doing that, here came the old man from down below. We didn't know whether he was the girl's husband or her father, but he had a great big knife and was screaming and yelling like a madman. The Japanese soldiers who normally guarded us on the ship were standing by L. D. who had made it to the top. They were laughing like hell and trying to force him back down, but he wasn't riding that net back down for anything, not even a dozen beautiful women—not even if they were sprawled naked on the deck!

The old man kept ranting and raving, and waving the knife around, while the guards teased him with comments we didn't understand. Finally, they took me off the barge too, and put on a couple of Japanese workers. Later on, when L. D. and I were working topside, I asked him what happened. He only grinned, shook his head. But he kept watching down below to see if the girl would put her head out or make any sign to him. The one time she did, we heard that yelling start up again, and her face jerked back out of sight before L. D. could even wave.

Getting enough to eat continued to be our chief preoccupation—the over-powering force that lay behind every conscious action or decision we made. I once read of a writer who described hunger as a demon in the stomach that took command of your life. This certainly was the case for us.

Scholars glorify evolutionary theory with discussions of the "survival of the fittest." The theory is silent about how you handle the situation where the guy who is less fit is your buddy. Survival of the fittest became, for us, "dog eat dog." We talked constantly about survival—how we would all come back and fight the Japanese, next time with better odds.

As each hour slipped into the next in an endless succession of days that dis-appeared permanently from my life, I told myself I have survived, I have existed, I have endured. But there were times when we were driven to extremes, reduced to mere shadows of human behavior, almost to an animal's existence. How can anyone understand the innermost feelings of a person who suffers such an experience—a person reduced to barely being able to communicate love and emotions to other beings? For years afterward, I felt I had lost this ability—felt that I'd left something behind in Japan, and because of it I was unable to convey the ordinary feelings that exist between normal people. A torch had seared my soul and burnt out love, hope, charity. Animals we were at times, but I'd like to affirm that there was a higher human spirit that kept us going, kept us helping each other nonetheless. Faith was part of it.

Fried rice brought out the animal in me on one occasion. After a couple of weeks in Osaka, as we sat at the tables under the bleachers eating our evening bowl of rice, I noticed that one of the chiefs had fried rice in his bowl. All of the rest of us had the ordinary steamed rice.

At the time, I didn't think much about it, being too tired and hungry to care much whether it was fried or steamed or smoked or raw. You have to realize that we went out each day and performed hard labor, while the chiefs—as our ranking officers—stayed behind and did paperwork, making out work schedules, seeing about "pay" for us (we got a few yen in those days, enough to buy cigarettes, when they were available). So, they had an easy life, compared to those of us who were out on the docks burning up the calories.

One night—after an especially rough day of shoveling coal and breathing filthy coal dust, I sat down at our evening meal and stared at my coffee-cup–size portion of rice. I had the shits pretty bad and anything I ate seemed to go right through me without doing any good anyway. Across the table the chief was joking and talking in a loud voice. It looked to me like he was feeling pretty good. Then I looked again. The sonofabitch had that fried rice in his bowl again. That was when the animal in my belly grabbed hold of my brain and I lost control. I leaned across the table and grabbed the chief's arm to get his attention. "Hey, chief, every night you've got fried rice and we get plain rice. I'd like to know how come?"

He stammered for a minute, pulled his arm away, made some wisecrack to the guy sitting next to him. Real calmly I said, "Chief, I'm taking half of your fried rice and I'm going to give you half of what I've got." Our table got real quiet, as the other guys started noticing what the chief was eating. "The hell you are," he said. I jumped up on the table and grabbed his bowl away, and then he grabbed my arm, and I popped him one in the chops, and pretty soon we were going at it. Everybody grabbed their rice and got the hell out of the way. Someone even picked up our bowls so they wouldn't get knocked over in the shuffle.

He was bigger than me and healthy; I was sick, but he'd been sitting on his ass all day while I was out working mine off, which evened things up. No one tried to pull me off of him, so I figured I had passive support. The fight didn't last too long. I punched out his lights and then we split the rice my way, and after that we didn't see any more fried rice. He may have kept eating it—since he was the guy who decided who cooked and who worked on the docks—but at least he didn't eat it in front of us. I wonder—which of us was the "fittest"? Hell, neither. We were both just poor dumb animals, frightened, half crazy, both trying to survive anyway we could.

After three months at Osaka, we were given the word that eighty of us were going to be moved again. The chief selected the men for the transfer, forty sailors and forty marines. After my experience with him, I was not surprised to find that once again I was in the group selected to leave. Navy Chief D. W. Barnum was appointed to be in command of our group; Marine First Sergeant Ercanbrack was second in command. We got an unforgettable send-off from Osaka on October 17, 1942.

The camp commander—Colonel Sotaro Murata—thought it would be an opportune time to let the public witness firsthand the overpowering strength of the Imperial Japanese Army. Consequently our poor, bedraggled, underfed, and poorly clothed group of eighty prisoners was marched through the streets of Osaka. Naturally, as we went, a group of curious citizens gathered and followed us. For many, it was the first time they'd ever seen an American.

By the time we reached the railroad station, a large crowd had gathered. At this point, we were lined up, made to stand at attention, and then made to go through a series of ridiculous drills in front of the crowd. We were publicly humiliated, embarrassed, and made to look ludicrous in front of the civilians. Meanwhile, Colonel Murata strutted back and forth, while his ragtag band of pint-size guards slapped us around if we did not turn precisely on command, or if someone staggered. (None of us were in good shape at this time.) The colonel alternated between screaming at us and lecturing the crowd, no doubt telling them how the victorious Japanese troops would easily overcome the physically larger Americans, because we had no "fighting spirit."

Under his urging, the crowd—which now numbered in the hundreds—became ugly and began jeering us, throwing things, crowding in and spitting on us. Stones began to fly. I was hit on the head with one. Others were hit in the body or face. Those who were not hit, stood next to their buddies and helped keep them on their feet; some men had blood running down their faces. After a quarter of an hour or so, the colonel screamed another order, and the crowd divided in front of the guards to let us enter the station. The guards were all smiles and laughing once we were inside. Such was the discipline of the Japanese people that there was probably not a single moment when the colonel did not have full command of the situation. Still, it was a terrifying and humiliating ordeal, painful because there was nothing we could do to resist or defend ourselves.

Once again we faced the uncertainty of a new camp, new regime, new guards. While waiting for the train we learned that we were headed for Hirohata—destined to be our last and toughest camp. We learned from the guards that Hirohata was near the town of Himeji, just southwest of Kobe—and around 130 miles away from a place called Hiroshima.

CHAPTER 13

JHT JHT JHT

HOUSES IN THE JUNGLE

SIMON: During those last desperate years of the war, Lydia and I had a succession of homes in the jungle. We left the Hugheses' place in early 1944, feeling that we could no longer burden them with our care, because Mrs. Hughes was struggling just to feed her family. We moved nearer the coast, thinking maybe life would be a little easier there, closer to the sea, away from the guerrillas who were harassing the Japanese. Unfortunately, many others had the same idea, and food was just as hard to come by there as anywhere. We jumped from one spot to the next to avoid either the Japanese or the guerrillas. We alternated from day to day, trying to decide whether the Japanese were preferable to the guerrillas or the guerrillas to the Japanese.

As food got scarcer, people ate anything. I tried snake, all kinds of seafood—even insects. Lydia wouldn't eat some of these things. We learned to do things we never imagined we'd be able to do. For example, our neighbors near the Hughes plantation grew corn. We helped them care for it, and they shared some with us. Then one day we heard about another farm where locusts came and started eating the crop.

"Never mind," I said, "We'll do something." So we watched carefully for the locusts, while I thought about ditches filled with water, burning green grass to make smoke, or some kind of herbs to poison them. Before long, the locusts were at our place eating everything in sight. We tried the measures I'd planned, but nothing worked well.

My best idea was to burn old tires, which seemed to slow them down a little—maybe the sulfur bothered them. But more and more came, and they laid eggs, and small ones hatched out and then moved across the ground until it looked like a wave, like the ground was moving. They were unstoppable. Before we knew it, the plants were stripped bare, down to straight stalks with no leaves, so we picked the corn—even though it wasn't ripe yet—and got what we could from it.

The only way we could collect the rest of our corn was by eating the locusts! The Filipinos showed us how to "French fry" them, and they weren't bad, especially after they'd been fattened on our corn.

Lydia became an expert at preparing cassava, a starchy root we dug up. She'd slice it, dry the slices, and then grind them. Eventually she made a white flour, somewhat like tapioca—which in turn could be baked, made into pudding, or cooked like porridge. Lydia was clever at cooking and once baked me a beautiful sponge cake in an old gasoline can. She rigged up a stove using two bricks and a few pieces of reinforcing steel. We ate using sections of banana leaves as dishes just like the Filipinos. From the locals, Lydia learned which wild plants and fruits were edible. One wild plant that we ate was a spinach-like leaf that grew wild, called "tankum."

Finally we decided we'd be safer nearer the coast, so we went to Pantukan and stayed in the city. The Pantukan mayor was a relative of the Hugheses—a man named Mr. Legal. He was well educated, a kind and polished gentleman. Across the street from Mr. and Mrs. Legal's house, an old couple lived. On Mr. Legal's introduction, they let us stay in their home. There was a wooden platform for a bed. Eventually we found an old cot and used it for sleeping. Life was difficult in the city, but people were kind and helped us.

One day the Legals had a party for their friends and invited us to join in. They roasted a pig and prepared other special dishes. Lydia tried to bake some muffins for it, but she didn't have the right ingredients and they didn't turn out well. That was the way it was those days. No one had much. Everyone made do with whatever they could get and shared with the others. We were taking care of our crops up in the hills and brought things down into the city. We shared whatever food we had with our Filipino friends.

Mr. Legal still had a couple of horses at that time. The guerrillas came and told him that they needed his horses to fight the Japanese. He didn't trust these guerrillas. So he said, "Okay, you can have the horses, but I want to go with you to see your leader and find out how we can help fight the Japanese." That was the end of him. He didn't come back and nobody ever saw him again. We felt terrible about what happened, because he'd befriended us and helped us find a place to live.

Another time I was walking on the beach, when I saw a big crowd gathered around a tree. They were yelling something. When I came up I saw there were some guerrillas and they had a Japanese tied to the tree. They were torturing him, mutilating him. They'd already cut off one of his ears, and blood was running down the side of his head. I knew him, and he was a good man, a kind person.

Jungle House

He'd lived there all of his life, and his sons were in the Philippine army. I wanted to help him, so I yelled at the guerrillas, "Why torture this man? He is a good Japanese, he's done nothing to hurt you."

The mob got ugly, because so many of them had suffered at the hands of the Japanese. They told me, "Shut up, Russo, or we'll tie you up there with him." There was nothing I could do—it was mob violence, and I was afraid for myself, even though I knew many of the people there. So I left, and a little while later they killed that innocent man.

The Japanese had a submarine base not far from Pantukan. At night the guerrillas would come down from the hills and take some potshots, sometimes kill a sentry or a Japanese soldier who was drunk or who walked a little bit too far from the base. After this happened a few times, the Japanese came in and shot up Pantukan and drove some of the people away. Whenever guerrillas would attack the Japanese, the Japanese soldiers would make reprisals on the villagers.

One day when the artillery shells started falling on the village, it seemed like they were only a short distance away and must soon hit us, so we moved again. We decided we'd be safer if we moved a little ways away from the city, but still stayed on the coast. The next place we found was an abandoned plantation.

There was an empty house, a ramshackle, run-down place. All the windows were broken, the screens were torn and falling off, and the roof leaked. It had a living room with a high ceiling, a bedroom, a kitchen, maybe another room or two.

This house was full of birds. There were bird nests all over the living room. We left them alone and stayed in the bedroom and kitchen. We moved in our cot, a few makeshift rattan chairs, and that was it. We stayed there for a while, and then one day some guerrillas came and confiscated some of our belongings—chickens and an old bicycle I had patched together. They said they'd received a telegram from General MacArthur authorizing them to take whatever they needed! I recognized some of them as former workers from the mine, but that didn't help us at all. Once again, we decided we'd better move.

This time we fled into the jungle to find a safer spot. It seemed as if we were running all the time. Some Filipinos showed us a place where they thought we'd be safe. It was hidden away, next to a small creek, but with open areas where hemp had been grown. We decided to build a house there and got some of our Filipino neighbors to help us build it. Our grass hut wasn't much of a house. It consisted of four poles, a thatched roof, and nothing else—no walls, no floor, no windows, and no door. Even with these hardships, we had a strong desire to survive.

As the war dragged on and food got even scarcer, life became extremely hard for us. No longer could we live off of the hospitality of our neighbors. Realizing that we were really on our own now, I sat down under a tree to contemplate our situation. I said to myself, "Simon, you graduated from the university with high honors, so now is the time to use your knowledge." Unfortunately, there were no courses on survival in the jungle in my curriculum, but I noticed that the Filipinos nearby were raising vegetables. I decided to plant eggplants, which seemed to grow well there. When they were fully grown, I collected two sacks of big juicy fruits and took them to the beach to exchange with the fishermen for fresh fish.

Nobody looked at my eggplants, since they could trade their few pitiful fish for much better things to the people starving in the villages and in Davao. However, they suggested, "If only you had grown some tobacco, that would be a different story." Anyway, they took pity on me and gave me a few tiny fish and I returned home to discuss my new plan with Lydia.

Once the eggplants were done blooming, I pulled them out to plant some tobacco. Every morning I would go through the field and by hand pick off the worms that ate large holes in the leaves. When the tobacco was ripe, I went down to the beach to make arrangements to sell all my tobacco for a supply of fish, but by that time everybody was raising tobacco and my tobacco had absolutely no value. Again, the fishermen took pity on me and this time gave me some fish heads.

Once again I said to myself, "Simon, you graduated with high honors, so you have to think of something to survive." I then noticed that nobody had soap. I knew little about inorganic chemistry because it had not been an important subject for civil engineers. Lydia, on the other hand, had studied chemical engineering. For days we tried to visualize chemistry on the blackboards of our minds, trying to remember the chemical reactions of saponification. Little by little it came back to us.

We made our own coconut oil by asking little kids to knock off coconuts from the tops of the palm trees, but they grew tired of that chore and stopped passing our shack. Then, after a few attempts and falls, I managed to make the climb myself. Once we had the coconuts, we had to break them open, grate the meat, and boil it to extract the oil.

Next we collected seashells, burned them, and used the calcium carbonate to make calcium hydroxide, which in turn we heated with salt water to make lye (sodium hydroxide). The process was complicated since the seashells had to be burned at high temperature. We split dried bamboo and stacked it up in layers, each layer alternating in direction. We put the shells on each layer. In this manner, we constructed a pyre that could reach a high temperature. After firing, we put the shells in an old oil drum and sprinkled them with water, whereupon they'd instantly crumble to a fine powder—calcium hydroxide.

We made salt by evaporating seawater. When the salt was added to the calcium hydroxide, the sodium displaced the calcium and made lye, which we separated from the calcium that precipitated out. We mixed the lye with the oil to make soap. Sodium hydroxide makes a liquid soap. You have to have potassium hydroxide to make solid soap. We were able to make potassium hydroxide by burning seaweed and other potassium-rich plants, and using the ash as a source of potassium. Finally, we produced a big block of beautiful white soap. We cut the block into bars using a hot wire as a saw.

We were able to trade the soap for other products and we did eat a little better. Interestingly, once we'd succeeded, the Filipinos started to come by and volunteer to help me with soap manufacturing. I innocently accepted their help, but then in a few weeks they quit and went away to open their own soap factories.

One interesting problem in soap production was the necessary water, which had to be carried from a neighbor's well one mile away. To eliminate this extra work, I decided to dig my own well, but the water was absolutely putrid with an offensive taste. I consulted with some people in the nearby village and asked one of them what to do. One fellow—as I recall, his name was Pedro—said he would get me a couple of mudfish (snake-like fish that dig into the ground during the dry season and swim in small streams in the wet season). The next day Pedro brought me two black fish, and I put them into the well. In a few days the water was clear and fresh. When I had dug the well, I'd cut through roots that rotted and fermented, and the mudfish ate these, making the water clear.

During the last two years of our jungle existence we did not see any butter, sugar, flour, meat, or bread. At one time we had raised geese, but they were long gone, as were the chickens we'd had. We subsisted on bananas, papayas, sweet potatoes, and rarely, a bit of fish. That's why, when I observed a water buffalo feeding her calf, I got a wild idea. If only I could milk a water buffalo, the milk would improve our diet.

I asked some Filipinos "How can I get a water buffalo?" A Filipino friend took me up into the mountains where the Mansakas, a pagan tribe of aborigines, lived. The Mansakas and a related aboriginal group, the Mandayas, lived in the northeastern Davao region, where they practiced a primitive agriculture. They were well known as silversmiths and made large breast ornaments worn by men and women. Occasional groups of Mansakas had visited us when we lived at the mine.

It took two days of travel before we arrived at the hut of the chieftain of this particular group. He was eighty to ninety years old, and his face was all wrinkled like a prune. On his right were six of his fourteen- to eighteen-year-old wives and on his left were another dozen or so. Through my interpreter, I told him that I wanted to rent a female carabao with a calf and would pay him with two bars of soap. All of them laughed and thought I was crazy. For one thing, nobody had ever heard of milking a water buffalo, and second, the female was no good for pulling a plow or a cart. This work was done by the males. Consequently, they could not understand why I would want a cow. He was more than willing to rent me the buffalo. I took the animals, and we made the long trip back to my hut, where I tied them in the pasture. In the morning I found that the calf had emptied her mother's udder during the night.

"Look here, Simon," I said to myself, "you got a diploma with high honors from the university, so think of something. There must be a way to get the milk!" The next night I tied the calf and the mother far apart. However, the calf cried all night and our neighbors complained bitterly to me in the morning that the noise had kept them awake. So then I thought, "Simon, you have to think harder!"

When the carabaos are young calves, the villagers put a ring in their nose so that they can control them. The next day I tied the mother to a tree using the metal ring through her nose and put two logs on each side so she could not kick me. Then I tried to milk her. She was able to kick the pail, however, and again no milk.

Then I remembered from my statics course that the tripod is a stable structure but a two-legged piece of furniture will fall down. So I tied one leg of the carabao up under her stomach. Every time she wanted to kick the milk pail, she fell down. As soon as I tried to milk the animal, though, I found out that she wouldn't produce anything but tired hands.

"Where is your academic distinction now, my friend?" I asked myself, since I knew that all our Filipino neighbors—and by now, even Lydia—were probably laughing at me and wondering when I would abandon this insane operation. Finally we figured it out. We let the calf drink some milk first, and when the flow was established, we removed the calf (for this I needed Lydia and another man). Then I directed the flow of milk into the pail. By repeating this operation as many times as needed, we had plenty of milk, which was so thick that it took three parts of water to thin it down for drinking consistency.

Somehow, by these measures and the goodness of the Filipinos, we survived. Beyond a doubt, the Hughes family and other unknown Filipinos are the reason we lived—they saved our lives, not once, but many times. Most of the details of those terrible days have faded, because if you distill our experiences to the essential, we had only a single preoccupation: food. How could we get enough to eat? By the end of the war, my weight had dropped down from 150 pounds to about 100. Lydia's was also about 100 pounds. Almost everything else faded into insignificance. Who worried about furniture, clothes, all those other things that formerly had seemed to be such an essential part of our lives? We thought only of our empty stomachs.

We went barefoot for two or three years. I had some tattered pants and a shirt; Lydia, some shorts, shirts, and a few other things. Outside the shack, we constructed a latrine; a palm frond partition provided some privacy for Lydia. Or, we'd simply walk a few dozen paces into the denseness of the jungle. We had no great need for privacy since we were virtually alone, and only rarely saw other people unless we went to the village or the coast. Bathing was simply stepping into the creek, or sometimes using a bucket for showering.

After food, our next greatest concern was to stay healthy. There were insects everywhere, and we both contacted malaria, but were affected in different ways. Lydia alternated between fever and chills, and suffered terribly before beginning to recover. In my case, the malaria seemed to go to my head, and I became delirious and lost all track of time and where I was. The Filipinos in the area also were victims of insects, parasites, leeches, boils, fungus, dysentery, malaria, and other diseases. There was a Filipino doctor in the village, but of course no one had any medicine.

After the lack of food and the illnesses that we experienced, the next worse challenge was the terrible loneliness, the lack of contact with other Europeans, or with any other human being, for that matter. Our contacts with anyone were limited—even with our Filipino friends—during those terrible final days of the war. We found ourselves living an animal's existence, almost without hope, barely surviving from day to day. We began forgetting English, speaking pidgin to each other, or mixing Cebuano with Spanish, with English, or with Russian. We scarcely knew what it was like to talk about something other than food.

There were moments when we'd hear shooting off in the jungle, and all we could do was slip away from our shack into the abaca groves, and remain still until whoever it was went away. We always worried that someday they'd come shoot us to retaliate for something done by the guerrillas. Yet, somehow we survived. Later, as we looked back, our survival in itself seemed a miracle. What we went through together was the "glue" that joined us together as no marriage ceremony or legal document could ever do. We looked at each other, and we knew if we could survive this, we could survive anything.

CHAPTER 14

‖‖ ‖‖ ‖‖

A RIOT AND A MARRIAGE

MITZI: The riot grew out of a division in sentiment within the camp that had existed from the beginning. The majority of people in Manzanar were loyal Americans who viewed their incarceration as a necessary evil associated with the war effort. They were willing to accept the loss of their homes and businesses—as wrong and painful as this was—because their country had told them they must, and because they knew that others were making even greater sacrifices, giving their lives in many cases.

Still, this was a painful time for everyone, because not only were two nations at war, but the heritage of the Issei was brought into the conflict. Nearly everyone had relatives in Japan, and even if they had never gone back to visit them, it was natural that there would be concern for the welfare of family members overseas. But this concern—for most of the internees—would never cause them to be disloyal to the United States.

Within the camp, there was a small minority who held pro-Japanese sentiments. One group—that called itself the Black Dragons—passed around leaflets supporting Japan. They and others attempted to play upon the emotions of the internees to win support for Japan. They also were determined to take action against the moderates—the pro-U.S. camp leaders.

It began one December afternoon in 1942—perhaps with an argument. I'm really not sure what triggered it.[41] There was a rally where arguments flew back and forth between the moderates and those who wanted to revolt. That evening, one of the pro-U.S. men was badly beaten. That night we stayed in the barracks, frightened. Outside we could hear yelling, shouts, the sounds of people running back and forth.

The next day more trouble broke out. People were being chased. A number of the pro-U.S. leaders were singled out as targets for mob violence. I was working in the hospital, and at one point we hid several of the pro-American men in

Manzanar Guard Gate and Tower

laundry carts to protect them from the mob. One man was the one who'd been injured the previous night. They stayed in the hospital until it was possible to sneak them out to a safe barracks in a laundry truck.

The mob surged through the camp, from the hospital to the police station to one of the mess halls. The camp police were unable to deal with the crowd and the MPs were called in. We could hear the MPs yelling over the public-address system, trying to restore order. Finally, the situation deteriorated—somebody threw a rock and the MPs fired into the crowd, killing two and wounding a number of others. One of the victims was just a boy, shot down near the mess hall. Then there were soldiers everywhere, searchlights, and curfew. The authorities clamped down hard to get everyone under control.

The pro-Japan internees eventually were separated from the rest of us and placed in a special camp at Tule Lake. They were permitted to renounce their citizenship—if they were U.S. citizens—and were allowed to sign up for repatriation to Japan. Mostly it was the Japanese aliens who wanted to be repatriated. For example, my friend Rosie Ishi—an alien who worked at the bank with me—went to Tule Lake, and then to Japan. Those who were returned to Japan went on the *Gripsholm,* the same ship that brought some of the American noncombatants home from Japan.[42] I wrote to Rosie several times, but my last letter was returned and I have no idea what happened to her. After the pro-Japan internees were moved out and other problems within the camp were resolved, peace slowly returned to Manzanar. Over time, camp life took on a hybrid mixture of American and Japanese culture. We would not have called it "normal," but barrack homes were slowly made more comfortable, gardens were planted, occasionally we were treated to Japanese food, kids were in school, and we settled into a routine. The next two years crept by as I wondered about my future.

My mother was strict in the old Japanese way—no boyfriends. There I was, still single. By 1944 we'd been in the camp two years, and I guess mother was beginning to worry I'd never find a husband. One day a woman came to talk to her. She was a friend of the Yoshinaga family, who lived in Block 27 at that time. It turned out that their son Henry wanted a wife.

The Yoshinaga family was from northern California. Henry was born in Walnut Creek, attended schools in Sacramento, and worked on the family farm. In the camp, he was working in the mess hall. He was a happy, carefree person, well liked by everyone.

So, my mother told this lady, "We'll see." Then she talked to me about whether it was time for me to get married. By then I'd given up hope and hadn't thought much about marriage. Anyway, he came to see me—and promptly got me mixed up with my married twin sister—that made us all laugh, poor guy!

But the important thing was that my mother looked him over, and he must have passed her scrutiny, because he was invited back. After several such meetings we were allowed to do things together—to go on picnics, or to see movies, but always in the company of other people. Meanwhile, behind the scenes, our respective parents completed the arrangements for a marriage.

Our wedding on July 8, 1944, was nice—a big one, with many people. Henry had many friends from the mess hall, I'd met lots of people through my job with the public health department, and of course, we invited all the friends of both families. The total was about 350 people. One of my mother's friends made me a beautiful white wedding dress. To make the dress, we had to have one of the Caucasian ladies on the camp staff make a trip to Lone Pine to buy the materials. Somehow, mother's seamstress friend was able to locate all of the rest of the things necessary to make an extraordinary dress. Another friend found flowers—some from the camp, some from Lone Pine. The decorations were magnificent, and transformed the drab prison camp. For a few hours, it was as if we were once again living among the warmth of our family and friends in Malibu.

Mitzi and Henry Yoshinaga, Manzanar, 1944

We were married in Manzanar's Buddhist church, located in Block 18, the ceremony performed by Reverend Nagatomi, who was the minister at that time. Following the ceremony, we had a reception in the mess hall. It was beautifully decorated with flowers and jammed with people. The cooks worked miracles, making all kinds of special dishes, some of which we hadn't seen for the past two years. I have no idea how they found—or improvised—the ingredients necessary to prepare the food.

After dinner, there were speeches by friends, some wishing us well and others making comments of a more suggestive nature. Everybody was in a good mood, glad to have a chance to forget about the war and the hardships we endured. Another friend arranged entertainment—there was a well-known young singer in the camp who performed for us that evening.

We had photographs of the wedding taken by Toyo Miyatake, a photographer who later became world famous. Some of his photographs of Manzanar received broad circulation after the war. The ones I treasure show Henry and me in the church—I in my white dress, holding a bridal bouquet, Henry looking stiffly formal in an unaccustomed suit. I still have the flowers, pressed and dried, tucked away in the photo album with the wedding pictures. The party lasted until late in the evening. Finally, as the last guests prepared to depart, Henry and I left the mess hall for the short walk to Block 27, where his family lived.

Thus a new phase of my life began within the barbed wire confines of the Manzanar War Relocation Center. I was twenty-six, and my husband had just had his twenty-seventh birthday. After we were married, we first lived in the barracks with Henry's family. This arrangement was hard on me, trying to adjust to married life, and at the same time working and trying to please my mother-in-law. Eventually we were able to move into a small apartment of our own in the barracks, where we had some semblance of privacy and moments to ourselves.

We really never had a honeymoon. There was really no place we could go, and besides, we both had to go to work on Monday morning. Henry continued working in the mess hall, while I had my job with public health, working with Dr. Togasaki, Josephine Hawes, the public health nurse, and others.

At home my new life was difficult. Everyone was under stress in the camp, and many of the usual Japanese family customs were either not possible or were warped to accommodate the requirements of our situation. One could not say that we lived in a model Japanese community, pulled up from Southern California and transposed to the Owens Valley. Instead, ours was a distorted, hybrid society, part of which clung to the old ways, and part of which had new ways forced upon it, ways which could neither be described as American or Japanese.

Many of the circumstances in the camp were shocking to the older Japanese, because they ran exactly opposite to ancient and deeply held traditions.

One of these traditions was that a new daughter-in-law moves in and assists her mother-in-law, who is the absolute authority in the family. A bride's value is measured by her acceptance by her mother-in-law, the respect she shows her in-laws, and her efforts to support her new family. I tried hard, but in many respects I fell short of what my mother-in-law expected of me. I worked, I was independent, I was many things that went against the grain of our culture. I was a victim, not only of the situation in the camp, but also of an age—of a period of sharp and painful cultural change.[43]

Even in a perfect setting, the transition from a single working woman to a traditional Japanese wife would have been difficult. In the twisted, crazy environment of the camp, it became another heart-rending burden I had to bear. There were nights when I lay awake in the barracks, listening to the wind swirl the dust under the floor and dreamed that I was once again a carefree child roaming free on the ranch in Malibu.

CHAPTER 15

〢〢〢

HAPPY LIFE BLUES CABARET

LYDIA: We had our problems, but our American friends in the Happy Life Blues Cabaret prison camp were worse off. At first there were no toilet facilities, little privacy, and no comforts in the camp. Water was turned on for two hours each day; otherwise there was none. Two things were abundant: cobras and centipedes. Simon and I had sent food to the camp whenever we could, and Simon also sent the money that he'd dug up near our old house at the mine.

Under these conditions, people were not at their best. The stress was compounded by babies crying all night, by illnesses that raged through the camp, and by the never-ending uncertainty regarding the fate of the prisoners.

Hugh Wills was still sick and was having trouble shaking it. He never really recovered from the hardships of his long trek to Malaybalay and was weakened considerably by dysentery and by malnutrition. All of this we learned from Filipinos who visited the camp and talked to some of the prisoners. Through the Filipinos, we made arrangements to send food to the prisoners whenever we could find something extra for them. We tried to keep track of our friends in the camp and do what we could do to help them. But we had problems of our own.

Slowly some organization was brought into the camp operation. Prisoners were assigned to work details to carry out the necessary chores. We learned that Jane was on a cooking detail, peeling vegetables and cooking rice and soup. Hugh was part of a wood-gathering detail that left the camp once a day under guard to cut wood for cooking.

Working on the firewood detail was the way the Willses finally got a house. After five months of living in the open compound with many other families crowded together, Hugh spoke to the guards about bringing some bamboo into the camp and was able to get their permission. Bamboo poles were placed in the ground, and the Willses and their friends wove palm fronds together to make walls and a roof. In this manner, five shacks were constructed using only a single

nail. Among the prisoners were American workers from the Del Monte plantation in northern Mindanao. One of them happened to find a nail among his possessions. This nail was used to drive a hole in the bamboo. Then a sharpened
piece of wire was pounded in the hole to serve as a nail. The wire was actually
straightened "barbs" from the barbed-wire fence, which were removed surrepti-
tiously when the guards weren't around. As crude as they were, these shacks
added immensely to the comfort of the prisoners with families since they could
now have a small measure of privacy.[44]

We knew that all the prisoners were having a struggle to get enough food.
Some of them had money and bought food from the Filipinos whom the Japanese allowed into the camp. These purchases were limited to a few *camotes*,
bananas, maybe a chicken or two.

Jane and Hugh buried their money and valuables at one of their last camps
near Malaybalay, just before the Japanese captured them. Consequently, they
had no way of purchasing food. A lady in the camp told them about a Chinese
man in Davao who was willing to lend money to the prisoners. The moneylender
lived in the city, near the dentist's house where I had been forced to stay.

By convincing the camp commander that she had a terrible toothache, Jane
was able to secure a pass to go into town. After a brief visit with the dentist, who
told her there was nothing wrong with her teeth, she slipped away to the moneylender's house. There, seated in a small neat home heavily shaded by dark green
trees, taking in the faint aroma of incense mixed with the wonderful smell of
food cooking, sipping pale green tea in a delicate cup, she borrowed $250 on her
verbal promise that she and Hugh would repay $1,000 at the end of the war.
She concealed the money within her clothes and began the long dusty walk back
to camp.

Her next worry: Would the guards search her, perhaps confiscate the money?
With the occupation, the Japanese had outlawed dollars and all other foreign
currency, and substituted military script. Everyone hid their dollars, which were
used in the black market. The fact that thousands of these types of loans were
made demonstrated the confidence of most Filipinos that the Americans would
someday win the war and return.

Fortunately, reentering the camp was uneventful, and with this money she
and Hugh were able to buy some chickens from a Filipino. Everybody wanted
hens for the eggs. But you had to be careful—the Filipinos would cut off the
cock's comb when the bird was young and try to pass off roosters as hens. To the
unwary, it came as a great shock to learn after four or five weeks that their "hen"
wouldn't lay eggs, and moreover, was usually up at dawn crowing.

Once the prisoners accumulated a few chickens, they kept them in a special pen in the compound with the knowledge and permission of the camp commander. Outside the camp a Japanese farmer also raised chickens. The prisoners kept a careful watch on the movement of these chickens at all times, meanwhile setting aside a few scraps of food for use as bait. When one of the outside chickens strayed near the fence, they would send children with food to lure the chicken near enough to be snared and added to the prisoners' growing flock.

Finally the Japanese farmer realized that he was losing chickens and came to the camp commander to protest. The commander ordered several guards to go with him to search out his chickens. The prisoners argued that they'd bought all of "their" chickens. The guards then asked the farmer to point out which ones were his, which, of course, he was unable to do. The soldiers yelled at him, mocked him, slapped him around for being so foolish, and told him to take better care of his business. Then they kicked him out of the camp empty-handed. But everyone was watched much more closely after the incident, and almost no chickens came near the fence from that day on.

That was the way the social order worked with the soldiers and citizens. The senior officers lorded it over the juniors; they in turn slapped around the enlisted men; and the enlisted men beat up civilians and anyone else on the slightest excuse, and many times with no excuse whatsoever. We all walked in fear that they would suddenly turn on us, sword in hand, and that would be the end.

In 1942, when Christmas and New Year's arrived, no one felt like celebrating. Simon and I scarcely noticed the coming and passing of the holidays. In the camp, it was an even more dreary time for the prisoners. Some people organized a program. The priests held a Christmas service, followed by singing of Christmas carols, along with a few pitiful decorations, and some hand-made gifts were exchanged. But the ceremony depressed everyone, and the prisoners resolved not to have one the following year.

In 1943 conditions began to get much worse in the camp. Food was limited to a few camotes, rice, sometimes soup made from fish heads or tails, or from the tops and green leaves of camotes. Occasionally there was a little fruit.

We were not much better off, but we continued to send food into the camp via Mrs. Hughes or other Filipinos whenever we could. It was never much—a few eggs, some eggplants, some fruit. Whenever someone was going to the camp, we sent the prisoners whatever we could find. I did not go; I was too conspicuous, and Simon was afraid the Japanese would accuse me of spying and would arrest me.

From the Filipinos we heard many examples of brutality—slapping, beatings, even beheadings. Two prisoners who'd escaped were captured a few days later. They were beheaded, and their heads were placed on posts by the camp as a warning to others. The civilian population of Davao was forced into a certain number of days of "voluntary" labor to help the Imperial Japanese Army. In Davao City, no one, young or old, was exempted from working in the fields or on the docks to assist the Japanese war effort.

Rumors floated through the town and villages all the time. We heard that some of the American soldiers had escaped from the Davao Penal Colony and were picked up by an American submarine after guerrillas helped them elude the Japanese and make their way to the coast. There were rumors of American soldiers hiding in the jungles, leading the guerrillas. It was evident to all of us that the Japanese hold was tenuous, especially outside the main towns. They rarely ventured away from the towns except in force.

After the war, we learned that the American military forces had been able to discover the location of many of the prison camps and in some cases were able to communicate with people inside them. Beginning in 1942, teams of Americans were brought to the Philippines by submarine from Australia. They were put ashore at various locations throughout the islands to work in conjunction with guerrilla groups. These teams operated clandestine communication stations that monitored Japanese plane, ship, and troop movements. The guerrillas were active in Mindanao. These teams harassed the Japanese, watched them, and waited for an opportunity to strike a telling blow. Unfortunately, they lacked the strength to attack the camp and release the prisoners.

Near the end of 1943, a few days before Christmas, the camp commander suddenly announced that the civilian prisoners would be moved. As before, they were given twenty-four hours' notice and were permitted to take two packages per person. For the Willses, the most important thing was the powdered milk for Trudy, who was now two and a half years old. Several of the Del Monte workers agreed to carry her milk as their baggage.

The prisoners were marched back across the river, through Davao, past the school that served as the Imperial Japanese Army headquarters, and down to the Santa Ana wharf. From there they were taken in small boats to a rusty Japanese freighter. They were loaded aboard and forced to stay in the hold, where the heat and stench were overpowering. The ship was full of rats. It remained at anchor in the harbor for five days, and then joined a convoy sailing to Manila. At night the prisoners were allowed on deck for a while. The ship had mechanical difficulties and could not keep up with the convoy. Slowly it fell farther and farther behind, until the rest of the ships merged into a small speck on the horizon many miles ahead. The Willses were aware of this and worried about the possibilities of submarines in the area. Fortunately nothing happened and they made the trip safely. Later, when the Japanese started transporting military prisoners north to Japan in crowded freighters, the loss of life was great. Thousands of prisoners died when the ships were sunk, and even if the ship made it to Japan, conditions on board were so terrible that these transports were known as "hell ships."

We did not learn about the transfer until later, when some Filipinos got word to Mrs. Hughes that her husband was no longer in the camp. It was not until after the war that we learned they'd been taken to Santo Tomas, the infamous camp in downtown Manila. Later the Willses were moved to the Los Banos camp.

The year 1944 began on a dreary and depressing note. We were on our own in the jungle. Most of the people we knew were gone from Davao. Our friends from the mine had all been moved from the Happy Life Blues Cabaret camp. Occasionally we'd hear reports of American military POWs working in Davao. They were gaunt skeletons. We were told that, of 2,000 men, one-third were too sick to work.

The Japanese were crueler and more brutal than before, and life was becoming difficult for the Filipinos, because the naval blockade effectively stopped movements in and out of Mindanao. We became isolated, not only in terms of medical supplies, food, and necessities, but also in terms of human companionship and news. We had no details about the war except that it was clear that the momentum had shifted. No longer were the Japanese bragging about their big victories. Instead they beat up on the Filipinos, just to prove they were still in control. The guerrillas became more audacious, which meant, of course, reprisals on the Filipinos whose homes were in the vicinity of the attack. The guerrillas could fade away into the mountains, but the townspeople were left behind in their homes to bear the consequences.

In June 1944, we heard rumors that the military prisoners from the Davao Penal Colony were put on ships and taken to Manila. Although we didn't realize it at first, moving the prisoners north could only signify one thing: the Japanese knew the Americans were getting closer!

CHAPTER 16

𝍷𝍷𝍷 𝍷𝍷𝍷 𝍷𝍷𝍷

HIROHATA

GARTH: We went to Hirohata by train from Osaka, arriving in October 1942. The train went through Kobe and on down to Hirohata. The camp was about seven miles from the town of Himeji, and about 130 miles from Hiroshima. At Himeji, there was a big Japanese army camp—not a training camp like Zentsuji, but an army camp full of soldiers. There was also an aircraft factory nearby. Overlooking Himeji, perched on the top of a hill that dominated the surrounding area, was Himeji castle. Built in the fourteenth century and occupied by a succession of shoguns, it had so far escaped damage from the war.

In Osaka my prisoner's number was *hachiju*—eighty. In Hirohata I became number fifty-seven—*goju-nana*. These were numbers we had to sing out at *tenko* in the morning, and at any special lineups, like when they called a surprise shakedown. If you didn't pronounce your number properly, you were slapped.

Hirohata was a company town serving a huge steel mill and dock complex. The camp commander was a Lieutenant Takanaka. Later he was transferred and replaced by Lieutenant Muto. There were two interpreters, Tahara and Uchinaka. The camp was similar to the other ones we'd been in—the same drafty unheated barracks, the same meager food rations, the same growing sense of wondering when the goddam war would end.

The main differences were in the brutality of the guards at Hirohata, the declining fortunes of Japan during the final two years of the war, and the shortage of food, which got steadily worse. In 1944, and especially in 1945, we stole anything edible in order to stay alive, including garbage, stuff that we found on the ships, trains, or docks, anything that even looked edible. At this time, for eighty men doing hard labor, the Japanese authorities provided thirteen kilograms (about twenty-nine pounds) of dry rice and six heads of cabbage per day.

When we first got to Hirohata—forty sailors and forty marines—I wasn't feeling too bad. We'd left Osaka, we were off by ourselves, and they weren't really pushing us too hard at this point. Our group of eighty now had a nickname: we were known as the "Eighty Eightballs," in reference to our reputation as trouble-makers. Navy Chief Barnum was in charge; Marine First Sergeant Ercanbrack was second in command. The chief was extremely fair, spreading around the soft work details and trying to see that food was rationed equally, down to a single grain of rice. He tried so hard that he went crazy worrying about being fair and had some sort of breakdown. Then he asked the first sergeant to take over.[45]

The chief was a Mason. One time in the middle of the night I heard him crying out, saying something that I know today was a cry for help from a brother Mason. They were secret words that only the Masons knew. Unfortunately there was no way we could help him. Eventually he pulled out of it, survived the camp, and went home with the rest of us.

When it was time to get up in the morning, a Japanese bugler would blow the horn announcing tenko. At Hirohata it was the worst sounding bugle I ever heard—like it was out of tune or something. Before we were captured, there was a popular song called "Ride, Red, Ride," a crazy song, but anyway, it kind of stuck with me. When they blew the bugle in the morning, I'd get up and start hollering "Ride, Red, Ride—up and go," to get everybody out of their racks. The shoes would come at me from every which way in the room, because it pissed the fellows off. However, they'd get a laugh out of it later on in the day. After a while, even that wore off, and I stopped singing.

After roll call we'd line up for breakfast—now just a cup of rice, sometimes tea. After eating we had a community wooden bucket for washing rice bowls. You dipped your bowl and spoon into the water. I always tried to be first in line for this. We had a canteen cup for tea, and I had the bottom half of a mess kit, which I carried from camp to camp. That was the extent of my personal belongings, other than the clothes I wore and my little address book with the names of all the prisoners.

At the docks we worked at unloading trains and ships. Later some of us worked in the steel plant, where we were forced to help the Japanese war effort. The steel mill—seitetsu in Japanese—was built on a man-made island extending out into the bay. Nearby a river emptied into the sea. We called the plant the "island steel mill."

As the end of 1942 approached, I celebrated my first anniversary in captivity. I'd now spent twelve months in four prison camps, counting the Catholic church in Guam. I'd lost a lot of weight and had been sick about half the time. We worked hard and the authorities constantly threatened us, but we had learned how to stay out of trouble. In spite of the radio broadcast I had been allowed to do at

Zentsuji, I still had not received any communications from home. I did not know whether my family knew where I was, nor if they knew I was still alive.

In 1943 my health began to deteriorate in several ways. Of course, I was not alone, and was neither better off nor worse off than the others. I developed a painful case of hemorrhoids. Looking back, I suppose this condition was brought on by a long period of constipation when we were first captured, and then was aggravated by the strain of heavy physical labor. I eventually reached the point where I could not walk without extreme pain.

We were fortunate to have an excellent medical officer with our group, Captain Sidney E. Seid. He was much more capable than Akiyoshi Tsujino, the Japanese medical orderly who was an army corporal with little medical training. Tsujino had the power to countermand Captain Seid's orders and would make sick men work, refuse them medicine, or cause them to be beaten. Captain Seid frequently confronted the Japanese authorities at great personal risk to try to better our treatment. Many of us survived due to his efforts.[46]

Captain Seid checked me over and decided that I'd reached the point where it was necessary to make an incision to reduce the swelling. He did this with a razor blade on a cold winter night, having me drop my pants outside so the cold would deaden the pain and lessen the bleeding. The Japanese gave no assistance, claiming no anesthesia or antiseptics were available. After this operation — which had to be repeated later on — I felt much better, and was again able to do my share of work.

Later in 1943 I began suffering from the effects of beriberi (vitamin B_1 deficiency), which many of us contacted as a result of malnutrition. I had both the "dry" and the "wet" types. The wet type was characterized by swelling of the limbs brought on by fluid buildup in the tissues. My left leg was most severely affected; my left knee ballooned to several times its normal size. It was extremely painful and difficult for me to climb ladders or work, but of course I had to continue to do both. The penalty for not working was not eating.

As my condition worsened, our surgeon made incisions in my leg to drain the fluid and reduce the swelling. This was performed with the tools at hand — a razor blade — and without benefit of anesthesia. This time Captain Seid was able to get a small amount of hydrogen peroxide from the Japanese to use as an antiseptic. A week or so later the operation was repeated. My condition seemed to worsen, rather than improve. One night the doc came to see me and said, "Garth, we may have to take that leg off."

At first I was speechless. I thought about football, working, hell, I can't even say what all went on in my mind. But I had a lot of respect for him, knowing how hard he tried for us and how badly he suffered seeing us sick and not being able to do much about it, even though he constantly risked his own neck fighting for us. Finally I said, "You're the boss, captain. If you say it goes off, off it goes. But I've got one request."

"What's that?"

"You wait until I can't drag myself in the barracks, crawling on my hands and knees. At that point get L. D. to conk me on the head, and then do it. Don't tell me ahead of time."

Captain Seid said, "We'll do all we can first. But I don't like the looks of that leg, and I think you should know all the possibilities."

Eventually he drained the leg two more times—four in all, making incisions progressively higher on my thigh with his razor blade as a scalpel. Finally, I began to recover and was able to keep my leg.

It was funny how the lack of food affected us in strange ways. Some people had vision problems. Every minor ache and pain seemed to be aggravated by hunger. I developed a toothache. It started driving me crazy. I went to Captain Seid to have it pulled. He looked at me and said, "Hell, there's nothing wrong with that tooth." Another month went by and it still drove me crazy. I went back to him and told him to pull the sonofabitch. He took some pliers and yanked it out. Afterward, he showed it to me. "Shit," he said, "there's nothing wrong with that tooth." He checked the gum, the bleeding socket. "I don't see anything there either." There I was, minus a tooth. At least it didn't bother me anymore.

Somehow, in spite of these difficulties, we survived. In recounting these experiences, I hasten to repeat that I was no better and no worse off than my comrades. We each had our afflictions and burdens to bear. There were times when we were tempted to yield to self-pity, to feel sorry for ourselves, to give up. Undoubtedly there were moments when we probably did feel sorry enough to give up, but we didn't let them last long. Each of us developed our own ways of combating these feelings.

In my case, I gave myself a mental "kick in the ass" and started thinking about what I'd do to the guards once the war was over. I had a little saying I used to tell myself. If you think about it, you'll see it isn't irreverent: "If you want your prayers answered, when you're done praying, get off your knees and hustle!"

A year later, on December 20, 1943, I received a package from home, sent through the Red Cross. I recall this as one of the finest Christmases I'd ever celebrated. I was now 22 years old. I could recognize my father's distinctive handwriting on the two customs declarations attached to the package, listing two pairs of socks, one toothbrush, a deck of playing cards, a jar of malted milk tablets, soup, a miniature chess set, a pencil and leads, chewing gum, vitamin pills, cod liver oil—it went on and on. My god, what a treasure trove!

I took everything out, and looked at each item every night. My friends looked at them, sharing this faint link to our distant home, the world we'd left behind. Better yet, the world that had left us behind, that had made us the sacrificial lambs on our island post, without bothering to let us know we were about to be sacrificed.

During the day, the box sat in our barracks on a shelf by my sleeping mat while I was away working. Such was the sense of honor among us that nothing was ever taken from that box. I followed the instructions that accompanied the vitamins religiously, and immediately, my health improved noticeably. Unfortunately, they were soon gone, along with the rest of my little store of delights. Still, the impact of that package on my spirit was incalculable. Coming as it did at the low point of my existence, it certainly helped prepare me for the difficult time that lay ahead—1944 and two-thirds of 1945. We had a saying: "In '44 we'll stay alive, make it home in '45." Without that package, who knows if I would have made it home?

For as long as I could, I saved every scrap of it—anything, however trivial or mundane, that represented a link with home. The paper, the string, the empty malted milk tablet jar, foil from the gum—even the customs declaration tags—I saved them all. The tags were one of the few things I managed to keep throughout the remaining months of my captivity, and I brought them home with me. I've still got them.

As the war progressed, conditions in the Japanese home islands had become extremely difficult. We knew the U.S. Navy had pretty well bottled up the islands so there weren't many ships getting through. Food shortages were widespread and the Japanese were beginning to experience these shortages themselves. Bombings occurred almost daily. The severity of the Japanese situation had a direct impact on those of us at Hirohata and on other POWs struggling to stay alive in prison camps scattered throughout the islands. In 1944 and 1945, prisoners started dying from the cumulative effects of disease and malnutrition. As the tide of the war changed and an invasion of the Japanese homeland appeared likely, the Japanese treated the prisoners even more brutally.

When I arrived at Hirohata, in October 1942, I'd lost about 35 pounds—down from 175 on Guam to around 140. The last time they weighed me in Hirohata, which was in July 1945, I was down to 118 pounds. I would have been a lot skinnier if I hadn't been working on the docks where at least we had a chance to steal food.

By the end of the war, there were nearly 500 men in Hirohata. They were eating anything that was even remotely edible. The diet included rice (almost always full of weevils), seaweed, grasshoppers, frogs, silkworms, ants, roaches, dogs, cats, rats, rotten vegetables, tangerine peelings—literally anything. Some of these we stole from the docks and warehouses where we worked. For example, the silkworms were a delicacy collected after the silk was unwound from the cocoons. Someone found packages of' the dried larvae in a warehouse and smuggled them into camp. One glorious find was containers full of dried banana chips, many of which found their way into the camp in the hidden recesses of our prisoners clothing.[47]

One day we were able to steal a bag of brown sugar and smuggle it into camp. L. D. and I removed a piece of floorboard beneath our sleeping mats and hid the bag under the floor, hung there in an old stocking, which served as a sack. At night we'd pull the bag out and eat a little brown sugar to give ourselves a few additional calories. Eventually some sailors crawled under the barracks from the outside and came across our sack. It was too tempting. Even though they must have known it belonged to a prisoner, they stole it.

On another occasion we were able to steal some whole tobacco leaf which we hid in the same place. We traded this for rice with fellows who were dying—literally—for a smoke.

One incident that happened near the end of the war—I guess it was sometime in June 1945—was typical of our food-stealing efforts. Maybe it was even a little better than most. L. D. and I were working on the dock in a blacksmith shop at the island steel mill. I was pretty sick with diarrhea, but I was assigned to a good detail thanks to the first sergeant. There were six of us there, and we alternated off and on swinging a twelve-pound sledge on an anvil to the rhythmic tap of a Japanese mechanic's hammer, making steel tools. The Japanese foreman was an older man, well educated, had a trade, knew what he was doing. He usually left us for lunch.

One day a ship came in and we could see that it was loaded pretty heavy. They unloaded a bunch of stuff, and then we saw these shiny tin cans—something like gallon cans. They were stacked up pyramid-style on the dock, right by the blacksmith shop. At noon, while the foreman went to lunch, the Japanese guards would also go off somewhere, eat, and take a nap. So we decided to go down and see what was in those cans. To our surprise, it was Japanese navy butter.

Can you imagine what fat—of any kind—meant to us at that time? Sure, we knew it would give us the shits since our systems couldn't handle it. But taken a little bit at a time, it would do wonders for us. Remember, I was pretty sick then.

So we grabbed two cans and hid them in the crane shop where we were working on the anvil. Naturally they had everything counted in Japan at that stage of the war, since starvation was pretty close for the Japanese people as well as for us. Sure as hell, they discovered that some of the butter had disappeared.

They made quite a fuss about the missing butter, but they couldn't find it, even though they searched us, searched the Japanese stevedores, searched the building—hell, they looked everywhere. A week later we knew they were still looking, so we just laid low. We'd hidden it well—on the bottom shelf of the honcho's locker, which he never used.

After another week or so had passed, fortune was good to us a second time. A shipload of rice came in and we were able to steal an entire fifty kilogram (110-pound) bag. The ship was loaded so heavily the rice wasn't missed. L. D. just rolled the bag onto my shoulder while I was standing on the dock, and I carried it to a new hiding place. There was an underground conveyor system that ran through the shops. We took the sack of rice down to the conveyor system and hid it underneath the conveyor, way in the back. We intended to use it every day at noon. Get a can, boil some water, throw in a couple of handfuls of rice, and put some of that navy butter on top, while the Japanese guards were out sleeping. What a banquet!

For a good week, or maybe two weeks, we were having a nice big can—like a big tomato juice can—of buttered rice. On an open fire, the water boiling, the guard thought we were making tea, so he went off somewhere for a snooze, and then we would slip down into the conveyor and bring out some rice. We found it didn't take long to steam rice that way. Once the rice was cooked, we'd toss in a big piece of butter and watch it melt and flow right down through the rice and then we'd eat it. Jesus, we were getting well—it was like a feast! I was living and beginning to feel alive again!

But then one day, another prisoner caught on to what we were doing. He saw us getting the rice out of the conveyor system and decided to help himself. He was on the crew, but he didn't pitch in like everybody else did—consequently we weren't sharing with him. The sonofabitch wasn't any good.

One afternoon he crawled down into the conveyor and filled up his pants legs with our rice. When he came back up, L. D. spotted him, and you could tell in a minute that he had something in his pants. So L. D. just raced across there and tackled him. When the two of them fell to the ground, the strings he had around the pants legs under his outer pants broke and rice poured out all over the ground—I mean all over! I was right behind L. D. and we were pounding the shit out of him when the guards came.

It was unusual for one prisoner to steal from another. That was fundamental law number one. You just didn't do that. We also had fundamental law number two—that if you got caught stealing, you had to step out and take your beating. There was no stepping out on this one, however, since they knew who it was. When they got us back to the barracks, they proceeded to beat the shit out of all three of us, and then they searched and got the rice. But they didn't get the butter—not yet.

Not long after that, however, a smart Japanese civilian dockworker—maybe a little better educated than the others—found it. He knew something was going on; he knew we were doing something at noon each day, but he wasn't sure what. Then one morning when we came down to go to work, he took us right in to the back end of the shop and he opened up the locker, where we had hidden the stolen butter. He didn't speak any English, but as best he could, and as best we could understand, he explained to us that we had stolen something from his navy that was valuable and that there was nothing that he could do but turn us in. From the look on his face it seemed like he just hated to do it, but he had to because we had broken the rules and he was an honest man. He may not have been in favor of the war—especially at this stage when things were getting pretty tough for all the Japanese—but he had to turn us in.

We never got such a beating as we got that time. I mean, they really beat the holy shit out of us. They were experts at beatings. I think the torture we got at Hirohata was the most highly developed form of physical abuse—maximum suffering, short of being incapacitated or dying. Their method was to strip you down, and then they'd put two guys behind you. They had fake Samurai swords that had several angles on them and were made out of wood, which they used like baseball bats. They would also put a guy in front of you with a leather strap—something that resembled a razor strop.

When they were ready they'd tell you how many times they were going to hit you. If you could stand there and take the beating, without making too much noise, that ended it. They'd give you the required number of swats and stop. If you fell down or if you yelled or screamed too loud, they started over. If they were going to give you a lot, and you fell over, then you were finished. You just weren't going to make it, that's all there was to it.

They stood behind us with those baseball bats and just beat the living shit out of us until we were both grunting and groaning and swaying forward from the force of the blows. If you went too far forward, the guy in the front would take that strap and hit you right on the balls, so you could get it from both sides. When they were done, we were black and blue, bruised—our bodies swollen in every conceivable place. I suppose we were as close to death then as any time since the shooting had began on Guam forty-three months before. Fortunately, somehow both L. D. and I made it through that beating. I'm sure the army didn't give that butter back to the navy. Those bastards kept it for themselves!

Another time, as we were walking to work at the steel mill, a little brown-and-white puppy ran out of nowhere and entered our ranks. It was jumping here and there in a playful mood. A tall thin marine stooped down and scooped up the pup without breaking stride. Then we all looked around to see if anyone was chasing the pup. The guards in front had not noticed, the ones at the rear of the column were too busy talking, and we were alone on the road, apparently in the clear.

Meanwhile, the pup, glad to be warm in the marine's shirt, was sticking his head out and licking the marine's neck, as any friendly puppy would do. The marine's fingers closed tight on the pup's neck and strangled it before it could make a sound. Once we were working, the pup was hidden under some refuse near the spot where we boiled water for tea at lunchtime. As soon as the guards left to take their noon nap, the pup was retrieved, skinned, cleaned, and tossed in a tin can full of boiling water that we heated over a wood fire. Before the guards returned, every trace of that dog was gone. Walking back to camp, the dog became a topic of conversation. "Hey, I feel bad. After all, it was a cute little thing—so friendly."

"Oh yeah? Just think of it as a Japanese dog, and you won't feel so bad."

"I always wondered what dog meat tasted like."

"Dog, cat, who cares? I just told myself that was chicken soup at its finest."

On another day, walking the same road, we came upon tangerine peelings scattered along the side of the road. We picked up handfuls and ate them, ignoring the fact that it was a windy day and there were rice paddies on both sides of the dirt road where we found them. Of course we knew the rice paddies were fertilized with "night soil"—human excrement—but hunger overcame any qualms we might have had.

As the end of the war approached, the brutality of the guards increased. Perhaps they feared that we would be emboldened to revolt if the discipline slackened, or perhaps we were just scapegoats for their feelings about the disaster that was overtaking Japan.

There was another time when L. D. got beaten up and damn near died. They beat up on him when he was sick. He had to stand there naked while they hit him with a wooden club on the butt and lower back. Each blow caused him to step forward a foot or two. He had to step back in position for the next hit. After a few of these he couldn't take it anymore; he passed out and fell down. When that happened they beat him some more, then put him in a fire protection tank. These were wooden tanks, buried in the ground, full of water, and covered with a metal grating or latticework. When they lifted off the grating, there was about twelve inches of air space above the water. The guards just stuck him in there and left him for the rest of the night.

They pulled him out about a half an hour before it was time for us to go to work. I'd been waiting for him, and once they'd pulled him out and dumped him on the ground, I dragged him in the barracks and tried to warm him up before they made us go to work. He was totally blue and half comatose from the cold. Once we got out on the island, we found a railroad car that was plenty warm from hot slag, and we tucked him away there where he could get a little rest and stay warm. The Japanese guard didn't even watch him too closely. I'm sure they didn't want to kill him, just maim him enough that he didn't give them any more trouble.

L. D. was a truly unique person. He had a singular appearance. He had red tissues that ran from the corner of each eye up to the pupil. They were bright red, and looked like a little red muscle. Also, he had bad acne; his skin was really messed up. He had a way of cajoling the Japanese so they believed that mentally he wasn't all there, and in this way he got away with a lot of things that would have resulted in a certain beating for anyone else.

There was another guy who was with us all the way through the three camps— C. D. Stansberry, from Nebraska. His wrists were big and powerful. In camp he was a kleptomaniac—I think the good Lord put the guy with us because he could open any Japanese lock. He would just take it in his hands and twist it until it popped open. Shortly after our transfer from Osaka, he got spinal meningitis. We isolated him and took care of him as best we could. At this point it really seemed as if God was helping us, because he recovered and no one else contacted the disease. He broke many more locks after he got well.

He was usually the first guy into a storeroom. When it was opened up, he'd come back and tell L. D., who would go in, and then it would be my turn. We'd take whatever we could find that was edible—canned fish, rice, or whatever. We'd eat it right where we were working, if the guards weren't too close. Otherwise, we'd go off to the *benjo* and eat as much as we could while we stood in the toilet. Then, if there was more, and we couldn't hide it, we'd take it back to camp. This was where we ran the greatest risk of getting caught.

The guards were unpredictable. They didn't search us every time. Usually, if they discovered something was missing, when we got out on the road in front of the barracks, they would have us open ranks for a search. Here they were funny. They would start at the end of the rank—we were in threes—and they'd have one guard stand up at the end, while another would come down the line. But the hell of it was they would search you in the same place, from one end of the line to the other. In other words, if they were searching armpits, that's all they would search. So, if you had something in your armpit, you moved it to your crotch. If they were searching crotches, you moved it to your armpit, or you'd put it somewhere else. After they'd gone down the whole column, that was it. You went on in. They didn't go back and search the other locations for some reason.

Many times, if there was something stolen, and they'd had a shakedown but couldn't find anything, and they were really adamant about finding it, they took the next step, which involved taking us into the courtyard where we had to stand at attention. At that point the guy who'd done the stealing had to step out. If he didn't, all of us suffered. In those cases they'd bring in some sections of railroad track. The rail portion—the top part that the train wheel normally rolled on—had been cut off with a torch. Since the rail had been cut off with a torch, the remaining web had a sharp, jagged edge. They laid down long lengths of these cut up rails and rows of us had to kneel on two of them, one underneath our knees and the other under our ankles, so that no part of the body touched the ground. All of our weight was then supported by these two points, resting on these narrow pieces of sharp steel. We had to stay there until whoever did the stealing owned up to it, or until the Japanese decided to let us out of it.

Now supposing the guilty party didn't step out, and the whole group was punished, we didn't tell on the guy, or turn him in, but we had a way of getting even. The way we handled it if the guy didn't step forward was to give the miserable sonofabitch the silent treatment. In the prison camp, if nobody would talk to you, or acknowledge you, that was a pretty powerful punishment. I can only remember one guy who got this. He stole rice from a Japanese out on the job and he wouldn't own up to it when we got back to camp. Consequently we were all punished. We wouldn't talk to him from then on. It drove this one guy nuts, absolutely nuts—after about a month, he just went around mumbling to himself. When he got out of the camp he went to a psych ward.

In Hirohata we suffered more at the whims of the guards than in the other camps. Some of them were poor enlisted grunts who plodded through the daily routines as we did and faded from the scene and our memories as quickly as they'd arrived. The others—those who brutalized us—were less easily understood. We never knew if it was because of an intrinsically sadistic nature or because they had a warped sense of the prerogatives of military duty. Presumably we'll never know, but we can at least hope that the rewards and punishments of such men are decided in another time and space by the higher authority that rules on such matters.

We had nicknames for all of them that reflected their most obvious characteristics. Shinichi Motoyashiki was one such guard. Rumor had it that he'd served in the navy, so his nickname became "Kaigun"—the Japanese word for "navy." He was taller than the average Japanese—close to my height. He had a fair complexion with deep, penetrating eyes and wore his dark, full hair in a close-cropped military cut. He was every inch a military man, fastidious dresser, immaculate regulation uniform, every crease and fold straight. He bore the marks of an old war wound—a stiff right leg, perhaps suffered in China, or possibly in a Pacific naval battle. Maybe the injury resulted from an encounter with U.S. forces, which might have explained his hostility to us.

He was crisp, serious, vicious. We never saw him smile, even when he was beating prisoners. But it was when he was pounding on them, or causing them to be beaten, that his eyes glowed, seemed to come alive, brighten with pleasure.

Then there was Sadie the Sadist. He was an older man, short, about four feet six inches, weathered, tough as nails. He was obviously an army man, who took sadistic pleasure in beating prisoners for almost no reason. His method was to "windmill" you, or slap you on both sides of the face with both hands as fast as possible until your face was bright red. Throughout the course of such punishment, the prisoner could not speak, complain, cry out, or fight back. Complaints inevitably lengthened the punishment, and resistance could lead to a quick death.

It was forever a contest of wills: the prisoner trying to remain expressionless so Sadie would tire of it and go away, against Sadie who seemed bent on eliciting a response, however minor, which would justify further punishment. Such beatings were always performed in front of the assembled prisoners, who were forced to watch. Occasionally one of us would score a minor triumph in this tug-of-war of wills. Our victories were minor and infrequent, so each one assumed a special significance. Since Sadie was short, he would usually stand on a bench to administer his beatings. This put him on eyeball level with the American prisoners.

On one occasion he began working over Harris Chuck, a tough marine from Chicago, one of the Insular Patrolmen. Harris kept moving forward until Sadie could no longer make full arm-length swings. As a consequence, Sadie began leaning backward so he could get maximum leverage in his blows. Harris continued to inch forward until finally Sadie fell off the bench and landed flat on his back, which caused the assembled prisoners to break out in guffaws of laughter. Infuriated, Sadie leaped back on the bench and really gave it to poor Harris to save face. But both sides knew that Harris had triumphed in the battle of wills this time.

There was Jerkoff, another guard whom we intensely disliked. He was short, just about four feet tall, wore thick glasses, always dressed in a sloppy, baggy uniform, and was barely able to carry his heavy Arisaka rifle without falling down. His nickname had its origins in our toilet paper rations. Once a month we were issued thirty notebook-size sheets of rough, porous, brown paper. As we joked: "Thirty sheets for thirty shits." Since all of us had ongoing bouts of diarrhea, this was never an adequate supply. This guard would walk up to prisoners at random and hand them an extra five sheets of toilet paper. "For masturbating," the little bastard would say. If you didn't take the paper, he'd probably beat you for being ungrateful or insubordinate. If you did take it, he'd come beat you later. There was no rational explanation for his perverse behavior. We all tried to stay clear of him at all times.

One day while unloading boxcars, the door—which we'd propped up and were using as a working platform—collapsed. I was dumped to the ground and cut a long gash in my shin, clear to the bone. I wrapped it up as best I could with a strip of cloth torn from an old rag and kept working. Walking back to camp that day was painful, and I began to fall behind. Normally stragglers were beaten. Pretty soon I saw Jerkoff headed my way. He knew I'd been hurt, so he didn't beat me. Instead he handed me five sheets of toilet paper, smiling like he was doing me a big goddam favor. Hell, I took it. I was sick, and I needed it, no matter what he thought or did. Then he started goading me, saying he knew all the prisoners masturbated, and he was giving the paper to me so I could use it. I knew I was in trouble no matter what I said or did. I wanted to punch the little fart, but he'd kill me if I laid a hand on him. So I did the only thing I could do—I closed my mouth and kept walking. Pretty soon he wandered off and left me alone. The next day he found me somewhere and demanded to see the toilet paper. When I told him it was gone, I'd used it, he screamed at me. "Masturbator," he said and then screamed more insults in Japanese. He walked away without slapping me that time.

You might think at our age, with a long imprisonment, that sex would have been foremost in our minds. But in our half-starved condition, other physical desires diminished or were sublimated to the one overriding thought that dominated our waking hours: our stomachs. There were a few exceptions, but usually we didn't have any opportunity to get near women.

On the docks we worked with Koreans who were on ten-year or longer contracts—or at least that's what they told us. As far as we could see, they never got back to Korea and they were practically slave laborers, working with us at the island steel mill. The Koreans worked at night, and we worked in the day-time. They were prisoners as much as we were. We began to work as a team, once the Koreans somehow found out that we were breaking into storerooms. They would leave word about what was in certain storerooms. After we broke into the storeroom, they would go in and help themselves. They didn't take the initiative—they left that to us.

We had contact with both Korean men and women, working alongside or down in the holds with us. You could hardly tell the women from the men. They wore baggy, nondescript clothes and they didn't speak to us. They didn't dare to, because the Japanese watched them very closely. The contact we had with the Koreans—those who worked the docks—was virtually our only interaction with people other than our captors. Rarely, there might be a ship with a Chinese crew member who would say a word or two of English to us, and then scurry off be-fore the Japanese caught him. Otherwise we were limited in any contacts fast with the outside world for four years.

All through prison life, I don't think any of us were getting enough to eat to get a hard-on. Hell, there were times when guys slept together, but that was when we had no blankets and it was so damn cold we could hardly move. We all huddled together sometimes just to survive. Sex became something we thought about—like ice-cream sundaes, hamburgers—that was impossible at the moment, but something we looked forward to overindulging in when the war was over and we returned home!

We badly wanted to get back at the worst guards—especially the sadistic ones—but it was dangerous, particularly at the end of the war when we were weak and they were more on edge than usual. There was one time, however, in the hold of a ship, when we settled some scores. I saw it happen, although I didn't participate myself.

We were shoveling coal out of the hold of a big cargo ship. It was hot, dirty, dusty work, and slow going. We'd fill up a cargo net, they'd hoist it up, and then we'd repeat the process. They were really screaming at us to work faster. I don't remember why—maybe they had another ship coming in, or maybe they were worried about an air raid. Anyway, finally a Japanese guard came down in the hold to make us move faster. He was one of the big, mean ones. He yelled and screamed and kicked a few of us. Then he noticed one of the sailors, a guy who was sick and who had passed out from all the heat. He was lying back in a dark corner, trying to recover, and the other guys were covering for him. The guard ran over there and started kicking him in the face and stomach. The sailor was a big guy, but by then he was nothing but skin and bones.

At first the prisoners just stood there and watched. Then somebody looked around and saw the guard was way back in the corner, where he couldn't be seen from up above. So one prisoner stepped over behind the guard and let him have it in the head with a shovel. Blam—down he went. Then a bunch of them jumped on the guard, and beat the crap out of him with their shovels, while the rest of us worked like hell so no one would think anything unusual was going on. Dark red blood was splattering on the deck behind us, out of sight from the hatch above, running little rivers with spots of black coal dust mixed in. The guard never made a sound. Before you knew it, he was dead and buried under a pile of coal dust in the darkest corner.

By some miracle, they forgot about him, and apparently he wasn't missed before the ship sailed. When we were done working, we got out of that ship and marched back to camp. All night long I lay awake, expecting to hear the barracks door crash open, and see the guards come in with fixed bayonets. Sure as hell they would muster us out and start beating everyone until someone talked. No one would step forward on that one, because it would mean a certain beheading in the courtyard. But nothing happened. Days went by, and I couldn't believe it, but they never came after us for it. We never heard a damn thing, so I suppose they thought he'd gone AWOL, or they never found him, or maybe the ship got sunk. Christ, we were lucky on that one.

Out of our original group of eighty guys who went to Hirohata, we only lost one: L. R. Bustamente, a marine from New Mexico. He died March 16, 1944, in Hirohata. He got a carbuncle on the top of his spine, just seemed to give up, and died in two days. Nothing we did seemed to help him. Afterward, when we went to clean him up, the poor guy was nothing but skin and bones, and he was covered with lice. No telling what complications he may have had. He was the only one we lost from our group of sailors and marines, but we lost a lot of army men. All told, twenty prisoners died at Hirohata.[48]

One of the sailors, Bob Epperson, worked the burial detail. He told me that when a prisoner died they placed the body in a wooden barrel, butt down, head folded against knees. A lid was placed on the barrel and it was taken to a local crematorium where it was burned, barrel and all. Then, in accordance with Japanese custom, the ashes were shifted and a bone from each part of the body, seven in all, was placed in a small white box. To this were added dog tags, letters, and any other personal belongings that would fit in the box. After liberation these boxes were returned to Eighth Army headquarters for shipment to next of kin. The ashes and the rest of the bones were thrown into rice paddies for fertilizer.[49]

I think about those white boxes when I remember the men who died in our midst. In my opinion, the reason why we lost more soldiers was twofold. First, most of them came from the Philippines, where they'd had dysentery, dengue fever, and a lot of diseases that we didn't have on Guam. Guam was a pretty clean island. Second, they didn't seem to take care of themselves the way the marines and the sailors did. Even in freezing weather, we would go out to the wash rack and rinse ourselves off with cold water, and if we had an undershirt, we'd rinse it out to keep the lice and the bugs off. Most of us kept our hair skinned, so there was nothing there for the bugs to hide in. But the soldiers—especially in the wintertime, when it was doubly cold because we weren't getting enough to eat— wouldn't go out and clean themselves as much as they might have. I want to stress that they were in a lot worse condition than we were, because they'd seen more fighting and horrible stuff in the Philippines. They told stories about the enemy kicking a guy's teeth out to get the gold, or the terrible dysentery they had. Their dysentery was so bad that when one of them fell on the road the guards would just roll the guy over in a pit and walk on without him.

The first soldiers who joined us at Hirohata had received several Red Cross shipments, and they looked okay. In fact they told us that when they first saw us, they thought we were Korean workers, because we were so skinny and weathered from working outside all the time. When they first came into the camp, I remember that the first thing I asked them for was a bar of soap.

Eventually we got some Red Cross packages of food at Hirohata. Packages were received earlier at the other camps, but we always managed to get transferred just before the time they were distributed. The Red Cross sent enough for every prisoner to have several a year, but they were either pilfered or destroyed. I'm sure the Japanese guards got their share of what came through.

In Hirohata we got Red Cross packages once or twice. As I recall we got two Red Cross boxes, but we never got a whole one to keep; the boxes had to be split four ways. They had things like powdered milk, coffee, butter, dried prunes, grape jelly, canned meat, cheese, chocolate bars, cigarettes, and other stuff we really needed. But some of the prisoners were crazy—they'd take a thing like cheese and trade it for rice, instead of slicing off a few slices and stretching it out for a week or two. In quantity, you knew it was going to make you sick, since your system couldn't handle anything that rich all of a sudden. But some guys would take the whole block and trade it for rice or something else. Those cigarettes that came with the packages—they were like gold! I ate rice for a long time by trading those cigarettes for food.

Working at Hirohata was rarely pleasant. Besides doing hard labor, we were often forced to work under unsafe conditions without proper tools. I had to work as a welder's helper without goggles or a mask for face protection. We frequently had to go in dusty ship holds or railroad cars without any respiratory protection, and we worked around hot slag at the steel mill.

Injuries and burns were common. One day two of us were breaking concrete. One man held the chisel with a pair of steel tongs while the other swung the sledge. The guy swinging the sledge lost his balance and the blow went wide, catching me on the end of my index finger. It split and flattened my finger, which bears that shape to this day. No medical care was available. All I could do—all any of us could do—was bind up the injury and go back to work.

I had barely recovered from my June beating over the theft of the Imperial Japanese Navy butter, when I had a run in with Sadie. I guess I wasn't moving fast enough for him, because he jumped on me one day at work. He made me stand at attention while the other prisoners carried over a crate for him to stand on so he could reach my face comfortably. When I saw him undo his belt knew I was in for it. He wore a broad leather belt with a heavy metal buckle, and used a marine fighting technique when he hit you. He wrapped the leather belt around his fist several times, leaving about twelve inches of the belt (the buckle end) free. Thus prepared, he punched me a good one on the left side of my head. At the same time, the belt snaked around my head and the buckle smashed into the opposite side, just below the ear. That was it for me. I dropped like a stone, out cold.

That was the only time a Japanese guard had been able to knock me down. When I came to, I staggered to my feet, so he could windmill me for a while with both hands. Then I went back to work. By the time I reached camp that night, my ear had swollen to unrecognizable proportions. My ear and nose bled on and off for hours and my sinuses were messed up. Eventually our surgeon, Captain Seid, lanced the wound to get it to drain and heal. I have a permanent indentation on the right side of my face as a result of this blow—another souvenir from my time at Hirohata.

It was too risky to try to escape from Hirohata—there was nowhere to go, and we were too conspicuous to last more than a day away from the camp out in the Japanese countryside. However, Stansberry found a way to get out from under a corner of the fence that surrounded the camp. After he'd made an opening, he covered it up with a big rock. On good nights, when there was no moon, he'd leave the barracks with a couple of other guys, and they'd sneak out through the

hole by pushing the rock away. Then they'd go down into the town, steal cigarettes and candy and stuff from the little shops, and then come back. Well, in a
small community, you're not going to get away with it for long. But there were
quite a few guys who went under that wall. I went once, but I chickened out—
and came back. I guess that was the only time I went out of Hirohata without an
escort until the end of the war.

॥॥ ॥॥ ॥॥

After hearing Garth's description, I wanted to see Hirohata for myself. On
my next business trip to Japan, I set aside a few days to visit Hirohata. I
took the bullet train from Tokyo to Kyoto, then passed through Osaka and finally
arrived in Himeji. I knew that the prison camps where the POWs had been held
were long gone. But I wanted to get a sense of the area, try to imagine what it
would have been like to be there during the war. As the train flashed through
Osaka, I imagined the train station in a different time, thought about the POWs
lined up outside the station, being abused by Colonel Murata and his guards, a
crowd of jeering civilians throwing stones at the bleeding and hapless prisoners
waiting to board a train to their next camp.

In Himeji I stayed in the Banryu (Dragon), a small, pleasant, Japanese-style
hotel. Kimono-clad attendants made up my bed on a large futon in the traditional manner. While there I spoke with Akira Imai, the manager of the hotel, and
asked him about his wartime memories.

He was a university student in Tokyo in 1942 and recalled when the first
bombers came over during the Doolittle raid that April. In 1943 he was drafted
and sent to Singapore. During the firebombing of July 1944, 60 percent of Himeji
was destroyed. He believed that this attack was due to the military base at Himeji
and because there was an airplane manufacturing plant not far from the location of the hotel. He was aware of Korean and American prisoners of war working at Hirohata. Nippon Steel and Mitsubishi heavy industries had plants on the
island. He did not know where the prison camp was located.

It took fifteen years to rebuild the town. The steel mill on the island was also
rebuilt. I took a taxi to the gate of the steel mill to see what it looked like. There
was a sign that read "Photographs and Entry Not Allowed." I got out, took several
photographs, walked around. I could see the tall, rusty red stacks of the steel
mill, piles of slag, train tracks, the canal around the island, a haze of smoke—just
about what you would expect for a steel mill. Working there in 1944 would have
been a special kind of hell. From one point I could look out through the haze and

see the waters of the Inland Sea. I knew that somewhere off in the distance—about eighty miles to the southwest—was Zentsuji, where the POWs' pilgrimage to Hirohata had begun.

I also visited Himeji City, the museum, and Himeji Castle. The museum had some wartime photographs. They showed the devastation of the bombing—wide swaths of the city gone, a few buildings standing. One picture taken during an air raid showed a stretcher and injured people on the ground. Another picture showed children, women, soldiers, and bore the caption "Daddy is in the Army, Mommy is working in the factory."

In the distance, Himeji Castle stood high on a hill overlooking the town. The Japanese say the castle resembles a great white heron about to take flight. The castle was spared by the bombers. For more than 500 years it has been a silent, ominous guardian of the city. Below the castle, small parks came to life with the whiteness of cherry blossoms in the springtime. There is also an impressive monument to the civilian war victims in Himeji, but none for the POWs who died at Hirohata.

On the train ride back to Tokyo, I could not help but think about the differences I'd observed between the Japanese and American POWs who had survived the Pacific War. Garth and his comrades continued their resistance to Japanese authority to the end of the war. Likewise, Simon and Lydia had preferred the risks of the jungle and Filipino guerrillas to living in the comparative safety of Davao under the control of the unpredictable Japanese. They had a deep-set belief in individual freedom that army boots and bayonets could not stamp out.

The situation was different with Itoh, Sakamaki, and even Mitzi to a lesser extent. On the crowded islands of Japan, the individual was subverted to the greater good of the group. Compliance, rather than independence, was a virtue in most cases, although Japan had its share of rebels who revolted against the oppression of peasants and farmers by the ruling classes. In the military, the requirement to follow orders without question was beaten into the recruits and the fatalistic concept of death before surrender was ingrained. Surrender thus became a dishonor to avoid at all costs, even at the cost of one's life. Sakamaki clearly reflected his Japanese military training when he initially begged his American captors to let him commit suicide. This training also influenced the treatment of American POWs, whom the Japanese believed had dishonored themselves by surrendering.

Itoh's situation was different. His last order was to not commit suicide, but to hide in the jungle, continue to resist, and wait for the Japanese army to return.

As time passed and he eventually realized that Japan had lost the war, he still did not surrender, preferring to allow his family to think he'd died in the fighting, rather than dishonor them by surrendering.

Once imprisoned, for the most part the Japanese adapted passively to their captors and caused no problem. They made few attempts at escape. The military POWs soon realized that propaganda about the Americans was not true. Japanese prisoners were not tortured nor killed; they were well fed and received medical treatment if needed. It was evident that Japan was going to lose the war. They would have to accept the new circumstances until free to return home and start the rebuilding process.

This same thought process characterized the American occupation of Japan. Within weeks bitter enemies lived side by side. In a remarkable transition, rancor and hate faded as the Japanese people accepted defeat and turned their energies to rebuilding their lives and country.

Mitzi and most of the other Japanese Americans interned at Manzanar and the other camps reacted the same way as the Japanese POWs. They accepted the circumstances of their imprisonment and made the best of it, especially the first-generation Issei. With very few exceptions, they did not revolt or attempt to escape. Mitzi's generation, the Nisei, had already begun to change from traditional patterns of thinking. They still respected the Issei beliefs of their parents, but at the same time expected the individual freedoms of American citizens. They felt the injustice of their imprisonment most severely.

CHAPTER 17

╫╫ ╫╫ ╫╫

THE BATTLE FOR GUAM

The early years of Guam's occupation did not bring terrible hardships to most Guamanians. During the period of the Japanese occupation, the native Chamorros did not show much interest in collaborating with the Japanese. For the most part, they retreated to their farms and ranches in the interior of the island, and kept out of the way of the Japanese.

After the invasion, the South Seas Detachment that had wrested the island from the United States was deployed to New Guinea, where its commander and many of the soldiers were killed in the ill-fated Japanese attempt to cross the Owen-Stanley mountain range and invade Australia. With the departure of the 5,000 invading troops, a small governing force of about 500 naval personnel stayed behind in Guam to administer Japanese policy. Like people in other liberated territories, the Guamanians were promised great benefits under Japanese leadership, once they were integrated into the Greater East Asia Co-Prosperity Sphere.

Matters continued more or less in this vein until early 1944, when the tide of the war had turned and it became apparent that the Americans were drawing closer and closer to Japan. It was only logical that Guam would eventually become a target, so Japan began reinforcing the island. Seasoned troops from China and Manchuria were sent to Guam, bolstering the island's defenses with an additional 18,000 fighting men.[50] A soldier named Masashi Itoh was among the reinforcements. He kept a diary in which he recorded his experiences.

In February 1944 Itoh and his hometown friend Fumiya Aihara were stationed in Manchuria. They were informed that their unit was moving again, but they were not told where it was going. They traveled south by truck to Harbin, Manchuria, finally arriving in Korea on March 4. After several days of loading a ship with troops and supplies, they sailed from Pusan to Yokohama. Even though the soldiers longed to visit the homes they had not seen for the past two

Japanese Bunker on Guam

years, their ship joined a convoy of twelve vessels and sailed from Yokohama after just one night in port. While they were at sea, they learned that their destination was a small island in the Marianas group called Guam. They arrived on March 21, 1944.

Itoh's group was first sent to Inarajan, the area where Garth Dunn had spent time in the Insular Patrol outstation three years earlier. The Japanese constructed fortifications there and at other locations nearby for the next several months. They were hampered by lack of materials and equipment.

With the arrival in 1944 of hardened Japanese combat troops from China, life for the Chamorros became much more difficult and conditions deteriorated rapidly. These troops were harsher than the administrative group who previously ran the island. By June 1944, all Chamorro men fourteen years or older were forced to work for the Japanese army. At this time, the Chamorro population was estimated to be a little more than 20,000 people.

In June the first American air raids began. On June 11, 1944, American bombers struck Saipan, Tinian, and Guam simultaneously as part of the preparatory action to invading Saipan. At first the Japanese did not realize that Saipan was the immediate target and thought Guam was about to be invaded. Terrified, many Guamanians fled to the hills. Just before the American invasion a month and a half later, all of the Guamanians were rounded up by the Japanese and placed in prison camps near Asinan, Manengon, and Talofofo.[51] These camps were identified by American fliers, and the Chamorros were spared greater casualties since they were concentrated in locations that the American planes avoided. In mid-June the Japanese on Guam learned of the invasion of Saipan. Air raids increased in intensity up until the date of the American invasion. Itoh's friend Fumiya Aihara was injured during a bombing raid on July 19, 1944 and died from his wounds a few days later. Itoh later noted in his diary that "Aihara now sleeps in a coconut grove near Ordot."

Following the June bombings, the U.S. Navy carried out a heavy naval shelling of the area around Agat, just south of the Orote Peninsula. This action caused the Japanese commander, General Takeshi Takashima, to suspect that the landings would take place there. Consequently, he redeployed the bulk of the Japanese forces to the area between Tumon Bay and the Agat beaches. He had two other commanders under him. General Kiyoshi Shigematsu was responsible for the Agana sector (Piti to Tumon Bay), where the Japanese had themselves landed three years earlier. To the south, Colonel Tsunetaro Suenaga was in command of the Agat sector. From the hilltops around Agana, Japanese artillery commanded the beaches where, in a matter of time, they knew the Americans would eventually arrive.[52]

The Japanese battle plan was to destroy the invaders on the beaches. Due to the rapid advance of the American forces across the Pacific, they did not have sufficient time to prepare fortified positions in the interior of Guam, from which they could fight a delaying action. Even if they had time, they lacked the essential materiel to do so.

Days went by, and news of the fall of Saipan on July 9th and the heavy bombardment and certain invasion of Tinian made its way to the Japanese forces on Guam. This news, coupled with the ongoing bombing and bombardment of Guam, seriously sapped their morale. However, the month-long delay from the initial bombing of Guam until its actual invasion had terrible consequences for the Chamorros. After rounding up the native population into prison camps, the Japanese began a program of brutal repression and committed atrocities on the Guamanians, possibly because these soldiers were veterans of the fighting in China, or perhaps because they sensed that they might never return home from Guam. Besides being forced into labor, people were beaten, priests were killed, civilians were raped and beheaded, and there were mass executions.

On the morning of July 21, 1944, the long-awaited blow finally fell. Following a tremendous, three-hour naval bombardment, the U.S. Third Marine Division landed on Asan Beach, establishing the northern beachhead, while to the south the First Provisional Marine Brigade, along with the 305th Regimental Combat Team of the 77th Army Infantry Division, landed at Agat Beach. Both forces secured the beaches; the northern force had a harder time than the southern force, due to the unfavorable terrain.

General Takashima had 18,500 Japanese troops under his command. In order to defeat the entrenched Japanese, the U. S. military put 50,000 personnel ashore during the invasion. After the American landings, Japanese groups waited for orders to counterattack once the positions of American strength were identified. On the night of July 21, the first counterattacks were launched. Despite fierce efforts by the Japanese, the American lines held. In the intense fighting, Colonel Suenaga was killed.

After the landings, the Third Marines came south, while the 22nd Marines and the 305th Infantry Regiment of the 77th Infantry Division moved north, to cut off Japanese forces on Orote Peninsula. The Fourth Marines remained behind to guard the flank and the southern beachhead. As the American forces moved north, they came under fire from Japanese artillery on Mount Tenjo. By the 24th of July, the Orote Peninsula was sealed off. On the nights of July 25 and 26, the Japanese launched suicidal counterattacks at Orote and in the north. These attacks all failed, and in the process, General Shigematsu was killed. By the evening of July 26, General Takashima knew that his only recourse was to move his forces inland and fight a delaying action as long as possible. By July 28, the American forces had recaptured the bombed-out shell of the marine barracks at Sumay. The Japanese still held Mount Tenjo and other high ground, but knew they could not resist at these locations much longer. General Takashima began making arrangements to move his headquarters, but was killed before he could get off the mountain. The 77th took control of Mount Tenjo. The last Japanese general, General Hideyoshi Obata, now took command.[53]

By the 29th, the Americans had recaptured the entire Orote Peninsula. Bands of Japanese were silently fading away to the north from Mount Tenjo and other former strongholds. They hid in the jungle and retreated in the direction of Barrigada, avoiding American patrols and the aircraft, all the while feeling the relentless pursuit of the opposition forces, who were determined not to let the Japanese forces regroup or reorganize.

At this time the American commander—Major General Roy S. Geiger— believed that the Japanese would retreat north, but sent a number of patrols south to verify that the main body of the Japanese had not gone in that direction. By the first of August, the Americans had sealed off the bulk of the Japanese

Marine Barracks, Guam, 1944

forces on the northern one-third of the island. At this time, a Major S. Sato met a group of about 250 Japanese soldiers trying to retreat north. Sato gave the order for these troops to disperse to the southern areas, continue fighting, and wait for the return of Japanese forces. This group of soldiers, which included Masashi Itoh, slipped back through the American net and proceeded south, losing about three soldiers per day to the American forces.

During the first week of August, the Japanese troops were harried to the northern tip of the island. On the 8th of August, organized resistance came to an end. On the 11th, General Obata was killed. Major Sato and Colonel Hideyuki Takeda attempted to rally stragglers to continue the struggle, but the battle was essentially lost.

In early August, with the main fighting over, American patrols searched for the remaining Japanese troops. An estimated 5,000 Japanese soldiers had slipped through the encircling American forces and fled into the Guamanian jungles. By the middle of August, Guam was declared secure, although skirmishes with stragglers continued for another year.[54] Patrols canvassed the area, searching out the remaining Japanese troops. A group of Chamorros joined this effort and served as scouts and guides. Many of these volunteers had either suffered themselves at the hands of the Japanese or had close relatives who had been beaten, raped, or killed in the frantic months before the invasion.

〜 〜 〜

Itoh kept a diary describing his experiences on Guam. In July it had become obvious to him that the Americans were about to land on Guam. His diary tells what happened next.[55]

ITOH wrote:

July 21, 1944

At around 0300 hours, it appeared that the enemy invasion was imminent. Our regiment started to move toward Mount Alutom, located behind Agana. We kept off the roads and traveled through the jungle. When we arrived at the mountain, it was still dark. We could see about 600 assorted enemy warships anchored off of Agana Bay. Even though it was still dark, they were bombarding the island. At around 0830 hours, the enemy started landing on the beach at the east side of the bay.

Later that day our group was given orders to move. In the evening we became separated from the rest of the battalion in the darkness. We searched and looked for a long time, but could not locate our group. While we tried to locate them on the radio, our lieutenant went out to scout. Finally, the battalion was located and our lieutenant started to lead us to it. On the way he got lost. All around us we saw unexploded one-ton bombs lying on the ground. By then it was almost dawn. The enemy was advancing toward us. In daylight there would be many airplanes overhead. If they found us we would not survive.

We had no choice but to hide in the jungle. We spent the daylight hours there. During the daytime, no Japanese planes flew. All of the soldiers and commissioned officers were frustrated and bitter about this. We all felt that if we had some air support, we could defeat the Americans, although we did not know at that time that our air bases had been destroyed.

July 23, 1944

At around 1800 hours, the division attacked the Americans. We all took part in the attack. There was a plan to make the final attack on July 25—a suicidal attack where we would all fight to the death. This plan was transmitted to Japan by radio. The high command in Japan did not approve the plan; instead we were told that additional men and supplies would be sent.

Japanese World War II Tank

⫟⫟⫟ ⫟⫟⫟ ⫟⫟⫟

During one of my Guam visits, Don Farrell, the public relations officer for the Guam legislature, introduced me to Jack Eddy, who had participated in the Guam landings. As a first lieutenant, Jack was a platoon leader in F Company, Second Battalion, Ninth Marines, Third Marine Division.[56] His unit had taken part in the fighting at Bouganville, returned to Guadalcanal to be refitted, then embarked for the invasion of Guam. They landed at Asan Point. The Asan battle was touch and go for five or six days until July 26, 1944. On the night of the 25th there was a big push by the Japanese, "Do or die time," as Jack put it. They tried to get to the beach and cut off the marines' supplies. A few got close, some actually got into the division hospital, but they were beaten back. During August and September 1944, there was a sweep to the north part of the island. In fall of 1944, after the sweep was done and the island declared secure, Jack's group went to Inarajan for a month, patrolling for stragglers, which they encountered in small groups. When they found campsites, food remains, or discarded Japanese cigarettes that were evidence of stragglers, the marines dropped off three or four men on nearby jungle trails and set up night ambushes.

The Ninth Marine Regiment camped on the beach between the Ylig and Togcha Rivers. This time was used for training and replenishing the platoon—

Jack said there were only seven men left from his squad of fourteen. Eventually, there were 3,000 men in tents in that area. The camp included an outdoor movie screen set up for the troops near the beach and a large dump for trash and garbage. The marines practiced battalion-size maneuvers near the Windward Hills. Their tanks and motor transport were up near Yona. The marines and army had patrol sectors around the area and kept watch for Japanese stragglers.

Occasionally Japanese were seen at the garbage dump and night ambushes were set up. On one occasion a straggler was observed in camp watching the movies. He escaped. When stragglers were killed, the troops did not bury them immediately—burial details later verified and buried them. The stragglers usually were not inclined to fight. They were not in good condition: some of them had lost their weapons, and a number of them were support personnel rather than combat troops. At one point, the marines went up the Togcha River, looked in caves, and found a camp of huts and shacks near Talofofo. There hadn't been much bombing in the area, and it was relatively undisturbed. The stragglers had been at the camp but had left.

The Ninth Marines pulled out of Guam in February 1945 to go to Iwo Jima. After Iwo Jima, Jack Eddy was shipped back to a hospital on Guam, then to the United States in April 1945. He remembered the date; it was just before President Roosevelt died.

The U. S. marines' rapid advance and superior logistical support kept the Japanese defenders off balance. They were severely hampered by the lack of adequate communications and confusion caused by the loss of many officers. The invaders relentlessly pressed the Japanese toward the northern end of the island. Organized resistance on the part of the Japanese began to crumble. Soon the fighting was restricted to scattered pockets of soldiers. Itoh's diary described the end of organized resistance by the Japanese.

卌 卌 卌

ITOH wrote:

July 27, 1944

We hid in the jungle near Barrigada and harassed the enemy before moving on in the direction of Mount Barrigada. Some soldiers disappeared in the jungle, either casualties or lost. We established a position about two kilometers from Mount Barrigada. There we saw some tanks drive through a nearby village. They stopped not far from us. I went with another soldier to investigate. We found one tank stopped by the side of the road, with seven soldiers eating dried biscuits in the rain, others inside the tank.

"Eat this instead," I thought to myself, as I threw a grenade at them. The explosion killed four and wounded three of the seven. The remaining soldiers put some white papers on the dead men, loaded the wounded soldiers into the tank, which was called *Lori* or *Loralei*, and then drove off. This was my first experience with killing someone.

After the tank had gone, we dragged the dead bodies into the jungle and took cigarettes and dried biscuits from the pockets of the enemy soldiers. I smoked a cigarette and found it to be good. I also took a carbine from one of the dead soldiers.

There were about 250 of us left in our group, including Second Lieutenant Osada and Warrant Officer Myodo. Before we left for our last move to the north, we assembled with two staff officers, Major Sato and Lieutenant Colonel Hideyuki Takeda. Lieutenant Colonel Takeda told us: "Refrain from suicidal attacks. Survive as long as possible and kill as many of the enemy as possible. Even if you are the only one to survive, you must not die." This speech was the beginning of our jungle life.

While in the jungle, we encountered enemy scouts. At each encounter they lost two or three men, and we suffered about five casualties. On average we were losing two to three soldiers every day. I kept thinking that any day the next victim might be me. In spite of these hardships, I didn't die. It appears that writing a record of the fighting in Guam might be my destiny.

Middle of August 1944
It was raining every day, and we were wet to the skin. Americans were patrolling constantly. We moved to another area we thought might be a little safer. At that time eleven of us were together, all under the command of a sergeant major.

August 19, 1944
First-class Private T, also from Kofu, committed suicide with a grenade. He had been sick. Corporal S. also killed himself by grenade. He had been a model noncommissioned officer. August slipped away. For many days we had nothing to eat but papaya.

Beginning of September 1944
An enemy ship for prisoners of war came to the beach near Barrigada. For three days they used a loudspeaker to tell us that we had finished our duties and we should surrender. The appeal didn't succeed. No one in our group surrendered.

We all promised each other that we would resist at all costs, even if we had to "eat stones," that is, to fight to the death.[57]

‖‖ ‖‖ ‖‖

Itoh and four other Japanese soldiers managed to sneak back through the American lines and head south along the eastern side of the island. By October 1944 (two months after the Americans had declared the island secure) they were near Pago. As they passed through thick jungle near a road guarded by Americans, Itoh paused, bent down, and started to tie a loose shoelace. At that instant heavy firing broke out. Two of his comrades fell dead. The other two were hit and crawled into the dense brush. Itoh managed to avoid the ensuing search and fled deeper into the jungle. For the next two weeks, alone and half dead from hunger, he made his way south through nearly impassable jungle.

Around the middle of October, as he was hiding in thick brush, he saw two Japanese soldiers emerge from the jungle and enter a cave. He went out to meet them and learned that they were Tokujiro Miyazawa and Bunzo Minagawa. From them he learned that more than twenty other Japanese soldiers were hiding in the same general vicinity. Itoh and his comrades decided it was safer to remain in a small group, and so they separated from the others. For the next seven months, until May 1945, the three soldiers moved from bivouac to bivouac in the jungle, rarely staying in one spot for more than a few days, and subsisting on coconuts, wild fruits, stolen food, captured chickens, and an occasional wild pig.

Near the end of May, they decided to build a hideout in a remote section of jungle near the Togcha River. The location was near the coast. The river had freshwater shrimp, and the site was close to an unoccupied farm owned by a man named Shimizu. Breadfruit, papaya, taro, bananas, and coconuts were plentiful. At this time the surviving Japanese stragglers were having a difficult time. They were constantly harassed by American and Guamanian patrols engaged in mopping-up operations and were forced to stay on the move. Every day saw more of them killed.

‖‖ ‖‖ ‖‖

ITOH wrote:

May 1945

Once again in the jungle, we were hungry. Private Minagawa and I went out to pick some papayas. We saw about fifty American soldiers patrolling. We went to their abandoned camp and found the butts of many cigarettes.

Over the next few weeks we would go out in the moonlight and pick taro and bananas. In addition, we also went to Shimizu's farm, and sometimes got a pig or cow. We spent two months in this location.

One day, early in May, we found footprints at the Talofofo plateau. We traced the steps and found seven Japanese soldiers. They had been stationed in China before being sent to Guam. There was also one elderly man who had come to Guam with the South Islands Development Plan before the war. We stayed with them for a while talking about our experiences and listening to theirs.

Then, on May 20, we left them, and moved to a section of jungle along the Togcha River where the land was relatively flat. There we built a shack of old galvanized, corrugated sheet metal we'd found in the cave. Shortly after we'd moved into our new house, Private Minagawa decided to leave us and join the group of seven we'd met earlier.

Private Miyazawa and I spent the next few days making furniture, building a table from an old oil drum, and so on. Finally the place was something we could call a home.

JHT JHT JHT

They built a crude lean-to with some old sheets of galvanized iron, and improvised some furniture and a rainwater collection system. Then they settled in to await the return of the Imperial Japanese Army. By now the strain of their jungle existence was beginning to tell on the three. Arguments arose about the division of work, food, and other matters. That was when Minagawa decided to leave.

In June 1945 Itoh and Miyazawa feasted on a cow they had stolen, but then hard times began in August as food became harder to find. At the same time, unbeknownst to the two soldiers, Japan had surrendered, and the Pacific War was over. Itoh and the other stragglers did not know that in June, Major Sato himself had surrendered along with thirty-four men, and a few weeks later, Lieutenant Colonel Hideyuki Takeda surrendered with sixty-seven men. In September, Itoh and Miyazawa were near starvation, existing solely on a few coconuts, papaya, and bamboo shoots. In October the rains came; they caught some chickens, Itoh shot another pig, and the food situation improved.

Itoh made daily entries in his diary, always mentioning the weather, almost always describing what they had eaten. In his entries, he rarely allowed himself to become pessimistic or depressed. He managed to maintain a positive outlook, exulting over the food they found, even when it was meager fare. His skill at

Major Sato Surrenders Thirty-four Stragglers, Guam, June 1945

making tools, mending clothes, and building wild animal traps provides further evidence of how he survived. In the succeeding months, life settled into a routine, but Itoh noted his frustration in his diary.

卌 卌 卌

ITOH wrote:

October 3, 1945 (Rain)
It has been clear and cloudy the last few days. I cannot bear too many rainy days. A small plane has been flying overhead. In the distance I can hear the Americans playing music all day. What is the Imperial Japanese Army, the enemy of America and England, doing? Where is our relief? They should consider our mental state. We have not eaten rice and miso for one year and three months. After all the hardships we've endured, I suppose we can get used to this.

October 6, 1945 (Clear)
I took my overnight trip but no cows or pigs appeared. I did find some clothing and food, and I got some cigarettes and sweets from the American's trash dump. I rested well and I'm looking forward to tomorrow.

October 8, 1945 (Clear)

An off day. I rested in the morning. In the afternoon I collected some firewood. The banana tempura dinner I had was delicious.

October 11, 1945 (Clear, then cloudy)

It was clear in the morning. On my way home from picking bamboo shoots, I encountered some pigs. They were wary. I took three shots but got none. Dinner tonight was the enemy's canned food; it was delicious. I'm looking forward to tomorrow.

October 13, 1945 (Clear, cloudy)

After breakfast I went to the Shimizu farm to build a pig trap. I found three chickens in the chicken trap I'd placed there. I brought them back and made a chicken coop for them. Now we have a total of fifteen chickens. The ones I caught earlier are tame enough that I let them run free.

October 18, 1945 (Cloudy, clear)

In the morning I did some more work on my pants and also made some other clothes. Every day at noon a siren blows. Today when it blew, I noticed five pigs in the valley below my house. I got my gun and managed to shoot one. It weighed about 330 pounds. I cut up the meat and carried it back to the house in my backpack. For dinner I had pork stew. The taste of meat was glorious—it has been fifty days since I had any meat.

October 23, 1945 (Rain, clear)

Last night I went to the enemy's trash dump, where I found a few sweets and some clothes. It rained and I was soaked as I came home in the dark. I saw the enemy's houses and automobiles passing by. I don't feel too good and I have a stomachache, possibly because I got so wet. For dinner I made a meat soup with wheat flour. It tasted like seasoned Japanese food. The occasions like this—when we have good food to eat—are like a holiday for us. Even with these hardships we are still alive. We are walking on the dark part of the road in the path of our lives.

‖‖ ‖‖ ‖‖

Back in August, Itoh and Miyazawa had heard gunshots in the distance. They went into hiding but no one came near their camp. September and October passed with no sign of the other stragglers. In November 1945 Itoh decided to pay a visit to the camp where the seven stragglers and Private Minagawa were living.

_卌 卌 卌_

ITOH wrote:

November 12, 1945
Early in the morning I went to pick some coconuts and breadfruit. After breakfast I took care of my gun, and in the afternoon, shaved. Tomorrow I'm planning to visit the hidden camp where the group of eight soldiers is living.

November 13, 1945
I got up before dawn, had breakfast, and then left for the site where our eight friends live. On the way I saw many shrimp in the Togcha River. I walked to the Talofofo mesa area and drank some coconut juice. When I arrived at the campsite there was not a sound to be heard. The camp had been destroyed and I saw two dead bodies. They must have been shot by the American soldiers.

One body appeared to be that of Private Minagawa and the other one I could not identify. The other six must have escaped. The corpses looked old and had decomposed. I heard some gunshots in August; possibly they were killed then. There were still many vegetables and fruits in their garden, which was growing beautifully.

I climbed a tree to see the coastline. From it I could see many admirable buildings built by the enemy. There were many automobiles going back and forth.

At times like this I think about my country and hometown and feel that something within me is going to explode. What future do we have here? What hope?

Later while we smoked, Private Miyazawa and I talked about our luck. Private Minagawa had left us to join the group of seven, causing his death. A small group like the two of us is less dangerous, because we are less likely to be spotted. We don't know what will happen to us eventually, but so far we are healthy. We just try our best to not be discovered by the enemy.

_卌 卌 卌_

At this point in time the war was over. Japan had surrendered back in August, around the time that Itoh thought Minagawa had been killed. The Guamanian authorities used aircraft to drop Japanese language leaflets over the jungle, telling the remaining soldiers that the war was over and they should surrender. Navy boats patrolled the coasts and used loudspeakers to broadcast the same information to inaccessible areas where the remaining Japanese soldiers were thought to be hiding.[58] Itoh and the other stragglers knew about these efforts but decided it was propaganda. From their training they felt it was dishonorable to surrender. After this lengthy time, there was another problem: their families had no doubt given them up as dead. To return now would dishonor their families.

The stragglers foraged for food early in the morning or at night. During the day they remained hidden in the hut, mending clothes, making tools, or performing other small chores. They became extremely wary, careful to leave no trace of their existence, and ready to flee at the first sign of a patrol. On December 31, 1945, Itoh killed five of their chickens for a New Year's feast. Renewed, the two soldiers prayed for their safety in the coming year, thought of the families they had not seen in more than four years, and wondered when relief would arrive.

After the island had been militarily secure for some months, the Americans sought the assistance of civilian authorities to track down and capture or kill the remaining Japanese soldiers. A special unit of the Guam Police Department was formed, called the Guam Police Combat Patrol. The combat patrol was a paramilitary unit of policemen who were familiar with the jungle and had prior combat experience as army scouts and guides. They were charged with hunting down the remaining Japanese stragglers, a few of whom held out for months or years after the war was over. The stragglers fell victim to the deep resentment toward the Japanese created by the atrocities committed during the final months of the occupation. Because of this antagonism, most of the remaining Japanese were killed outright or committed suicide; only a few were taken alive or persuaded to give themselves up. The combat patrol unit remained in existence until 1948. By then several hundred Japanese stragglers had been killed and a handful taken alive. The U.S. government subsequently decorated all of the original unit members.

In 1946, Itoh's diary begins to make frequent references to "native patrols." He recognized that there was something different about these patrols (compared to the marine and army patrols, which no longer came), but thought they were simply groups of native hunters—a misjudgment that would have fatal consequences.

In February 1946, Itoh and Miyazawa were visited by Minagawa and a fourth soldier named Tetsuo Unno. Itoh was relieved to learn that the body he'd seen when he'd visited their camp the previous November was not Minagawa. The two of them had escaped when their larger group was raided and most of its members killed. As a result of that experience, they were extremely cautious, even to the point of not disclosing the exact location of their hideout to Itoh and Miyazawa. The two groups went their separate ways, occasionally meeting to exchange food or cigarettes.

On February 19, 1946, Itoh noted in his diary that he'd found a paper stating that the war was over and that the emperor had ordered all Japanese forces to surrender and return to their homeland. The procedure for surrendering safely was described in this paper, which also stated that Japanese soldiers were currently being transported home by the Americans. Itoh copied the entire proclamation in his diary and then wrote:

> Japan cannot be defeated. We believe in our country and this belief sustains us. With divine power behind it, Japan will win; no doubt we will win. I will not be deceived by the propaganda in this leaflet!

Itoh's daily entries as the months of 1946 passed focused on weather, food, what he ate that day, and his constant preoccupation with the enemy who continued to hunt down the stragglers. He describes a typhoon that struck the island, nearly destroying their hut, several earthquakes, and the onset of the dry season in May and June, when food was scarce. He writes of making tools—needles, knives, and a saw; writing poetry; and carving objects such as a case for his chopsticks, which he decorated with a drawing of Guam. He tells of mending or making clothes and building furniture for their hut, also of making traps for rats, chickens, and wild pigs. He describes occasional injuries, headaches, dysentery, and food poisoning, and how much he misses his parents and sister in Japan.

卌 卌 卌

ITOH wrote:

March 14, 1946 (Clear)
Since early morning I've worked on my rat traps and completed two. We find a rat in the traps almost every day. They are delicious to eat. We bake them all morning.

May 26, 1946 (Clear)
Before it got light, I heard gunshots. It sounded like they came from the field, but I stayed in bed. Around noon I left to pick bamboo shoots and breadfruit. On the way I saw some footprints by the barbed wire around the enemy's barracks.

August 21, 1946 (Clear)

This evening I checked the pig trap and found it contained two pigs. To celebrate I brought one home so we can prepare some pork dishes. We invited Mr. Minagawa and Mr. Unno for a delicious fried pork dinner.

September 30, 1946 (Clear)

I finished my work on Mr. Unno's knife. Today we ate the last of the breadfruit for breakfast; also, we have no more fresh meat. In the evening I dug some *baraimo* [a small wild sweet potato]. This month is over. I pray that we live uneventfully in October. The white chicken laid an egg. I took it away just before the chicken tried to peck at the egg.

November 24, 1946 (Clear)

At noon I went out to dig some bamboo shoots. I encountered a patrol in the valley below our house and had to run from them. I'll enjoy dinner tonight.

December 11, 1946 (Clear)

Today I picked some corn. They've cleared the land around Mr. Shimizu's farm. We'll have a harder time now. [Note: The stragglers hung the corn to dry; see page 175.]

December 25, 1946 (Clear)

In the morning our friends returned with a stolen cow. We killed the cow, and ate some for dinner. It will make a great New Year's feast.

December 26, 1946 (Clear)

Since early this morning we've been working on cutting up the meat. We'll have barbecue beef tonight. I'm looking forward to it. 'Till tomorrow.

December 27, 1946 ( )

卌 卌 卌

Early in December 1946, the two groups of stragglers decided to join forces to stage a "raid" on Yona. They went out at night, passed many American barracks, but managed only to steal some clothing. Apparently they were observed by someone because the combat patrol records state that the Talofofo-Togcha area (where the stragglers hideout was located) was placed under increased surveillance after that date.

Several days before Christmas 1946, Unno and Minagawa again visited Itoh and Miyazawa to plan a foraging raid on the village of Talofofo to get food for a New Year's celebration. Itoh noted this in his diary. He did not realize that in his reckoning of time he had gained one day. His December 25 was actually December 24 and so on. In his methodical manner, Itoh had written in the date for the December 27 entry, leaving space for his weather report. That entry was never made, however. After dividing the meat, Unno and Minagawa took off, leaving Itoh and Miyazawa to cut up and cook their portion.

The stolen cow was reported to the combat patrol the day before Christmas. Before dawn on Christmas morning, a number of patrolmen gathered their weapons and set out on the trail. Fearing an ambush (several of their members had been killed or wounded in skirmishes with the Japanese), they proceeded cautiously through the dense bush. At daybreak they were near the hideout. They could smell meat cooking and heard Itoh and Miyazawa conversing in low tones. They silently spread out and surrounded the stragglers' camp. As they closed in, one of Itoh's chickens sensed their presence and started cackling. Startled, the stragglers jumped to their feet. There was a burst of carbine rifle fire, then silence.

The combat patrol searched the area and then returned to the hideout and found one dead straggler. They buried the body before burning the hut and its contents. Among the straggler's belongings in the hut they found an unusual item, a little leather-bound book bearing the name of an American soldier, First Lieutenant Philip N. Pierce, 155 Howitzer Battery, Fifth Amphibious Corps. Other than a few pages with notations in English, the bulk of the diary was written in Japanese. It included hand-drawn maps and sketches of airplanes. It was taken to police headquarters in Agana where a report was prepared.

The following is excerpted from the police report, which was forwarded to the commanding officer of the marine barracks (director of island security) at Agana:[59]

At approximately 1030, Christmas morning, 25 December 1946, after waiting several hours for any additional stragglers to appear at the Japanese bivouac area, the Combat Patrol walked in and demanded the straggler's surrender. When the straggler attempted to flee, he was shot and killed.

The straggler had been preparing breakfast only for himself, but there is evidence that indicates perhaps more than one straggler has been living in the hideout.

Guam Police Combat Patrol at the Stragglers' Hideout, Christmas 1946

The hideout consisted of an improved hut with a corrugated iron roof and a wooden deck. The hut is located in rugged terrain covered with thick underbrush. Besides a small stock of corn and taro root, there was evidence of a cow that had been slaughtered.

The straggler was dressed in khaki shirt and trousers of G.I. issue, and was wearing a pair of Japanese type sandals when killed. Also found in the bivouac area were 3 seabags containing 9 pairs of G.I. field shoes, 12 khaki shirts, and 10 pairs of khaki trousers. No identifying marks were found on the clothing. Eight diaries, ranging from good to poor condition were found with scraps of paper which are badly weathered.

The clothing on the straggler revealed no evidence to identify the person. Preliminary translation of the diaries and other printed materials reveals that only one diary is of value. This diary is the property of Sergeant M. Itoh.

The Guam Police Combat Patrol are continuing operations in the above-mentioned area.

The report, along with the diary and photographs of the dead straggler and the straggler's hideout, were eventually sent to Washington, D.C. It was filed in a box containing information concerning American POWs from Guam and sent to the U.S. National Archives for storage.

By chance, in March 1986 I found the diary buried in a file. At the time I was researching the American prisoners of war from Guam and the Philippines and was trying to find additional details in World War II documents that had been recently declassified. With the assistance of the Marine Museum, Washington, D.C., I was able to obtain documents from the U. S. National Archives on a loan basis. By pure coincidence, I found the police report and diary in a file box of reports, where it had been mistakenly filed with documents related to American POWs from Guam.

I was struck by the sadness of this reminder of the terrible fighting on Guam. First, who was Lieutenant Pierce, and what had happened to him? Had he been killed by this Japanese soldier? I decided to see if I could locate Lieutenant Pierce, or at least find out what had happened to him—find out why his small notebook had ended up in the hands of a Japanese soldier.

Then there was the needless death of the straggler, Christmas Day, a year and a half after the end of the war. More out of curiosity than anything else, I thumbed through a few pages of the diary. I was intrigued by the drawings of aircraft and the maps it contained. I could not read Japanese, but I quickly recognized one drawing as being a map of Guam. On a whim I decided to make a copy of the diary and have it translated. Once I became aware of the personal saga it contained, I decided to try to return it to Itoh's family. Based on the police report and information in the diary at that time, I assumed that Itoh had been killed, and I was certain that his family would appreciate receiving information about his final days on Guam.

CHAPTER 18

‖‖ ‖‖ ‖‖

MacARTHUR RETURNS

By the fall of 1944, the long island-hopping campaign across the Pacific had brought General MacArthur to the threshold of the Philippines. At this time the Joint Chiefs of Staff faced a decision: invade Formosa, as Admiral Earnest J. King recommended, or invade the Philippines as MacArthur desired.[60] Eventually, MacArthur's arguments carried the day, and planning began for the liberation of the Philippines. The initial target was to be Mindanao.

In September 1944, Admiral William F. Halsey suggested a bold plan: strike at Leyte, in the middle of the Philippines, where the Japanese would not expect it and where intelligence showed that Japanese forces were weak. This location was even farther north, closer to Manila than Mindanao. MacArthur agreed, and the invasion timetable was advanced by several months. On October 19, 1944, the Sixth Army came to Leyte.

Far away, on the southern corner of Mindanao, Simon and Lydia were unaware of these rapidly changing events as they struggled to stay alive into the new year.

In January 1945, the invasion of Luzon began. MacArthur's broadcasts to the guerillas caused them to intensify their activities throughout the Philippines, tying down additional Japanese troops. In February the first U.S. patrols entered the Manila city limits. In daring raids the prisoners at Santo Tomas and Los Banos were freed.[61] Jane and Hugh Wills and their daughter, Trudy, were finally at liberty, rescued by troops from the 511th Parachute Infantry, who parachuted into Los Banos behind Japanese lines, stormed the camp, killed the guards, and then carried the 2,147 prisoners to safety and freedom across Lake Laguna de Bay in amphibious tractors.

I was able to locate and interview Jane Wills at her home in California. She told me about life in the Happy Life Blues Cabaret camp, and then the trip by boat to Manila and internment at Los Banos. Her description of the rescue of the prisoners was electrifying. She recalled visiting some friends in the camp that morning. They heard planes overhead, saw the paratroopers coming down. Then the bullets started flying. There were 250 guards. Only five escaped; the rest were killed, including the camp commander. Warrant Officer Sadaaki Konishi, second in command of the camp, was one of the escapees. He was a tyrannical leader who withheld food and forced starvation rations on the POWs. The rescue was carried out by American forces with the aid of Filipino guerrillas. The POWs were put in amphibious vehicles, no time to pack anything, and then raced out of the camp under fire. In a tragic aftermath, Japanese forces led by Konishi returned the next day to find the camp empty. In retaliation for the raid, they attacked a nearby village. Families were shot or tied to the stilts supporting their houses, and the houses set on fire. An estimated 1,500 Filipinos died as a result, although they had been warned by the guerrillas to leave the area in case the Japanese returned.[62]

At this time, in Yalta, the Joint Chiefs informed the British that there were no plans for taking the other Philippine Islands. In March, MacArthur declared Manila secure, but in reality fighting raged on for another month. MacArthur, on his own authority, resolved to liberate the rest of the Philippine Islands.[63] His actions were approved retroactively by the Joint Chiefs of Staff. This decision saved many Filipino and American lives, and undoubtedly saved the lives of Simon and Lydia, because elsewhere in the Philippines, the Japanese were still in control, and people were dying daily from starvation or illness. On Mindanao, both Simon and Lydia were ill again.

⊥⊥⊥ ⊥⊥⊥ ⊥⊥⊥

LYDIA: We both had malaria. Things got bad at the end of 1944 and in 1945 because we were both extremely weak. Our house was by the road to the cemetery, and every day, two to three times per day, we saw people going up to the cemetery to bury their dead. Hundreds were dying by then. I had the normal kind of malaria. First you got terrible chills—you just couldn't get warm, even though it was ninety degrees outside. You wanted hot-water bottles or anything to warm up. These chills went on for a few hours, then you got a high fever, like you were burning up. During one bout of malaria, I coughed up worms, tapeworms or some kind of parasite. Simon tried to comfort me, saying that I was lucky—those worms couldn't stand hot-blooded Latvian women.

Simon's malaria was different. He had a fever, and it went to his head. He became delirious, didn't know where he was. He lost his appetite, became incoherent, rambling. I took care of him. He was the only husband I had; I didn't want to have to go to the trouble to get another.

卌 卌 卌

In January and February 1945, the Allies began bombing Davao. B-29s and B-24 Liberators flew over on both day and night raids. Filipinos constructed foxholes or found caves to hide in during the air raids. They watched in fascination as the Japanese searchlights sought out the planes, which were too high for the Japanese guns to hit.

MacArthur continued his campaigns to liberate the other islands. In April, in the last major amphibious operation of the Philippines campaign, Australian troops and the U.S. X Corps landed on Mindanao.[64] Through the last half of April 1945, U.S. troops fought their way toward Davao. They were assisted by strong guerrilla action, which kept the demoralized Japanese off balance. On May 2, 1945, Davao was declared cleared of Japanese forces. Remaining elements of the Japanese forces were pushed north toward Malaybalay, where they hoped to fight a delaying action in the remote mountains. Unfortunately they were running out of supplies, had little food, and many of their officers were dead or captured. On June 30 the Mindanao campaign was declared over. Many Japanese remained in hiding. After the war ended, more than 20,000 Japanese troops gave up, and about 10,000 Japanese civilians surrendered.

卌 卌 卌

SIMON: We were expecting the Americans. We'd heard about the liberation of Manila. One day we saw ships coming into Davao harbor, then small planes flew over, mapping the bay. There was an amphibious landing, but there was not much resistance at that time. Still, it was a month or more before the troops came to where we were.

Then began a dangerous time in the Philippines. There was no real law or authority. On one side there were the battle-weary U.S. troops, veterans of dozens of amphibious assaults and clearing operations during the past two years. In the middle were the retreating Japanese soldiers and marines—in some cases organized groups, and in other instances lone stragglers moving silently through the jungle, prepared to give their life for their emperor. On the other side, there were the guerrillas, increasingly bold and aggressive, harassing the Japanese, making their own laws wherever they went—laws of force.

卌 卌 卌

LYDIA: In May, we were both ill with malaria again, especially Simon. His weight had dropped to about ninety pounds.

I'll never forget the day the Americans came. We were just skin and bones. We heard gunshots and crawled into the abaca grove to hide from the soldiers. I distinctly remember a soldier coming right in our direction, ready to shoot anything that moved. As he approached, his face was tense, he had almost a grimace, he was a dehumanized robot, a killing machine. He saw Simon and lifted his gun, aiming it at him. I leaped up and shouted at the soldier, "Don't shoot him, he is dying of malaria, let him die in peace!"

Instantly the soldier's face changed, almost as if he had taken off a mask; his expression became human. He waved to the GIs behind him and shouted to them, "Hold your fire, there's a white woman here."

I looked at him and the other soldiers who materialized from the brush to stand beside him. "Are you Americans?" I asked. He nodded. "Thank god," I said, "you finally got here."

卌 卌 卌

SIMON: At that moment I became delirious and passed out. When I regained consciousness, I found myself in an army hospital. By the magic of modern medicine, administered by the Amercian army doctors, I was brought back to life. When I started to recover, they gave me an army uniform in which I looked like a scarecrow, because I was so thin. They also gave me shoes, but I could not keep a pair of shoes on my feet, since I'd been walking barefoot for the past three years.

On June 30, organized resistance on Mindanao was supposedly over.

After I had recuperated somewhat, I got a job working for the U.S. Army's Department of Enemy Property Custodians, where my responsibilities included engineering related to the restoration of schools, bridges, powerhouses, and communications.

With my new job, Lydia and I moved to the outskirts of Davao, where we found another empty house, and we just moved in. We didn't know who it belonged to. While we were there we still heard shooting far away—they said it was Japanese guerrillas, stragglers who didn't know about the surrender or who refused to stop fighting. After we'd been in Davao for a while, we met an army doctor at a party. He told us to come in to the clinic so he could check us. I had so much bacteria from malaria they couldn't believe it. They gave us atabrine and other medicines. Our health improved rapidly with better food. The first time we ate a little bread and butter from the army, along with some other rations, we got sick because we weren't used to such food. Slowly we adjusted to new foods and then began to regain some of the weight we'd lost.

After the fighting stopped, everyone was so poor that there were lots of thieves. People did desperate things to survive. Our house was a two-story house, but the upstairs window was broken. One night a burglar climbed up and slipped in, but Lydia heard him and woke me up. I chased him out of the house and would have caught him, but he had oil all over his body and slipped from my grasp. What would I have done with him? Poor fellow—he had nothing, and neither did we.

I made many dear friends with army personnel. One day my army friends wanted me to locate some Japanese souvenirs for them, particularly samurai swords. Consequently I took a group to the jungle where I knew one of the last battles had been fought. On the trail we saw the glittering metal of a Japanese sword handle with a pearl-covered design and a long scabbard. I bent down to lift the sword, but noticed it was attached to a wide officer's belt. When I lifted it higher, I noticed that the belt was still attached to a khaki uniform. At this point I stood up and pulled it up out of the dense undergrowth—only to watch in shock as human bones fell out of the uniform. I stood in stunned silence as my friends grabbed the sword and cut off the belt, and then went on looking for other mementos.

After the war, I received a letter from Hugh Wills. He sent me a map and asked me to go to Malaybalay to see if the stuff he buried was still there. I took a plane from Davao because the road was bad. When I got there, I asked the local constabulary to provide a guard for me while I searched for my American friend's belongings. I knew that things were still rough there because of guerrilla activity. They kindly provided me with a driver, a guard, and a jeep to assist my search. Hugh had given me specific instructions for finding the spot. We had to travel on a certain road until we reached a numbered concrete milepost, where we would find another road that branched to the left.

I found the milepost, but everything was overgrown and I could not see any trace of another road. Finally, on my hands and knees along the shoulder of the road, I was able to locate some asphalt and find the road described in his directions. We then followed this track, seeking a clearing he'd described, where they'd camped when hiding from the Japanese, and where they'd buried their money, jewelry, and other personal belongings.

As we searched, I saw a strange glittering in the thick jungle a short distance away. I took a few minutes off from the search to see what this was. It turned out to be the sun reflecting off of the windshields of jeeps and trucks left by the Americans at the end of some terrible battle. In the ebb and flow of the fighting, the vehicles had been forgotten. Everything was undisturbed. Some of the trucks were still full of supplies, packages of medicine, everything new, unopened. But plants had already grown up around the trucks, branches reached inside the windows and back, and soon everything would disappear to the jungle. I left this strange sight and returned to the search.

Finally we found the clearing that Hugh described in his instructions. There I was supposed to look for a particular large tree. I think I found the right tree, but after digging all day around the base of it, I found no sign of the box buried there. It was starting to get dark, and the constables were getting nervous, looking anxiously off into the jungle. Finally they said, "You do not want to stay here after dark." So with reluctance, I abandoned the search and we drove back to Malaybalay, where I found a cheap hotel to spend the night.

As I lay in bed in the small room, listening to the mosquitoes buzz around my net, I thought about my friends, and all the hardships they'd suffered with their ten-month-old baby, the camps they'd been in, how they'd lost everything—I couldn't sleep. Finally I dozed off, remembering the days before the war, the little dinners we had at their house at the mine, how cute their daughter was.

The next morning I went back and persuaded the constabulary to help me make one more effort, so we returned to the site and I searched and searched, but with no luck. So I had to return and write a letter to my friends so far away, to tell them that I'd failed. I still wonder—Was this the right place? Perhaps some Japanese soldier found their precious cache? Or was it another clearing, now totally overgrown, all recognizable signs disappeared?

Back in Davao, I was still working for the army. One day I was approached by one of the lieutenants I knew. "Simon," he said, "we're going to auction off some jeeps. Why don't you come and buy one?" I told him I didn't have any money, but he said to come anyway.

According to the rules, the jeeps were supposed to be in running order. Most were not, however. Some didn't have any tires, some wouldn't start, and so on. Hundreds of people showed up for the auction. But when the colonel in charge saw the condition of the jeeps, he got mad, told everyone to go home, and postponed the auction. Then he set a new date to get everything ready. When the next date came around, a few hundred people showed up, but the jeeps still weren't fixed, so he postponed the auction again. There were several more postponements, and finally everyone stopped coming to the auctions. Then the army decided to sell the jeeps "as is."

I told the lieutenant that I wanted to buy one. By this time he'd been put in charge of the sale. "Oh hell, Simon," he said, "why don't you buy them all?"

I told him, I didn't have enough money.

"Give me a down payment, and you can write an IOU for the rest," was his reply.

The next thing I knew, I owned a fleet of jeeps. I drove the ones that would run to a friend's place, and borrowed some trucks to haul the rest of them there. Then we fixed them up and sold them. Some we kept and rented to people, and some we cannibalized for spare parts to fix the others. Before long I paid off my IOU and had saved some money.

Time passed, but conditions were still bad in Davao—no jobs, little money, and seemingly, no future. Lydia and I decided we would sell everything, go to Manila, and try to get a visa to go to the United States. We picked out the best jeep to keep and sold all the rest. It was the money we got by selling the jeeps that helped us start a new life in California.

We made arrangements to go by ship from Davao to Manila, with our jeep and our other few belongings on the boat with us. Unfortunately, we did not know that conditions in Manila were worse than in Davao. Manila had been horribly damaged by the fighting—more so than most cities in Europe.

Once there, we looked everywhere for a place to live and finally found a small junky house on stilts with a few pieces of furniture. We rented it from a Russian woman we met. The devastation of Manila was shocking, appalling. Thieves were everywhere and they would steal anything they could get their hands on. I immediately got a length of heavy chain—ship's anchor chain—so I could chain the jeep to the stilts holding up the house. Almost every night as we slept, we could hear the chain rattle as thieves came under the house to try to steal the jeep.

We applied for immigration visas to the United States. A doctor examined me, took X-rays, and unfortunately found spots on my lungs which he classified as scars from tuberculosis. I was refused an entry visa. Next I went to a lung specialist who decided that the spots were the result of an earlier case of pleurisy. The secretary at the consulate refused to accept the verdict of the specialist. We then applied for and were granted visas to emigrate to Australia.

A week before our departure, I ran into the mine superintendent, Mr. Sundeen. He told me that he'd heard we were in Manila, and he'd been looking for me so he could repay the $200 dollars we'd given him to distribute to the American prisoners in the Happy Life Blues Cabaret during that depressing Christmas of 1942.

I was moved by this gesture, but told him we would cherish the idea that we had done something to help them all during the war. I asked him not to take that feeling away from me by returning the money, and finally he agreed. He then asked what plans Lydia and I had, and I told him we were leaving for Australia in a few days. Next he asked, "Why not go to the United States?" So I told him of my experience with the lung X-rays and the result: refusal of a U.S. visa.

At this story, he got all excited. "Just wait a minute," he said. "You go down the street, sit down and have a beer, and I'll meet you there in an hour or so." An hour later he reappeared and told me that a U.S. visa would be waiting for us at the consulate the next morning.

Apparently, when Mr. Sundeen was in the Santo Tomas camp, he met a fellow prisoner who became the American consul in Manila after the war ended. The consul invited Mr. Sundeen to work in the consulate to restore the records of U.S. citizens. My visa was arranged through this friendship, which overcame the red tape. This incident was further proof of the proverbial wisdom that anytime we do something altruistically without expecting something in return, providence will see that it comes back tenfold.

Once we had our papers, we got on the first available ship to the United States. I sold our jeep to get money for our passage out of the Philippines. On our last night in Manila, a thief came into our house and tried to steal our money and papers, but fortunately we awoke in time and chased him away. This was December 1946, and the vessel was a refrigeration ship, sailing to San Francisco via Okinawa. It carried only a dozen passengers.

During the short stopover at Okinawa, Lydia and I went ashore and toured the island. We were shocked at the total devastation we saw, the remnants of the horrible fighting that took place there. Even then, a year and a half later, the island was completely bare—there was not a single tree standing anywhere. Once again we were reminded of the great tragedy of war, and of the marvelous good fortune that permitted us to survive when so many others did not.

CHAPTER 19

HHT HHT HHT

FREE AT LAST

GARTH: The war began to escalate in the summer of 1944, after the United States captured bases within bombing range of Japan. The bombings intensified during the coming year. On the Fourth of July 1944, our fliers blew up Himeji. Himeji was close to Hirohata, so we could hear the bombers come over, see bombs bursting over the city. We were looking out from underneath the eaves of the barracks, watching them bomb it, cheering the fireworks, shouting and hollering. For us, it was the greatest Fourth of July we ever had. The Japanese came rushing in and screamed at us to get back in bed. You could sense their ambivalent feelings—they would have loved to see a few bombs hit our barracks, except that they were there too.

The only way we got any news in Hirohata was when a Chinese ship would come in loaded with bauxite, iron ore, or some other cargo. There were always Chinese who spoke English on the ships, but they had to be careful speaking to us because they couldn't let the Japanese find out what was going on. They would slip somebody an American newspaper, or maybe talk with one or two people, who would in turn spread the word. We weren't absolutely sure, but we thought that they were telling us the truth, and we certainly wanted to believe what they were saying—that the Americans were getting close, especially a month or so before the war ended. Then one afternoon in 1945, Navy Hellcats came over and "scissored" right over the Japanese antiaircraft guns near the docks and blew the shit out of them. We watched even as the Japanese were trying to hustle us back to camp so they could continue the illusion that they were winning the war.

We assumed the bombers were B-29s, or *B-ninju-ku*, as the Japanese called them. When the planes came over, the sirens would go off, but by then the planes were already gone. You could see the white vapor trails they left in the air in the daytime, but that was all. If the bombers had chosen to come our way, we'd have been blown to bits by the time the air-raid sirens had come on. The Japanese came to fear the sound of the air-raid sirens that heralded the arrival of the dreaded B-29s, against which they were defenseless. Their only recourse was to try to find shelter against the horrible punishment they received from the air.

One Sunday morning, a month or so before the end of the war, we were mustered out of the barracks, lined up, and marched out through the prison gates. We had no warning or explanation; since the bombings had become routine, we thought perhaps an air raid was imminent. We were marched north of Hirohata, then up a hillside trail until we reached an enclosed bamboo stockade. The walls were made of thick bamboo poles, sharpened to a point on the top. All around the top there were machine-gun platforms. The lieutenant had us stand at attention while he made a short speech.

"American forces will never invade Japan," he announced. "To do so will mean certain death to the invaders. The entire population of Japan is prepared to die in defense of the empire." He paused at this point. Previously, he'd been walking back and forth, studying our reaction. "If Honshu is invaded," he screamed, "all prison camp forces will be mobilized and sent to fight the invaders. But first, we will bring you here and all prisoners will be shot!"[65]

With that, he turned on his heel and marched back down the hill. We were formed up and marched back to the barracks, wondering why our captors chose to alert us to their plans. Did they think we were able to communicate with the Allied Forces, and that concern for us might alter invasion plans?

The guards were stricter than usual, jabbing their rifle butts in the back of anyone seen talking or edging closer to another prisoner. Still, before we reached the camp, a whispered message had traversed the entire column. It was a solemn vow, and every man was committed to observe it at any cost: none of us would ever climb that trail again. When it came to that moment, we'd take our chances with the guards, and at least take them with us. We would not return passively to this Japanese Gethsemane to be gunned down like sheep in a pen!

Near the war's end, we were still working at the island steel mill. One day we went to work and we could tell something big had happened. We learned about Hiroshima there in the steel mill, on August 7, 1945, the day after the bomb had been dropped. The Japanese told us that the Americans had dropped a bomb that had killed 100,000 people. There was a big cloud over the Inland Sea, and they told us that if the cloud blew our way we were all going to die. Now, you know what we told them—we'd been out of touch for years—so we told them they were crazy, America didn't have a bomb like that. Well, that created bad feelings, since they thought we were mocking them. Many of them had relatives in Hiroshima. For the first time, they were feeling some of the agony we'd felt for four long years, when we wondered if we'd ever see an end to our imprisonment. Of course, as soon as the war ended, we found out America did have an atomic bomb. There is no doubt that the bomb saved our lives. They kept watching the cloud and marched us back a little early that day.

The way the war ended was strange, sort of anticlimactic. It was August 15, 1945, and we stopped for lunch while working at the steel mill. Usually they gave us a half an hour. An hour went by, and still the honcho didn't come back. An hour and a half went by and he still hadn't shown up, so we were joking with each other, saying, "Hell, the war must be over!"

Finally the honcho came back, after more than two hours. He didn't speak much English, but he told us that the soldiers were coming to get us right away. We said to ourselves, "In the middle of the day? The war's gotta be over," still just kidding around.

Pretty soon the guards came in and gathered everybody up. They took us to the rendezvous place in the plant, and from there got us out on the road. They did the usual thing—running us the mile or two back to the camp, beating the stragglers just like they always did. Once we reached the camp, we were forced to stand at attention in the road until the lieutenant appeared. When we saw him, we thought, "Uh-oh, big trouble, it's a shakedown." But instead he stood at attention, and said in a formal voice, in broken English: "The war is over. America has ordered us to paint PW on top of all barracks."

And that was it. It seemed like an eternity before anybody reacted. Then, when realization finally settled in, we went through the gate like a crazed mass of humanity, right to the galley, right to the storeroom. In a second we'd ripped the locks off of the storeroom door, taken sacks of rice into the galley, and said, "Cook it up." We started eating as much as we could eat: rice, rice, rice. Naturally everybody got the shits, but still, we ate, ate, ate. Afterward, once we quit celebrating and restored some order, a couple of guys painted PW on the roofs of the barracks using ground-up atabrine tablets for paint.

The funny part of it was, here we were in prison, but the tables had been reversed—we were in charge. Sergeant Ercanbrack decided we needed some guards—not Japanese now, but Americans—so he put the guys like me who had been on patrol on Guam back on patrol again. Then, for two weeks, we sat there. Nothing happened. They told us to sit tight and our officers would get in touch with us.

Some of the guys couldn't wait. I remember a guy from Pasadena—he commandeered a train engine, put the flag up, and went all the way to Tokyo—took a bunch of guys with him. Others took trucks and headed for Osaka. Most of us stayed to find out what was going to happen. For a while, it seemed like we were still forgotten. Finally, one day some navy planes came circling over. We were waving at them, trying to get their attention. They kept circling, so we put a fellow named Brown up on the roof. He was a navy signalman and knew semaphore. He stood on the roof and signaled them who we were and what we needed. Then they took off. We thought, that's the end of that. A couple of hours later they came back, dive-bombing the barracks, dropping seabags of clothes, sugar, and other stuff. They damn near hit some people, so we waved them off.

About two days later, B-29s came over and dropped platforms full of food and clothing, using parachutes. They landed all around the camp and out into the rice paddies. Then we went out of the camp, got some Japanese and Korean workers, and organized working parties. They spread out into the rice fields and collected all this stuff and brought it back to our warehouse. Anyone caught eating or stealing anything, guess what they got—the same thing they had given us! Only worse!

Once we'd gathered the supplies, we called the workers and formed two lines. We put the Japanese in one line and the Koreans in another. We were going to pay them off for helping. We sent the Korean line through the storeroom first and gave them blankets, cigarettes, and food because they'd helped us all through the war. The Japanese could see them exiting with our gifts. Then we called in the Japanese line. As the Japanese came through the door, we kicked the living shit out of every one of them and put them out the back door so the next guy couldn't see. These Japanese lived in the area and were the same ones who threw rocks at us and beat the shit out of us.

One morning in September 1945, the day of the surrender ceremony on the USS *Missouri*, we had a flag-raising ceremony in Hirohata. I've still got a photograph of that magnificent day—one of the proudest moments of my life. The prisoners made the flag. The white cloth came from the parachutes used to drop supplies. The blue came from a couple of old sport shirts. The red came from the lining of the blackout curtains in the Japanese officers' barracks. Once the flag was ready, Ercanbrack mustered everybody out in front of the barracks. The photo shows us lined up there wearing a mixture of military clothing that had been dropped by the aircraft. We had an honor guard holding Japanese weapons as Ercanbrack raised the flag.[66]

Watching Ercanbrack bring that flag up, I thought back to my first meeting with him, more than four years before, on Guam. I had just reported for duty at Sumay. Someone came into the barracks and told me to report to the sergeant. When I walked into his office, the screen door—which had spring-loaded hinges—

Raising the Flag at Hirohata

slammed noisily behind me. Ercanbrack looked up from his desk and told me to go back out and come in without slamming the door. Then he chewed me out for not writing home. He sat me down and made me write a letter to my parents, which he then personally mailed.

Anyone who has endured the deprivation of liberties such as we experienced can understand the sentiments that were in our minds when we raised our flag at Hirohata. In retrospect it was fitting that Ercanbrack was the man to preside over such a moment.

Then there was the matter of the brutal guards. They quickly went into hiding, but we got some of them later. We caught one of them—a buddy of Kaigun, and one of the worst. A group of us commandeered an old Japanese army truck and took him up in the mountains near the camp. There we tied him to a tree so his feet wouldn't touch the ground, and beat him with sticks and rifle butts until he was unconscious. Then we returned to the camp so another group could come up in the truck and beat him some more. This continued three or four times until he died, hanging on the tree.

In telling this story after the fact, it sounds heartless and wrong, as though we were lowering ourselves to the level of bestiality of the worst guards. We were. At the time, we didn't worry about it—no one was the least bit sorry about that bastard. He had been responsible for too many deaths, and no one knew what ultimate system of justice would evolve after the war.

There were other guards we wanted to find. Several of us volunteered to stay behind and help the army find them. They finally let one prisoner stay—he spoke fluent Japanese and knew all the bad guards. After the war we learned that Kaigun had been located and was brought to trial. I don't know if any of the others were ever brought to justice.

Finally, after another week, the Eighth Army arrived. They picked us up in trucks on September 9th and took us to the railroad station in Himeji, where we traveled directly to Tokyo via Osaka. From there we were transported out into the bay and placed on an American battleship, the USS *West Virginia*, where we remained until they flew us out of there—navy personnel to Guam, army personnel to Okinawa.

One distinct memory I have of that ship was leaning on the rail, watching an LST—a large amphibious vessel for ferrying troops and equipment—run back and forth in the harbor. Somebody had rigged a loudspeaker on it, and it was playing American music: Glen Miller, Tommy Dorsey, and so on. I stared at the bombed ruins of Tokyo in the distance, while the melodies of "Pennsylvania 65000" and "Chattanooga Choo-Choo" drifted across the still waters of the bay.

CHAPTER 20

卌 卌 卌

PRISONER OF WAR NUMBER 1

Ensign Kazuo Sakamaki had the dubious distinction of becoming the first Japanese prisoner of war after his midget submarine ran aground and he was captured in Hawaii the day after Pearl Harbor. This became his particular cross to bear for the rest of his life. Once in a POW camp on the U. S. mainland, he suffered yet another distinction—he was the *only* Japanese POW for the first seven months of the war. It was not until July 1942, when nine more Japanese POWs were brought to the United States and placed in a different camp, that his singular status changed. From 1942 to 1945, Sakamaki was held in four different camps. He credits life in Camp McCoy, Wisconsin, with causing him to question the stern military beliefs that had been ingrained by his training and gradually changing his outlook toward committing suicide.

The United States constructed hundreds of POW camps as the war progressed, primarily to house the tremendous influx of German and Italian POWs from the conflict in Europe. More than 400,000 POWs were eventually brought to the United States. One such camp was constructed at Fort McCoy, an army training base located near the town of Sparta, in central Wisconsin. Japanese POWs were a rarity: at the end of 1942, there were only 52 in the United States; at the end of 1943, the number doubled to 116, and the total did not exceed 1,000 until September 1944. By the end of the war, there was a total of 5,424 Japanese POWs in the United States—a tiny fraction of the total POW population. They were distributed among five camps in the United States, with the largest number—about half—held at Fort McCoy.[67] Approximately 30,000 additional Japanese POWs were held outside the United States.

The small number of Japanese prisoners—compared to hundreds of thousands of Europeans—was due to two reasons. The first was the Japanese policy of *senjinkun* (never surrender). As this policy became known to Allied soldiers and as evidence of Japanese atrocities to military and civilians circulated among the troops, they became more and more disinclined to take live captives. The second reason was that the United States arranged to keep the bulk of the Japanese prisoners in Australia and New Zealand, and later, in the Philippines and Okinawa, simply because of the logistics: prison camps there were closer to the fighting.

The behavior of the Japanese prisoners of war was dramatically different from that of the European captives. Many stated that they wanted to commit suicide and lamented the fact that they had no means by which to do so. Under the Geneva Convention, a normal step in the processing of prisoners of war was for them to fill out a postcard that the Red Cross would forward to their families, informing them of the prisoner's status. In the case of the Japanese prisoners who viewed capture as a state of dishonor, they requested that their families not be informed.

The question of suicide weighed heavily on Sakamaki. Although he resolved this issue in his own mind early in his imprisonment, he saw it as an ever-present problem for the new arrivals in each camp where he stayed. The prisoners he encountered told the horror stories of battle, how they had fought hard, but survived and were captured, while so many of their comrades died in battle. They were the fortunate ones, those who died!

Sakamaki characterized their situation as follows:

Our life was one of dilemma. We wanted to die and yet we could not die. We wanted to kill ourselves and we could not. The dilemma had a decidedly deteriorating influence on us . . . When we were stripped naked behind the barbed wire, we were compelled to look at ourselves as we truly were—a picture of failure. But it was not entirely our fault, we said. Fate had something to do with it.

We had no hope for the future. We were at the very bottom of life. We despised ourselves. We were in a perpetual state of spiritual shock as prisoners of war. Death demanded our allegiance and yet life claimed our bodies. Images of past combat experiences kept coming back. The future was utterly bleak.

Strong-bodied men went out of their minds.[68]

Later, when new groups of prisoners came to the camps, Sakamaki met with them and briefed them on life in the camps. He urged them to accept conditions in the camp and to recognize that now they were no longer bound by military laws but by international agreements that pertained to POWs. He told how the prisoners were not living in isolation, but the eyes of the world were on them and their conduct had far-reaching implications for Japan. He bluntly confronted the issue of suicide, stating that there was "no more honor or freedom for suicide," now that they were in the camp. He urged the new arrivals to not dwell on the past but to take advantage of this time in the camp to reflect and to learn new things. He said, "The way to advance our nation is to increase our knowledge of the world's civilizations and apply what is best in them to our lives. If Japan is to progress, she must adopt the strength of the West and make it vital."[69]

Army interrogators soon learned that there were three phases in the life of a newly arrived Japanese prisoner. The initial phase was one of fear and a desire for suicide during which the prisoner would not cooperate in any manner. The second phase occurred after the first few days in captivity, when the prisoners realized they were not going to be tortured or killed, and in fact were receiving food far superior to what they'd received in the army. At this point they became cooperative. In a sense, this reaction represented a deeply ingrained aspect of Japanese culture. Their good treatment, the food and new clothing they received, all were gifts that must be repaid in some manner. During this period the prisoners were anxious to repay their captors and talked freely providing any information requested. The third phase occurred after several weeks or months when the prisoners became accustomed to their life in the prison camp and then no longer wanted to be bothered with interrogation. At that point they became less cooperative.[70]

Japanese prisoners of war were treated in accordance with the standards of the Third Geneva Convention, which dealt with prisoners of war. In part this action was motivated by the War Department's hope that the Japanese would reciprocate by treating American prisoners of war similarly, even though they had not signed the Geneva agreement. To reinforce this idea, each Japanese POW received a translated copy of the provisions of the Geneva Convention stipulating his rights. In the camps the prisoners lived in barracks. They had access to facilities and could play sports, cards, or read. There was a canteen where prisoners could purchase cigarettes, candy, and other personal items. Prisoners were paid; enlisted men received 80 cents a day at the camp to spend at the canteen. All officers received a monthly salary ranging from $15 to $35 per month with an increase near the war's end. Religious and humanitarian organizations, especially the YMCA, provided many amenities for the prisoners.

The Japanese POWs exhibited some interesting and occasionally challenging cultural differences. There was little or no rapport between the Japanese and German or Italian prisoners. Within the Japanese prisoner ranks, there was a pecking order based on the date of capture. Prisoners captured later in the war looked down upon those already in the camp because they had surrendered early in the fighting. Of course, they in turn were looked down upon when the next group arrived. There was also tension between the prisoners from the Imperial Japanese Army and those from the Imperial Navy. In most cases the army men had experienced greater hardships than the navy personnel. Upon receiving good treatment and food, the army prisoners were more compliant. The navy men were well fed, in better health, and tended to be more arrogant to other prisoners and to their captors.[71]

Under the terms of the Geneva Convention, officers are not required to work but enlisted men may be assigned to nonmilitary tasks. Working was not a problem for the German and Italian prisoners, who found that work took their mind off their imprisonment and gave them something to do. The Japanese prisoners, however, objected to working, and in many instances refused to work, creating discipline problems for the camp commanders. The public dislike of the Japanese created another issue. German and Italian prisoners could be taken to work outside the camp in small groups, but the public reacted negatively to the presence of Japanese prisoners. Consequently, most of the work that they did was within the confines of the prison camp or nearby army bases.

At the onset of the war, there was great concern about prisoners escaping from the camps, roaming through the countryside, and sabotaging American war efforts. Although there were a number of escapes, all of the prisoners were eventually recaptured, and there is no record of significant sabotage. As one might expect, by far the largest number of escapees were Germans and Italians. Altogether only fourteen Japanese escaped in the United States; all were recaptured within a period of a few days to a few weeks. There were no riots or uprisings in the American camps.[72]

The first serious riot of Japanese prisoners of war occurred at a POW camp in Featherstone, New Zealand. In 1943, several hundred prisoners refused to work. In the ensuing confrontation, a Japanese officer was shot and wounded by a camp guard. Other prisoners rose in protest and charged the guards, who opened fire on the prisoners. All told, more than forty prisoners were killed and seventy-four wounded.[73]

The largest escape of prisoners occurred from a camp near the town of Cowra, New South Wales, Australia. In August 1944, the Australian authorities announced that they planned to move the Japanese POWs to another camp several hundred miles to the west. The next night hundreds of Japanese stormed the camp fences and began breaking through the wire. With improvised weapons—

largely knives and baseball bats—they stormed machine-gun posts and killed two guards. More than 300 POWs escaped. All of the escapees were rounded up within the next ten days. In the melee, four Australian soldiers and 231 Japanese died. Many of the Japanese died of self-inflicted wounds.

At the end of the war, when it became time to repatriate the Japanese prisoners, authorities worried that the prisoners might resort to mass suicides rather than return home. There was also concern about public reprisals against the prisoners because information about Japanese atrocities was widespread in the Allied nations. Fortunately, neither of these concerns was realized. The repatriation of Japanese prisoners was largely uneventful and took place as transportation became available. Upon returning to Japan, the prisoners experienced a mixed response. Their families were happy to see them among the living, but other members of the public openly criticized the POWs for not committing suicide. Within a short time, however, the stigma of surrendering gradually faded. The returning POWs realized that they were not alone—the entire country had surrendered.

CHAPTER 21

⊞⊞⊞

HOME FROM MANZANAR

MITZI: In the spring of 1945, I discovered I was pregnant. By then I was working in the camp administration and knew all the key people. One of my bosses was Joe Winchester, who was head of food administration. Mr. Ralph P. Merritt was the man who had overall responsibility for Manzanar; he was called the project director. He later headed the Rapid Transit Authority in Los Angeles. Also, there was Mr. Harbach, assistant chief steward.

Working in administration, you knew everything that was going on. Fumi Sakuma, one of my girlfriends, ran the switchboard. She usually knew all the major developments even before some of the big bosses found out about them. For example, I learned that the government was giving money to pregnant women. At first I didn't think I was eligible, but then one of my friends in administration helped me.

I also learned that my friend from the State Bank Examiner's office was visiting the camp. I remembered him from those frantic days right after Pearl Harbor, when he was the person assigned to oversee shutting down Yokohama Bank. He helped people collect money they had coming to them from the bank—either money in savings accounts or interest that was due. He helped me collect the small amount of money due me.

In administration, we were first to know the camp was going to be closed. I first learned of it in August 1945 via other people who worked in administration. As the word spread, it caused turmoil. For many people, leaving became the second greatest disturbance in their lives, second only to entering the camp. People suddenly were faced with deciding what to do with their lives. We were not like other prisoners, now free to return to our homes and families. We had no homes, and our families were interned with us. We had to start over. This disadvantage, along with a fear of the reception they would receive upon returning to the outside world, caused consternation for many families. The uncertainty was aggravated by the fact that the government offered to pay relocation expenses. Some people decided to move east, away from California, to start over again in a new place, perhaps to avoid some of the old prejudices that they feared might still be in place.

A few fortunate people had been able to arrange for someone to take care of their house or business. But for most of us, this wasn't the case. I suppose my family was among the lucky ones because they were able to go back to the ranch in Malibu and pick up the pieces there. But this didn't help Henry and me.

Henry left a few weeks before I did to try to find a job and a place for us to live. By then we'd heard about the end of the war. For most of us, it was a time of mixed feelings—looking forward to rebuilding shattered lives and dreading the uncertainty of what awaited outside Manzanar's barbed-wire fences.

Finally, in the middle of September 1945, I said good-bye to Manzanar. I was seven and a half months pregnant. My government, which had loaded me on a train with two suitcases and sent me to Manzanar at the start of the war, saw fit to send me home in a different fashion. I was taken to Los Angeles in a car. I was provided with a driver and a public health nurse, who saw to it that I was safely delivered to the hotel on Bunker Hill where Henry had found accommodations for us.

Manzanar closed for good on November 21, 1945. After leaving Manzanar our real struggle began. We had almost no money—just a few hundred dollars we'd scrimped together a penny and a nickel at a time. Besides that problem, we had Henry's parents living with us because they'd lost everything and had no place to go. In Japanese families, tradition has it that the care of the parents falls to the oldest son. It was our obligation to help them. Moreover, they knew that I would soon need help with the baby, and this was something they could provide.

My parents were fortunate. They were able to go back to the ranch, where they were welcomed back by the Rindge family. With some effort, they resumed their life much as it had been before the war. But I noticed a big change in my mother as a consequence of being in camp. Before, she was a traditional Japanese wife—demure, not one to push her ideas, yielding to her husband on most matters of importance to the family. The camp changed her; she became more assertive and outgoing.

When it came time for our daughter to be born, I went to the county hospital, where the health services were free, so we could use the $250 the government had given me for hospitalization costs as money to live on. Masaye ("Masa") was born on December 6, 1945, exactly four years after that pleasant Saturday so long ago, when I'd gone home to Malibu to laze around and prepare for the bank's Christmas party. The next day the war had broken out, shattering every aspect of my comfortable, small world. Now, just four years later, it seemed to me that a decade had passed, that my old self had disappeared and a new person occupied my body.

After the baby was born, I started looking for a job. In February 1946, when Masa was almost three months old, I obtained a position working for Coast Trading Company, a Japanese wholesale grocer. Mr. Sakamoto was the manager. In addition, I worked part-time at the Bunker Hill hotel. Meanwhile, Henry and his father started a gardening business and gradually built up a group of customers around the Los Angeles area. One of these was the Thomas I. Smith family in Glendale. The Smiths had a baby boy named Andrew who was Masa's age, and Nancy, a daughter seven years older. On several occasions Henry took Masa with him while he worked, and she played with Andrew. From this initial contact, a long friendship, now embracing the third generation, has grown up between the two families.

A few years later, Henry's father became ill, and was forced to stop working. Henry continued the business for a while, but after his father died, he decided that he would rather pursue a career as an automobile mechanic. Eventually, he opened his own garage. As for me, I stayed at Coast Trading for a number of years, until I was offered a position as a bookkeeper at the Paladin Seafood Company.

These were hard times for us. We traveled a difficult road for many years, as did most of our friends. We started from zero, with scant resources other than our own determination. We were now five mouths to feed and five bodies to clothe. I accepted the need to work without question. I'd worked ever since I was old enough to help on the farm, and even the ordeal of the prison camp did not change the need to work. I suppose I will always believe that I was born to be busy. Somehow, in spite of these difficulties, we managed to get our lives established once again, and built a new future for ourselves.

𝍷𝍷𝍷 𝍷𝍷𝍷 𝍷𝍷𝍷

After interviewing Mitzi, I wrote up my notes and sent them to her. When we next met to go over her comments, she told me that in the spring there was a pilgrimage to Manzanar. Former internees and their families would visit the site and reminisce, as well as clean up any weeds that had grown up in the cemetery. I'd stopped and looked around the Manzanar site previously, while on my way north to the Sierras for skiing or fishing trips, but decided it would be worthwhile to make my own pilgrimage there with Mitzi as a guide.

Mitzi Yoshinaga, Manzanar, 1986

Shortly before Christmas 1986, Mitzi, my wife, Nancy, and I traveled to Manzanar. It was a beautiful, sunny December day, not cold in the Owens Valley, but in the distance the Sierra Nevada mountains sparkled with a sprinkling of snow.

We paused at the entrance gate to take photographs of the stone guardhouse and the memorial plaque. When you drive in through the gate, the site appears to be a desert, with dead trees and tumbleweeds. If you take time to park your car, get out, stretch, gaze at the snowcapped mountains in the distance, and walk around, you will see other things—the detritus of a sprawling community of 10,000 souls.

Mitzi took us on a tour through the site. As we walked the grounds, hidden remnants of the camp came to light among the weeds and brush. Long-hidden roads appeared, foundations of old barracks, uprooted water lines. We saw the remains of a neatly sculptured rock garden that once graced Block 12. Elsewhere there was a stone-lined pond. Though overgrown with weeds and tangled dead trees, this was obviously once a spot for meditation. We went to the area where her family and Henry's family had lived. At the site of her former home, she took a large stick and whimsically wrote in the sandy soil, "We were here!"

I could almost see the memories flooding back as Mitzi pointed out areas where others had lived and described some of the incidents of their daily lives. We visited the graveyard, not far from the site of the hospital where she had once worked. After several hours we drove out the gate to return to Los Angeles, silent much of the way home, each of us thinking about the hopes, fears, and broken dreams enshrined at Manzanar.

In 1988 Mitzi sent me a note. She'd gone to the annual pilgrimage at Manzanar. The bus was late and she missed the first part of the ceremony. Then they left early, right after a service for those who had died at Manzanar, because the wind came up and started blowing sand and dust. She sent me this litany, which was part of the ceremonies:

ON THE SANDS OF MANZANAR

On the sands of Manzanar
  there we sat down and wept
when we remembered the homes we left.
  On the steps of our barracks
we looked longingly home.
  There our captors called to us:
Sing of loyalty to the land of the free.
  Sing to us a song of faith.
In silence, the clouds wafted overhead.
  In silence, machine guns and barbed wires watched.

How shall we sing of loyalty?
  How shall we sing of faith?
Our voices are filled with tears,
  our hearts are heavy and broken.
From deep within our soul,
  A voice said: "Remember, remember."
And we remembered.
  Our sunlit homes, the open farms, and laughing children.
We gathered our flutes cleared, cleared our throats.
  We sang our songs of loyalty and faith.
The silent mountain is our witness.
  The machine guns and barbed wires are no more.

O! Let not these hearts forget.
  O! Let not these voices be silent.
Let not these eyes look away!

With voices strong,

We sing of loyalty, faith, and unity.

With tears of joy we lift our hearts saying:

"Remember, remember, Manzanar, Manzanar!"

On the sands of Manzanar, our heritage.

We stand, proud, thankful and free. Amen. Amen.

—Rev. Paul T. Nakamura

CHAPTER 22

STRAGGLERS: PRISONERS OF CONSCIENCE

At the end of the war, thousands of Japanese military personnel were stranded in remote islands and jungles scattered throughout the Pacific. This situation occurred in part due to General MacArthur's island-hopping campaign whereby entire Japanese garrisons were bypassed and left to wither and eke out survival as best they could, and in part due to the rapid advance of the Americans, who overran the Japanese positions and caused thousands of defeated soldiers to flee into the jungles. Surrender was not an alternative, although a few did. Suicide was the honorable way out, which many chose; the remainder became stragglers, hiding in the jungles, living a twilight existence, in their minds dead to families and relatives in Japan and deprived of any future that they could imagine. Some persisted in this practice because they were ordered to go into the jungles and continue the fight after the American invasion, "until the Japanese army returned." As the years passed, those who remained came to the gradual realization that Japan must have lost the war, but by then they knew their families must have given them up for lost. They believed that if they surrendered they would be killed, and at any rate they could not face the dishonor of capture. Defiant to the last, they elected to take their chances with a third form of death: living on in the jungle. So, the remaining few continued their Never-Never Land existence, prisoners of their own consciences.

Following the end of hostilities, calm slowly settled over Guam. There was still a large military presence, and American warplanes still flew in exercises. Troops, supplemented by the Guam Police Combat Patrol, still patrolled the island. The diminishing numbers of Japanese stragglers hid in their caves and deep-jungle hideouts, wondering when the Japanese army would return.

U.S. military records, which combine actions of army, navy, and marine patrols along with those of the Guam Police Combat Patrol, illustrate the difficulties faced by the stragglers. The combat patrol was disbanded in 1948. By the early 1950s, sightings of stragglers were extremely rare, although a few more stragglers turned themselves in.[74] By 1959 the world had largely forgotten about the Japanese soldiers. Indeed, the governor of Guam, responding to an inquiry from the U.S. ambassador in Japan, was emphatic in stating that it was highly unlikely that additional stragglers remained on Guam.[75] History was to prove the governor wrong.

In 1986, six months after finding Itoh's diary in Washington, D.C., I was again in Guam to carry out more research on POWs. I had been contacting people to gather information on the invasion and occupation of the island. Then one day in a casual conversation with Richard R. Williams, chief of staff of the Guam Legislature, I happened to mention that I'd found the diary of a Japanese straggler. I did not mention Itoh's name. "Stragglers," Dick replied, "how interesting. I remember reports of them in 1952, and then in 1960 those two came out—Minagawa and Itoh."

"Itoh?" I thought to myself. I wondered if it could possibly be the same guy. But surely he was dead, or was he? "So what happened then?" I asked.

"Oh, it was big news," Dick replied. "They were cleaned up at the naval hospital; the press made a big deal about it—after all, they'd been in the jungle for sixteen years by then. We made phone calls to Tokyo, they spoke to relatives who had given them up for dead years ago, and finally we flew them back to a heroes' welcome in Tokyo. Up until the time they landed and spoke with their relatives, they still thought it was a ruse and that they were going to be dumped in the ocean, that America could not have defeated Japan. Later a movie was made about their adventures."

This was electrifying news—what if Itoh was still alive? First, I had to make certain it was the same person. At the time, I didn't say anything to Dick. Instead, I returned to my hotel and got my notes. I rushed to the library and pulled the file copies of the *Guam Daily News* for May 24, 1960. Reading the article I saw that Itoh had spoken with his sister Kimiko—the same name that appeared in the diary I'd found. This was positive confirmation that it was the same person, and I had a copy of his long-lost diary. At this time, the original was back in the National Archives.

So it was Miyazawa, not Itoh, who had been killed in 1946. Instead, Itoh had gone on to survive in the jungle for fourteen more years, eventually returning to civilization in 1960. Later, I learned the story of what happened that Christmas Day 1946.

Unno and Minagawa had departed for their own hideout, leaving Itoh and Miyazawa behind, cutting up and cooking the rest of the stolen beef. Itoh was

Sergeant Masashi Itoh, Guam, 1960

kneeling down, cutting the meat into smaller pieces, while Miyazawa was standing up cooking. Itoh recalled hearing some sound, perhaps a twig breaking, and then a shot and Miyazawa going down. Itoh flung himself sideways and scrambled desperately into the thick brush to escape.

While in Guam I interviewed a number of people who told me stories about the stragglers. They included Major John Aguon, whose father, Lieutenant Juan Aguon, was head of the Guam Police Combat Patrol; George G. Flores, formerly a sergeant and group leader of the combat patrol; and Jesus Uncangco, one of the combat patrolmen who went out that Christmas Day 1946. The police reports I'd read stated that somebody had reported a stolen cow the day before Christmas 1946. I asked Uncangco what he remembered about that incident, if he recalled how the combat patrol had tracked the stolen cow, and if, as they approached the hideout, they had smelled the fire and heard low voices speaking.

卌 卌 卌

UNCANGCO: The Guam Police Combat Patrol was divided into three groups: the red, white, and blue. Each group, consisting of about ten men, was assigned a different area of the island. We had an office in Agana to respond to calls from anywhere on the island. If there was a call, we would go out and look into the situation.

Typically, we would go on patrol and stay in the jungle for two to three weeks. We had M-1 carbines and hand grenades. We took rations with us and we had a support group we could call on if we needed more supplies or additional manpower. But we could survive in the jungle without rations because we could live on papaya, bananas, and coconuts. Also we could hunt wild pigs. But the less noise we made the better off we were.

I remember one night we set up an ambush. It was planned for early daybreak, when the Japanese would be moving about. We got there late at night to set the ambush; we knew there was a regular trail coming down from Lamlam Hill. But that night, and that morning, none of the Japanese came down the trail, which usually they did. I think they were wise to us. By scouting we knew it was a man-made trail, and there had to be a bunch of them up in the Lamlam area. So we then proceeded to the Lamlam area and found where they had camped, signs of eating, a warm fire. We had missed them because they had the advantage of being on the high ground and must have spotted us. Usually we could not surprise them in the daytime, so we planned night or early morning ambushes.

We would cover four, five, six, seven mountains until we came across tracks. We could easily tell if they were one or two days old, or fresh. If we came across fresh tracks, we were always so happy! Boy, we knew we were going to have some excitement! When we found a recent trail, we started pushing, going after them. Once near the end of 1946, we stayed after a big group, giving them no rest. After the fourth day, a bunch of them—seventy-six stragglers altogether—surrendered in the Umatac district.

Oh, those days were fun. We were young and we didn't know any better. I was only sixteen years old—I lied about my age to get into the patrol. I lied about my age because I wanted to get back at the Japanese. During the occupation my girlfriend was raped while I was with her. They tied me to a tree, and four of them raped her. I became a fugitive from the Japanese because I went after them later, and I cut one guy's head off. This all happened in 1943, before the American invasion. My family was put in the concentration camps along with everyone else, but not me. I was still a fugitive, hiding in the jungle. When the Americans landed, a lot of us helped them as scouts and guides.

I remember that Christmas morning. We went out early—we made it a point to go early in the morning so the wet grass would give the stragglers away. We could follow their trail more easily. We found their camp where they were cooking. There was a volley of fire, one guy went down; then we called cease-fire and went in to check the place. At that point I saw a slight movement—just a blurry figure, a guy moving really fast, running down the hill toward an old taro patch. I was one of the ones who went after him, but he got away. Only one guy had been killed. But we knew that more than one guy had been there. We could tell this from the clothing and things left behind. We thought that the other guy might have been wounded.

卌 卌 卌

From the captured diary, the patrol assumed that it was Itoh who had been killed, when in reality it was Miyazawa. After the 1946 attack, Itoh formed a loose association with Unno and Minagawa. Unno got sick and died in 1954 and was buried by Itoh and Minagawa. For the next six years, Itoh and Minagawa were alone, fugitives from an enemy who no longer existed.

Farmers who lived in the area where the stragglers had their hideout remembered missing chickens and pilfered gardens. Itoh mentioned the Shimizu farm frequently in his diary. I was fortunate to speak with Frank, Joe, and Paul Shimizu, who shared their family records and gave me a tour of their property near Togcha.

In 1960 Itoh and Minagawa were living at a camp only 200 yards south of the Cross Island Highway, about 100 yards from an abandoned marine barracks. One Saturday morning in May 1960, Minagawa was captured after a brief struggle with two Guamanians who surprised him as he climbed a breadfruit tree. When he did not return, Itoh surmised what had happened and decided it was

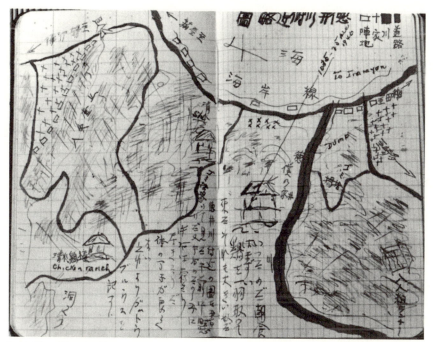

Itoh's Diary Showing Map

finally time to give himself up. The following Monday, Minagawa returned to their camp in a helicopter with naval and civil investigators and he called Itoh in. Although initially fearful and suspicious, the two stragglers finally began to believe that they would survive and the war was really over when they spoke by telephone to relatives in Japan. They received a series of medical tests in the naval hospital, were given haircuts, had their first warm bath in many years, and received a gift of new clothing. A week later the two returned to a heroes' welcome in Japan.

In April 1987, I returned to Guam—in part to conclude the arrangements for returning Itoh's diary, and in part to explore a number of caves in the jungle, in search of artifacts left behind by the stragglers. Using Sergeant Itoh's diary and maps as a guide, and using World War II target maps, combat patrol reports, and information I'd gleaned from interviews, I was able to locate a number of caves and hideouts used by the stragglers. I was assisted in this effort by my friend Don Farrell, and a contingent of U.S. Marines stationed on Guam who volunteered to help. My wife and I flew from California to Guam on a red-eye flight, met our group, and immediately went off into the jungle. We searched in vegetation so dense that you could literally not see a person four or five feet away.

In some of the caves we found live ammunition, Japanese army paraphernalia, and medical kit supplies. Some of the caves had apparently been used to treat the wounded. It was hot, sultry, and quiet.

The silence was broken by a marine shouting from a cave a dozen feet away from the one I had just entered. He emerged holding a crude rubber sandal, hacked from a truck tire by someone using a machete. My thoughts flashed back to the old navy photos I'd seen, and I knew we'd hit pay dirt. This was the last cave occupied by Itoh and Minagawa before they were discovered and returned to civilization in 1960. Remarkably, even though twenty-seven years had elapsed, we could readily identify the site on the basis of the old newspaper accounts. When we left the cave on that hot afternoon, we had recovered a knife, a rat trap, shoes, cooking utensils, animal snares, and a number of other artifacts left behind by Itoh and Minagawa. We found a unique system they had constructed to catch rainwater. It consisted of a bucket jammed in a crevice in the rock above their cave, with a hose leading down to a container inside the cave. As we trudged back through the dense green jungle, I tried to imagine what it must have been like to spend sixteen years living off the land under the noses of people perceived as hostile forces, while one by one comrades were either killed or grew sick and died. But *how*, I wondered, and *why* would a man choose to survive so long under these conditions?

With the assistance of the Guam legislature and the Japanese consulate on Guam, I learned that Sergeant Masashi Itoh was still alive and living on the outskirts of Tokyo. Then followed a lengthy series of long-distance phone calls, which established that Sergeant Itoh was willing to meet me and the Marine Museum was willing to let me return his diary to him.

A few months later, in June 1987, I met Masashi Itoh, and forty years after his diary had been captured by the combat patrol, a small ceremony was held on Guam to return the diary to him.[76] He was quite moved to get it back, and we became good friends.

I met Itoh and his wife at the airport as he arrived from Japan. The governor of Guam and other dignitaries also greeted him. Masashi Itoh was still tall and in excellent health despite his long ordeal in the jungle. With the aid of an interpreter, he patiently answered all our questions, described his jungle life in detail for all of us, and displayed the same sense of humor and positive outlook that had attracted me to the diary in the first place.

He was impressed when we showed him some of the artifacts we'd found and recognized them as things he'd made. He described the workings of a rat trap, how the door was closed by a rubber band made from inner tubes. Sections

Straggler's Tools, Clothing, and Weapons

of the same inner tubes were used as bladders to store rainwater for drinking purposes. Old tires were used to make Japanese-style sandals. These were carved from discarded truck or jeep tires and were given a unique shape. The bottoms were smoothed and rounded so as not to leave a distinctive footprint.

Itoh's description of his jungle life kept us on the edges of our chairs. He said the surviving Japanese soldiers became extremely wary. They stayed undercover in remote parts of the jungle during the day. Night or early morning hours were used for foraging for food and cooking supplies. They moved frequently, never staying in one spot for more than a month or so, and using caves only as hiding places for their belongings, not as hideouts. They had caches of food and utensils at remote locations, so if surprised in one spot, they could flee to another. They attempted to leave no visible trace of their existence—food scraps and human wastes were buried. Despite these precautions, Itoh had countless narrow escapes and was wounded once.

One of the highlights of meeting Sergeant Itoh was the opportunity to go back with him into the jungle to search for some other diaries and a pistol that he remembered hiding in a secret location. One morning a group of us followed him into the jungle—densely green, humid, silent. From one moment to the next, shadowed figures would disappear and reappear in the thick brush. Shrubs and trees filtered the sunlight overhead. In some places we walked in semidarkness. In others, bright shafts of light filtered through the dense foliage. We could imagine the tension that enemy soldiers must have felt as they probed for each other in hidden pockets of the jungle—just as they did during the Second World War.

Without map or compass, Itoh led us to a ridge honeycombed with caves, some of them large enough to conceal dozens of men. Our party included six young marines—all volunteers, under the command of Captain H. J. Schmidle— me, my wife, Nancy, John Lockwood, a photographer, and his wife Toshiko Lockwood, our translator. Here we were, following a sixty-six-year-old former Japanese soldier through tangles of thorny brush and head-high grass, beneath dark, shadowed glades, in search of a distant clump of breadfruit trees.

We looked in nooks and crevices scattered among the dozen or more caves, but failed to find the spot where he had hidden the pistol and the diaries. In retrospect, it didn't matter. What was fascinating was watching Sergeant Itoh move through the jungle, seeing him point out the edible plants, in one case pulling up one to show which part of the root could be eaten, or listening to him tell how the breadfruit ripened, first in one area, then in another. We listened silently as he described various places he'd roamed and showed us where he'd hidden and watched searching American patrols pass.

In no small way his survival was due to his adaptability and cleverness, but his mental strength also contributed significantly. He was a creative person, and his diary records inventions he devised to fight the boredom of solitary isolation in what he perceived to be an enemy-controlled jungle. He made pets of captured chickens, drew plans for a house he wanted to build, wrote poetry and songs, studied mathematics, kept several diaries, and carved objects from wood

Sergeant Itoh's Diary Is Returned

and deer horn. He maintained a remarkably accurate calendar by observing the moon and stars. Besides clothing and shoes, he made dozens of implements including needles, knives, scissors, tools, and cooking utensils.

I asked him how they been able to get enough food. Besides the fruits that grew wild, he and Minagawa gathered a type of wild potato and bamboo shoots. He told me about making snares for deer, about the foraging habits of wild pigs and how to hunt them, and catching freshwater shrimp in the rivers. When pressed as to how he obtained the things he needed, he replied, "Everything we required was readily available in the American army's trash dumps."

During our meeting in Guam, we also talked with Sergeant Itoh's wife. Just before his fortieth birthday, a friend introduced him to Miss Taeko Endo, and they were married on January 7, 1961. Taeko Itoh was a charming and good-humored woman who was strongly supportive of her husband. When asked about the early years of their marriage, she said that at first she worried about his health. It took a long time for certain habits to die out—for example, waking before dawn or being alert at the slightest sound or disturbance in the night or his sensitivity to various odors.

The survival of Itoh and Minagawa in a forbidding and hostile jungle environment for sixteen years after American forces recaptured Guam from the

Japanese is a remarkable accomplishment, viewed from any perspective. Like the other *horyo* in this book, they were survivors.

₩ ₩ ₩

Here is a sequel to this tale of stragglers. On the island of Saipan, Captain Sakae Oba finally, on December 1, 1945, surrendered with his fully armed group of forty-six soldiers. For a year and a half, he had successfully evaded capture by thousands of American troops searching for him.[77] The appearance of Itoh and Minagawa in 1960 was a surprise to all who thought that there could be no more stragglers hidden in an island the size of Guam. And yet, a dozen years later, in 1972, Sergeant Shoichi Yokoi was captured in Guam, presumably the last surviving member of his small group of comrades-in-arms who remained in the jungles of Guam.[78]

Next, there was Lieutenant Hiroo Onoda, who finally surrendered on the Philippine island of Lubang in 1974. He still possessed his Japanese army rifle and live ammunition. After he was located, he refused to surrender, but finally did when ordered to do so by his former commanding officer.[79] In 2005 there were reports of two more octogenarian Japanese soldiers coming forth on the island of Mindanao; this story was later determined to be a hoax. Then in 2006 a Japanese soldier named Ishinosuke Uwano, who had been stationed on Sakhalin Island, came forward in Ukraine and said that he wanted to visit his homeland.[80]

CHAPTER 23

卌 卌 卌

PICKING UP THE PIECES

SIMON: It was November when we arrived in San Francisco. We didn't really have any warm clothes. For the first week or two we stayed with a Russian friend whom we knew from the Philippines. My first requirement was to find a job. A friend working at Bechtel told me that jobs were scarce. He suggested that I take the streetcar downtown, get off at the ferry building, and start knocking on doors. I got off at the wrong spot, found myself at the Pacific Gas and Electric Company, and went in to see about employment. Amazingly—the first place I went, I had a job! I rushed home to tell Lydia the good news.

Now that our fortunes were improving, we found a small apartment that we could afford on my salary as a draftsman. This apartment, however, was a dark, dingy place—not pleasant. After a few weeks, we noticed that we both had continual headaches. Fortunately I discovered the problem: the gas heater was vented into an old fireplace, but the chimney had been sealed long before. We were fortunate we didn't die of carbon monoxide poisoning. Imagine—to survive all that we did, only to asphyxiate in a run-down apartment!

After a while I convinced my supervisor at PG&E that I was capable of doing engineering work, and I got moved from the drafting room to engineering, with much better pay. Meanwhile Lydia tried to find a job. One night, a friend suggested Spreckels Sugar Company, since Lydia had worked in a sugar factory in Latvia. A few days later I walked over to the Spreckels office from PG&E to see the general manager. He was gruff.

"What can I do for you?" he asked.

"I'm trying to help my wife find a job. I wondered if there were any openings in the sugar factory."

He looked me over and then said, "Tell me, what kind of an accent is that?"

"I was born in Russia," I replied.

"You goddam Russians. We help you in the war, and now look at all the trouble you're giving us."

He went on for some minutes. I listened for as long as I could stand it. Then I replied, "Look at Berlin. If the Americans hadn't been so dumb, the Russians wouldn't be where they are. You didn't have to hand it to them, no arguments."

He glared at me, speechless.

"Thank you for your time," I said, and I turned to go.

"No, stay," he said. "You made a good point. Nobody around here ever argues with me. I'm surrounded by 'yes' men. What can your wife do?"

Before I knew what was happening, we had an extensive political discussion about the war, the future of Europe, even the United Nations. Then he realized I was worried about being late getting back to work. To my amazement, he picked up the phone and called the factory and told them that Mrs. Solomaniuck would be reporting for work tomorrow, and to find a job for her!

We worked and saved our money, and before long we were able to buy a house in Redwood City. Lydia was happy to finally have a house that was really her own. A few days after we moved in, we stood outside as the moon rose and toasted each other with some prized Ararat (Armenian brandy) a friend had given me.

"Now we are really Americans, Simon. Only in America. Maybe it is a miracle," she said.

I had to think about it for a while. Then I had the answer. "America is full of miracles."

$$\text{JHt JHt JHt}$$

GARTH: On Guam, I went to field hospital 103, where they did some medical tests, mostly to see if I had any communicable diseases. We were supposed to get everything taken care of before they flew us back to the States. They gave me a clean bill of health; I could fly home. But some of us were late catching a flight, and the weather turned bad, so the latecomers had to go by sea on an army transport ship.

I was one of the late ones—and it was my own fault. I ran into a guy I used to play football with at Hoover High—Harry Chase—a chief pharmacist's mate. He came by in a jeep when I was supposed to be recuperating in the hospital. I started talking to him and found out that he was stationed out at the other end of the island. He had a great big squad tent where he held sick bay. He talked the navy nurse into letting me go with him, telling her, "Oh, it's okay, I'll look after him. I'll take care of him for a week or so, and then I'll bring him back."

I didn't know what he had in mind. He took me down to the squad tent where we hung out with the navy chiefs. He had some grain alcohol—190 proof or something like that—and a coke machine outside the tent. He'd cut the booze himself, then serve it to all of us. That was his idea of therapy. He used to ask me, "Garth, how many years has it been since you had a drink?" Before I could say anything, he'd pour me another, and then he'd launch into a new story about what had happened to the world while I was in prison camp.

I remember going in the navy mess several times and eating with the chiefs. God, it was heaven eating all you wanted. I put on the weight I'd lost in record time. Anyway, Harry kept me there for a week, drunker than hell half the time, and I never went back to the hospital. By the time I woke up from my stupor, the weather had turned bad, the last plane had left, and I had to go back on that goddam ship.

Since they wanted to get us all back as soon as possible, they really packed us on the ship. While we'd been on Guam we'd had plenty to eat but we were still hungry. The captain of the transport told us that since the ship was going non-stop from Guam to San Diego, they'd have to restrict rations to two meals a day. Naturally all the prisoners complained. So then the captain said, "Okay, we'll feed you three times a day, but you have to do the dishes," meaning the prisoners would have to do their own KP duty. We had those tin trays that they used in the navy ships—the ones with the little dividers that separated the vegetables from the meat and so forth. We'd get our food in those trays and take it up on the deck to eat. And then, when we'd finished eating, we'd throw those trays over the side of the ship as our way of cleaning up!

Pretty soon the captain made another announcement: "Hey fellows, please stop throwing the trays over the side, because we don't have enough left to feed you. We'll feed you and you don't have to do the dishes either."

It was a fifteen-day trip from Guam to San Diego. They also talked about us doing our laundry on the ship. Before we left, they issued us clothes on Guam, so we'd have enough to get to San Diego. Laundry? Shit. We didn't do any laundry. When something got dirty, we threw it over the side too. Hell, it had been nearly four years since we'd had a change of shirts!

Finally we arrived in San Diego, and we all got sizeable paychecks, since we had back pay coming. Then everybody went crazy.

When I arrived in the San Diego hospital for more examinations, I called home and spoke to my mom and dad. They were overjoyed to have me back from the war. My first request was for my mother to promise to go to church with me the first Sunday I was home. Then I asked my brother to come down to San

POW Garth Dunn, Home from the War

Diego to pick me up. James took me home, and we watched our brother Donovan play in a football game that evening. James was unable to play that night himself because of a shoulder separation. I had to return to San Diego for more tests, but managed to get transferred to Long Beach Naval Hospital for the rest of what I had to do, and I was discharged from the Marine Corps on March 19, 1946.

After my discharge from the service, I enrolled in a ten-week course at Glendale College to resume my education interrupted by the war. At Glendale I met and dated a former campus queen, a girl named Mildred Moore. She liked me (so she said) because I liked to dance.

When my brother James got married, Millie happened to be a bridesmaid, and I was the best man. I took Millie out a few more times, and we got engaged. I graduated from Glendale in June 1947; we were married on August 2, 1947. I entered the University of Southern California the following September, graduating with a bachelor's degree in business during the winter of 1950.

My first semester in college was pure hell. I had done no reading for four years and had to compete with kids fresh from high school. It took me awhile to get back in the groove of school, but I managed to graduate in the top 10 percent of my class.

It's fair to say I had some problems. I had not yet recovered my health, and sometimes had nightmares thinking back on what happened in the Japanese prison camps. There were times when I took it out on my family without meaning to do so. In that regard I don't think I was any different from other POWs. I just pushed all the memories into the back of my mind and tried to forget them.

After graduation I joined Brown Vintners and worked in sales in the Los Angeles area. In 1958, I went to work for the Stitzel-Weller Distillery and had responsibility for marketing operations in the five western states. At Stitzel-Weller I was fortunate to work for Julian P. Van Winkle Jr., who had been a captain in the Tank Corps during the war and was wounded in the Philippines. His friendship was important, because I found in Mr. Van Winkle a rare kind of support and tolerance that helped me reclaim my normal life. He understood the mental baggage that the returning veterans brought home with them. Today we have much more appreciation for the long-lasting effects of incarceration on an individual than we had following World War II—perhaps because of the Vietnam conflict.

I have to say I was treated fairly by the Marine Corps. I received $3,150 in back pay plus $1,500 for mustering out. At the time of my discharge, my salary was $69 per month. In 1950 I received $1,370 under Section 6(B) of the War

Claims Act of 1948 as compensation for inadequate rations, based on $1 per day of imprisonment. In 1953 I received $2,055 under Section 6(D) of the act as compensation for forced labor and inhumane treatment.

꜒꜒꜒ ꜒꜒꜒ ꜒꜒꜒

MITZI: Four or five years after we were released from the camp, the government offered compensation to those who were imprisoned. In most cases it amounted to $2,500 per family, although there were a few farmers and ranchers who'd lost large tracts of land and received more. My parents were eligible for compensation, and we helped Henry's parents apply. Henry and I were not eligible, because we were not a "family" prior to being sent to camp.

People often ask me what my feelings are about our treatment. Sometimes I feel as if I must remind my questioners that I'm an American citizen, and there was never any doubt in my mind where my loyalties belonged. For my generation, Japan was something our parents talked about, a curiosity perhaps, but not much in the thoughts of American kids growing up in Santa Monica.

What happened to us was not unique. Throughout the world today we hear of innocent people deprived of their liberties. It is too much to expect that this sort of injustice will end during our lifetime. My hope is that, by considering our experiences, others may better surmount their own difficulties and find reason for optimism in their situations—the inner strength to deal with adversity.

I'm expected to be bitter, but I'm not. We were luckier than most people. We were not beaten, not starved, generally not killed, although a few of us were. It was a terrible time—a time when all Americans suffered in one way or another. We were destined to do our suffering in the shadow of the Sierra Nevada mountains, in a setting where we sensed the presence of a higher power, and where the natural beauty gave us hope that a day would come when we would see both peace and justice.

꜒꜒꜒ ꜒꜒꜒ ꜒꜒꜒

Sergeant Itoh had a joyous homecoming with members of his family, although at first he was bothered by the constant attention of news media. Initially he had trouble sleeping at night—waking at the slightest noise, instantly alert, even though he knew there was nothing to fear anymore. One day, accompanied by his family, he visited the cemetery and read the inscription on the tombstone that his father had placed there. It said: "Killed in action on September 30, 1944."[81]

Upon mustering out of the army, Itoh received sixteen years of back pay, but due to inflation it was only slightly more than $100. Both he and Minagawa were given jobs by the movie studio that decided to make a film about their lives in the jungle. In June 1987, when I met Itoh and returned his diary to him, he was in good health and working as a security guard at a Tokyo bank. He and his wife, Taeko, had a daughter and a son. We corresponded for several years but I have lost contact with him.

JHt JHt JHt

Ensign Sakamaki returned home on January 4, 1946. In his book he noted: "As the repatriation ship approached the port of Uraga, I saw Mount Fuji, and I knew I was home."[82] The returning Japanese had varying reactions. Some were calm, some very emotional. The news media sought out Sakamaki as POW number 1 and asked him to describe his experiences in America. He tried to avoid the press, his father saying on his behalf that he wished to remain silent in humility to pay reverence to the victims of the war. But Sakamaki was too public a figure to entirely avoid the spotlight. He received hundreds of letters, some praising him, others condemning him for not committing suicide. One example came from a man who wrote several times:

> I cannot understand how you could return alive. The souls of the brave comrades who fought with you and died must be crying now over what you have done. If you are not ashamed of yourself, please explain how come. And if you are ashamed of yourself now, you should commit suicide at once and apologize to the spirits of the heroes who died honorably.[83]

Sakamaki accepted that, as POW number 1, public attention was inescapable. Regarding the letters, he wrote that most of the unfavorable ones came from men. He wryly noted that letters from women were more solicitous, possibly because he was a bachelor.

He was anxious to find a job but decided to not rush into a new career. Various opportunities were presented to him, but none felt quite right. Life was very difficult in postwar Japan, so initially he stayed and worked on the family farm. After a year of waiting, he received a job offer from Toyota, which became his future career path.

EPILOGUE: PRISONERS TODAY

𝍷𝍷 𝍷𝍷 𝍷𝍷

Simon and Lydia Peters (who changed their names after the war) are both deceased. They lived in their home in northern California after Simon retired from his position as a supervising civil engineer at Pacific Gas and Electric Company. Simon maintained an active interest in engineering until he passed away. Lydia eventually went to work at the Stanford Research Institute, and in later years took care of their home and Simon. Their home, which I visited many times, was surrounded by flowers and gardens designed by Lydia, which reflected artistic flair and beauty. No carabao roam the grounds, but there were fruit trees, vegetables, and spectacular flowers under immense, beautiful oak trees.

Davao is now a center for copra production and logging. The Central Elementary School on C. Bangoy Street, which was taken over to serve as the headquarters of the Imperial Japanese Army, was still there when I visited Davao in 1985, but the area has since grown, with new streets, more stores, and more people. Traveling southwest out of the city, one finds the Davao River and the rebuilt Generoso Bridge that Hugh Wills and others scuttled on December 20, 1941. A few miles past the bridge, on the MacArthur Highway, is the site of the Happy Life Blues Cabaret. The camp was razed after the war. Later the La Suerte cockpit was built on the site. On Sundays, Filipinos came from miles around to wager on the outcome of cockfights.

Several years after the war, the gold mine resumed operations under the name of Masara Mines. A road was constructed from Mawab south to the mine. The remains of the tram have long since disappeared to scavengers. Later an operating lease was given to APEX mines, and new gold finds in valleys below the mine led to a proliferation of small gold-panning claims.

The Santa Ana wharf still stands at the foot of Monteverde Street, and steamers and *bancas* tie up there to take on passengers to cross the gulf or to travel to other parts of the Philippines. Davao retains its reputation as a source of some of the best tropical fruits in the Philippines and is specially noted for its production of durian fruit.

After returning to the United States at the end of the war, Hugh and Jane Wills lived in Mexico and Central America, where Hugh had several other mining jobs. After they retired to San Diego, Hugh, in failing health, passed away. As Jane put it, "He never really recovered from that long trek to Malaybalay and his subsequent illnesses in Los Banos." On occasion, Jane and her daughter Trudy got together with the Peterses.

Warrant Officer Sadaaki Konishi, who was second in command at Los Banos, was executed in April 1949 for atrocities committed against the POWs and the Filipino villagers who lived near the camp.

Garth and Millie Dunn had a home in Southern California and raised two daughters, Lori and Nancy. Garth retired and was able to devote his full attention to trout fishing in the High Sierra and to improving his golf game. For years he maintained contact with some of his comrades from the camps. Garth passed away in 2006, and two years later, in 2008, his beloved Millie passed away as well. Garth's friend L. D. Orr died in an accident several years ago.

Major General Tomitara Hori, who landed troops on Guam and accepted Captain McMillin's surrender, went on to New Guinea with his army. There he and many others died in the first Japanese setback of the war.

Since the war, Guam has changed in some ways and remains unchanged in others. Today it is a popular spot for Japanese tourists and honeymooners. Nightclubs and hotels have emerged to meet the demand. The U.S. Navy and Air Force occupy huge tracts of land, consequently much of the island has been preserved with little change. Agana was destroyed prior to the landings on Guam and has been rebuilt. At the outstations—Inarajan, Merizo, Talofofo, and others—life goes on pretty much as before.

Postwar Japan has been extensively rebuilt and bears no resemblance to the desolate, shattered landscape of 1945. The Osaka camp burned down in the final days of the war. The camps at Zentsuji and Hirohata are gone, yielding to postwar economic development and the desire to remove all traces of the wartime militaristic regime. The island steel mill is still in operation at Hirohata. The town of Himeji has been rebuilt, and Himeji Castle is a popular tourist spot.

The Zentsuji camp commander, Lieutenant Yuhei Hosotani, was convicted of war crimes and sentenced to five years imprisonment. The camp doctor, Saito, was also convicted and hanged. Colonel Sotaro Murata of the Osaka camp was sentenced to life imprisonment for war crimes. From the Hirohata camp, Shinichi Motoyashiki ("Kaigun") was sentenced to twenty years for cruel and brutal atrocities. Akiyoshi Tsujino, medical orderly, was sentenced to thirty years at hard labor. Kitaro Ishida, quartermaster corporal at Hirohata, was sentenced to thirty years at hard labor for beatings and atrocities against prisoners.[84]

Following his return to Japan, Kazuo Sakamaki, POW number 1, received letters from women, many with marriage proposals, some including photographs and biographies. By springtime 1946, he felt that depression about the war had finally left him and he began to think more and more about some of the attractive females he'd met. Around that time, Sakamaki had observed a young woman named Sadako working in a neighboring field. Her family later approached his father with a marriage proposal. Sakamaki did not want to be rushed into something as important as marriage. Steeped in the formalities of navy tradition, he asked for her health certificate, academic records, a brief biography, her family history. After studying these documents, he decided to eliminate the go-between and wrote to her directly, asking for her friendship. They went to the city shopping, then to a picnic in the mountains. They found each other compatible and fell in love. A marriage contract followed and they were married on August 15, 1946. In September 1947, their first child, a daughter named Yoshiko, was born. Later they had a second child.

After starting in the personnel department of Toyota, Sakamaki rose in the company, and became president of the Brazilian subsidiary in 1969.[85] In 1983, he returned to Japan where he continued to work for Toyota until he retired in 1987. He passed away on November 29, 1999.[86]

In 1966, the town of Seto, Japan, erected a memorial in a park near Mitsukue Bay where the midget submarine crews trained. The front of the monument has this inscription: "Greater East Asia War Nine War Heroes Monument." The back of the monument lists the names of the nine midget submarine crewmen who lost their lives, but there is no mention of Kazuo Sakamaki, the sole survivor. The inscription on the rear of the monument pays this tribute to those who died:

> The nine war heroes, who loyally and bravely died for their country as a foundation for peace, attacked Pearl Harbor before dawn on December 8, 1941, as the vanguard of the Greater East Asia War. As characteristic of the first suicide squadron, they achieved brilliant military results.

The inscription goes on to describe their training and connection to the town and its people and states that Mitsukue Bay has now changed from a Pearl Harbor of war to a Pearl Harbor of peace, symbolizing peaceful relations between Japan and America.

Henry Yoshinaga passed away in 1982. Mitzi Yoshinaga, outlived her husband, helped support her daughter and then her granddaughter. Even as she approached seventy years of age, she worked sixty hours a week as a bookkeeper for a motel in Los Angeles. She continued to take Japanese lessons, to further improve her skills and remove any vestiges of her "farm-girl" Japanese. A woman full of the truest pioneering spirit, an archetype of the women who built countries like America, she was an inspiration to those who knew her. Sadly, she passed away at age 93 as this book was going to press.

Manzanar is gone. It was dismantled in 1946, and the property returned to its owner, the Los Angeles Department of Water and Power. The barracks were sold off to returning World War II veterans for $333 each, to be used as homes or shops. A number of these structures exist today, scattered throughout Lone Pine and Independence. Thousands of travelers pass Manzanar every winter or spring on their way north to the ski slopes at Mammoth or to the exquisite lakes and crystal-clear streams of the Sierra. The stone guardhouse at the main gate remains and can be seen from Highway 395. It bears the following inscription:

MANZANAR In the early part of World War II, 110,000 persons of Japanese ancestry were interned in relocation centers by Executive Order No. 9066, issued on February 19, 1942.

Manzanar, the first of ten such concentration camps, was bounded by barbed wire and guard towers, confining 10,000 persons, the majority being American citizens.

May the injustices and humiliation suffered here as a result of hysteria, racism, and economic exploitation never emerge again.
CALIFORNIA HISTORICAL LANDMARK NO. 850

The only complete structure still standing is the auditorium. Built in 1944, it was converted to an equipment storage facility for the Inyo County Highway Department when the camp closed. Today it houses an interpretive center constructed by the National Park Service. In the center, there is a scale model of Manzanar, 8,000 square feet of exhibits, and a theater where you can view a short film, "Remembering Manzanar." There is also a computer terminal where visitors can look up the names of internees and their barracks assignment in the camp.

On the far west side of the camp, and a little north of the rock garden, there is a distinctive white monolith—a marker honoring those buried at Manzanar.

Japanese characters on the monument translate as "Tower of Memory," or perhaps "Memorial Tower" is more appropriate. Fittingly, a barbed-wire fence surrounds the monument; within are the stone borders of a dozen or so graves. Other graves can be seen outside the fence.

When asked "How many people are buried in this cemetery?" Jim Matsuoka, another Manzanar internee who was there, replied, "A whole generation is buried here. The second-generation Nisei Americans lie buried in the sands of Manzanar." These things, and the memories, are all that remain of Manzanar.

Lieutenant Philip Nason Pierce survived the war. Lieutenant Pierce was another mystery associated with Sergeant Itoh's diary. After some research, I learned that Pierce, the original owner of the book that became Sergeant Itoh's diary, took part in the battles of Roi and Namur, Kwajalein Atoll, then participated in the battles of Saipan, Tinian, and finally was in the landings on Iwo Jima. Afterward he came to Guam from March to October 1945 and returned to San Diego in November 1945. Apparently he had discarded his small notebook, and Itoh found it in the trash. Pierce received the Bronze Star and several other awards for his military service. He went on to become a writer of distinction and international reputation, the author of three books. He is best known for his award-winning biography, *John Glenn: Astronaut*, a book club selection that was translated into seven languages. Pierce retired as a marine lieutenant colonel, having served in Korea after World War II. To my regret, he passed away in 1985, so I was unable to show him the notebook and to hear his story of what happened to it forty years before on Guam.

I finished the first complete draft of the book in 1986 to 1987, during a period when I took a three-month sabbatical from my company. Some parts were published—specifically, those related to the story of Sergeant Itoh and the return of his diary. At that time, the central characters were alive. In 1988, my life became more complicated when I became president of a Los Angeles–based architecture/engineering firm. I had very little free time for writing and research. This situation persisted through another major career change that took me to the presidency of DMJM, an even larger international architecture/engineering firm. As time passed, I never lost sight of the story and resolved to finish it at some point. I retired in 2003, did some more work on the topic of prisoners of war in 2004, and meanwhile published two books on other topics and wrote a third. Finally, near the end of 2008, I put other matters aside and began the final version of this book.

After I returned Sergeant Itoh's diary to him in Guam in 1987, he presented our party with three statues of Buddha, which he'd carved by hand from wood grown near his hometown. He stated that he was grateful to be welcomed back to Guam as a friend. "In a way," he said, "the island was my second home, and in spite of the hardships and suffering, I have many fond memories of my life in Guam." As we held the statuettes, the exchange of presents took on many shades of meaning. The gifts transcended differences in culture, religion, history, and age. Here, at the edge of the Togcha jungle, the ghosts of Christmas 1946 were silenced; former enemies met in friendship. To have been part of this healing was the finest gift one could receive.

Neither I nor the participants in this account have any intention to resurrect wartime hatred, racist feelings, ridicule of one race by another or of one nation by another. The bravery and dedication of the troops on both sides of the Pacific War is documented, as even the most biased soldier from either side could testify. Likewise, war engenders evil, evil men and women, and evil deeds. Again, no party to war is free of such people or such excesses, nor is any warring nation innocent of all wrongdoing. We do not choose to condemn any entire human society for the evil deeds of a few people, when there is ample evidence of goodwill and good deeds by others. Let us put all of that behind us.

In the perilous times of war, the unconquerable human spirit triumphs. This is the reason for retelling these stories—as a message to future generations, so they may know and emulate the courage and spirit of the prisoners, if ever they face a similar crisis in their own lives.

One final note–and the prisoners I've spoken to were unanimous and adamant on this point: they were strengthened by their wartime experiences. World War II was a unique time in their lives, and difficult as those years may have been, they feel that they benefited from their experiences. They seek no pity, and most defiantly, want no sympathy. They are the survivors.

END

MARINE CORPS MUSTER ROLL

卌 卌 卌

Guam, December 1941

NAME	RANK
McNulty, William K.	Lt. Col., Commanding Officer
Spicer, Donald	Major, Executive Officer
Starr, Marvin T.	Captain, USMC
Flournoy, Walter N.	1st Lt.
Todd, Charles S.	1st Lt., Chief, Insular Patrol
Dunsmoor, Earl W.	1st Lt.
*Ercanbrack, Earl B.	1st Sergeant
Knighten, Jese W.	Supply sergeant
Laser, Henry F.	Supply sergeant
O'Shea, John J.	Platoon sergeant
*Ford, Cecil C.	Staff sergeant
McMurry, Cloyd C.	Sergeant
Molloy, George D.	Sergeant
*Rossetto, Otto	Sergeant
Runck, John F.	Sergeant
***Shane, George J.**	Sergeant, Asst. Chief of Police
Sobey, William H.	Sergeant
Combs, Jay "B"	Mess Sergeant
Anderson, Harry E.	Corporal KIA
Copeland, Frank E.	Corporal

Notes:

Members of Insular Patrol shown in **bold**

*: Went to Hirohata

†: Died at Hirohata

KIA: Killed during Japanese invasion of Guam

NAME	RANK
Hagood, Fletcher M.	Corporal
Jaspits, John	Corporal
*Lee, Robert J.	Corporal
Legato, Albert	Corporal
Lufkin, Sewell R.	Corporal
Newton, Robert A.	Corporal
Nichols, Glenn E.	Corporal
Rybicki, Clarence J.	Corporal
*Shaul, Emmitt W.	Corporal
*Thiel, Robert A.	Corporal
*Thoren, Oscar L. R.	Corporal
*Wallace, Howard E.	Corporal
*Waller, Clyde R.	Corporal
*Ward, James S.	Corporal
Ritzhaler, Paul R.	Field cook
Andersen, Frank R.	Private 1st class
***Ankrom, Merlin W.**	Private 1st class
Babb, James W.	Private 1st class
Baggett, Ralph N.	Private 1st class
Bagwell, Woodrow L.	Private 1st class
Ballinger, Richard W.	Private 1st class
Barnett, Carroll D.	Private 1st class
***Bay, William R.**	Private 1st class
Bearden, Ivan C.	Private 1st class
Bender, Edward	Private 1st class
Bomar, William W. Jr.	Private 1st class KIA
*Bowman, Rupert O.	Private 1st class
Brown, Roy "T"	Private 1st class
***Budzynski, John J.**	Private 1st class
Buerger, Burdell O.	Private 1st class
Burt, William H.	Private 1st class KIA

Notes:

Members of Insular Patrol shown in **bold**

*: Went to Hirohata

†: Died at Hirohata

KIA: Killed during Japanese invasion of Guam

NAME	RANK
†Bustamente, Lawrence	Private 1st class
*Chuck, Harris	Private 1st class
Church, Ray H.	Private 1st class
Combs, Charlie A. Jr.	Private 1st class
*Crichton, Clint M.	Private 1st class
Desaulniers, Armand C.	Private 1st class
*Dunn, Garth G.	Private 1st class
French, Edward W.	Private 1st class
*Garrison, John B.	Private 1st class
Giles, Doyle B.	Private 1st class
Goebel, Daniel W.	Private 1st class
Golich, George "C"	Private 1st class
Hanson, Knute C.	Private 1st class
Humphrey, Herbert J.	Private 1st class
Huston, James L.	Private 1st class
Jones, Artie W.	Private 1st class
Jones, John H.	Private 1st class
Kauffman, John W. Jr.	Private 1st class KIA
King, Lloyd S.	Private 1st class
Kuonen, Charlie R.	Private 1st class
La Chappa, John E.	Private 1st class
*Maas, Edward	Private 1st class
*Meletis, Paul J.	Private 1st class
Mucciacciaro, John D.	Private 1st class
Nixon, Harbart "C"	Private 1st class
Ormseth, Russell B.	Private 1st class
Peak, Martin H.	Private 1st class
*Plummer, Nathan S.	Private 1st class
Redenbaugh, Carl E.	Private 1st class
Ross, Howard DeF.	Private 1st class
*Rucker, John D.	Private 1st class

Notes:

Members of Insular Patrol shown in **bold**

*: Went to Hirohata

†: Died at Hirohata

KIA: Killed during Japanese invasion of Guam

NAME	RANK
Schlegel, Alfred A.	Private 1st class
Schubert, Arthur G.	Private 1st class
Seymour, Charles R.	Private 1st class
Seeger, Harold A.	Private 1st class
Smalling, Hollis	Private 1st class
Taylor, Marion A.	Private 1st class
Turk, William H.	Private 1st class
Van Horn, Ray E.	Private 1st class
Watts, Willard W.	Private 1st class
Weaver, James W.	Private 1st class
Wickham, John E.	Private 1st class
Law, Phinas A.	Private 1st class
Manning, Don M.	Private 1st class
*Frederick, Ravich, N.	Private 1st class
*Moreno, Alfonso J.	Private 1st class
*Bryk, Chester J.	Private
Cutler, Jack M.	Private
*Dalrymple, Russell E.	Private
Darter, Harold L.	Private
Drolette, James A.	Private
Emch, Robert W.	Private
*Erdman, James	Private
*Hinkle, Robert M.	Private
La Grone, Harry J.	Private
Larsen, William K.	Private
Lewis, Cecil W.	Private
*Ligon, Lane E.	Private
Martin, Max H.	Private
Miller, Albert R.	Private
Moore, Richard K.	Private
Morrow, Clifford V.	Private

Notes:

Members of Insular Patrol shown in **bold**

*: Went to Hirohata

†: Died at Hirohata

KIA: Killed during Japanese invasion of Guam

NAME	RANK
Moss, Wynn T. Jr.	Private
Neal, Gayle	Private
Nettles, Howard	Private
Ordoyne, Eulice J.	Private
Perkins, Elbart S.	Private
Pogue, Bill B.	Private
Shively, David T.	Private
Smith, Elwood	Private
Smith, John M.	Private
Smith, Lee T.	Private
*Spellman, Edward J. Jr.	Private
Standlea, William D.	Private
Dupuis, Edward C.	Private

Marine Corps Reserve

Marks, Mortimer A.	1st Lt.
Morgan, Glenn D.	1st Lt.
Stone, Frank M.	Platoon Sgt.
Vonton, Sherwood R.	Sgt. Class I(e)
Honan, Thomas B.	Sgt. Class III(b)
Lyles, John H.	Sgt. Class III(b)
Damon, Walter LeR.	Mess Sgt
Boyle, Martin	Corp. Class I(e)
Podlesny, John R.	Corp. Class I(e)
*Moore, Howard C.	Corp. Class III(b)
Ramsey, Edgar A.	Corp. Class III(b)
*Cohen, Sam L. Jr.	Pfc. Class III(b)
*Higgin, William D.	Pfc. Class III(b)
Kozlowski, Leonard B.	Pfc. Class III(b)
Mueller, John A.	Pfc. Class III(b)
Summers, George R. Jr	Pfc. Class III(b)

Notes:

    Members of Insular Patrol shown in **bold**

    *: Went to Hirohata

    †: Died at Hirohata

    KIA: Killed during Japanese invasion of Guam

NAME	RANK
*Trascher, Floyd L.	Pfc. Class III(b)
Dixon, Vernon G.	Asst. Cook
*Herd, Leo	Asst. Cook
Danielson, Davey C.	Field music
*Hernandez, Pedro B.	Private
*Kallgren, Harry M.	Private
*Nichols, Frank Jr.	Private
*Orr, Luther D. Jr.	Private
Obborm, Max B.	Private
Roslansky, Marvin A.	Private
*Wood, Jeff C.	Private

Notes:

Members of Insular Patrol shown in **bold**

*: Went to Hirohata

†: Died at Hirohata

KIA: Killed during Japanese invasion of Guam

ANNOTATED BIBLIOGRAPHY

卌 卌 卌

Adams, Ansel. 1944. *Born Free and Equal.* New York: U.S. Camera.

Photos of internees at Manzanar internment camp.

Agawa, Hiroyuki.1979. *The Reluctant Admiral: Yamamoto and the Imperial Navy.* Tokyo: Kodansha International.

This book, written by an ex-Japanese navy officer, describes the complex life and death of Admiral Yamamoto, who planned and led the Pearl Harbor attack.

Bailey, Ronald H. 1981. *Prisoners of War.* Chicago: Time-Life Books.

Stories of POWs, mostly European. Describes some mass killings of American POWs by the Japanese after the Japanese surrender was announced.

Bosworth, Allan R. 1967. *America's Concentration Camps.* New York: W.W. Norton.

Boyle, Martin. 1963. *Yanks Don't Cry.* New York: Pocket Books.

Description of life in various POW camps by a marine ex-POW.

Brines, Russell. 1944. *Until They Eat Stones,* New York: J. B. Lippincott.

The author is an Associated Press correspondent who was imprisoned with his family by the Japanese, first in the Santo Tomas camp outside Manila and later in Shanghai. He documents the Japanese militaristic philosophy and how it affected the conduct of the war.

Brown, Joseph R. 1982. *We Stole to Live.* Cape Girardeau, MO: Missourian Litho and Printing.

Description of food and conditions in the Zentsuji POW camp. Includes photos of POWs and of the camp.

Chase, Gen. William C. 1975. *Front Line General—The Commands of William C. Chase.* Houston: Gulf Publishing.

General Chase tells what it was like to take part in the capture of the Philippines, including his successful rescue of the 3,700 civilian internees in the Santo Tomas camp.

Crowl, Philip A. 1960, 1978. "Campaign in the Marianas," in *United States Army in WWII, the War in the Pacific,* vol. 9. Washington, DC: U.S. Government Printing Office.

The official version of the recapture of Saipan, Tinian, and Guam by the United States.

Daws, Gavin. 1994. *Prisoners of the Japanese: POWs of World War II in the Pacific*. New York: Quill/William Morrow.

A detailed treatment of POWs captured by the Japanese in all theaters of the Pacific War including extensive interviews.

Dos Passos, John. 1946. *Tour of Duty*. Boston: Houghton Mifflin.

Describes visits to Philippines and Guam near end of war, including a trip to meet Philippine guerillas with Lee Telesco.

Dower, John W. 1986. *War without Mercy: Race and Power in the Pacific*. New York: Pantheon Books.

The Pacific War quickly became a violent struggle characterized by bitter fighting and a "take no prisoners" mentality by both sides. Yet, at war's end, Americans and Japanese worked together peacefully to rebuild Japan. Dower analyzes the racist views of both sides, how they affected the conduct of the war, and how they changed at war's end.

Drinnon, Richard. 1987. *Keeper of Concentration Camps: Dillon S. Myer and American Racism*. Berkeley: University of California Press.

An in-depth study of underlying racism behind the wartime internment of Japanese Americans. The War Relocation Authority (WRA) was first headed by Milton Eisenhower, who found that rounding up American citizens and putting them in concentration camps "made it hard for me to sleep at night." He turned the job over to Myer, a career bureaucrat from the Department of Agriculture. Myer instituted the policies of illegal imprisonment, forced labor, breaking up of families, and the other dark horrors of the relocation camp cynically rationalized on the basis "that we were protecting Japanese Americans from reprisals." When the camps were closed, Myer became commissioner of the Bureau of Indian Affairs and brought his racist policies onto the reservations.

Dull, Paul S. 1978. *A Battle History of the Imperial Japanese Navy (1941–1945)*. Annapolis: U.S. Naval Academy Press.

This unique book tells the story of Japanese naval operations from the viewpoint of the Japanese, using captured Japanese documents and records.

Eads, Lyle W. 1985. *Survival amidst the Ashes*. Winona, MN: Apollo Books.

A fictionalized account of the capture of Guam and subsequent treatment of POWs. Eads was a navy man stationed on Guam and was captured when the Japanese took the island.

Embrey, Sue Kunitomi. 1972. *The Lost Years, 1942–1946*. Los Angeles: Moonlight Publications: Gidra.

Description of life in the Manzanar internment camp, including a chronology of the evacuation and relocation.

Epperson, Robert B. 2004. *A Sailor's Story*. Privately published.

The author was stationed on the *Penguin* when the Japanese attacked Guam. He survived the sinking of the ship and describes the attack and subsequent life in Zentsuji, Osaka, and Hirohata POW camps.

Farrell, Don A.1984. *The Pictorial History of Guam: Liberation-1944*. Tamuning, Guam: Micronesian Productions.

The early history of Guam, including the Japanese occupation and liberation in 1944.

Flanagan, Edward M. 1999. *The Angels Came at Dawn*. Novato, CA: Presidio Press.

In a daring raid behind Japanese lines, paratroop infantry rescue Jane Wills and other prisoners in the Los Banos camp.

Frank, Benis M., and Henry I. Shaw. 1968. *Victory and Occupation: History of U.S. Marine Corps in World War II*. Washington, DC: U.S. Government Printing Office.

Appendix A has a detailed description of Marine POWs during World War II. A total of 2,274 marines were taken prisoner; all but 4 were captured by the Japanese.

Frankl, Viktor E. 1984. *Man's Search for Meaning*. New York: Simon & Schuster.

Originally titled *From Death-Camp to Existentialism*, this book describes the dehumanizing process experienced by POWs and explores how some survived. The author survived a German concentration camp.

Fukubayashi, Toru. (no date). *POW Camps in Japanese Proper*. Translated by Yuka Ibuki. Tokyo: Research Network Japan.

A compendium of POW camps in Japan, with descriptions of facilities, Japanese officers in charge, number of POWs, work done, number dying, etc. Research conducted by Japanese volunteers. Report can be accessed at http://Homepage3.nifty .com/pow-j/e/index.html.

Girdner, Audrie, and Anne Loftis. 1969. *The Great Betrayal: The Evacuation of Japanese Americans during World War II*. Toronto: Macmillan.

A history of Japanese Americans and the bigotry that led to their imprisonment, including conditions in the camps where they were held.

Greenfield, Kent R. ed. 1959. *Command Decisions—20 Crucial Command Decisions that Decided the Outcome of World War II*. New York: Harcourt, Brace.

This book describes the decision to invade the Philippines rather than Formosa.

Hane, Mikiso.1982. *Peasants, Rebels and Outcastes: The Underside of Modern Japan*. New York: Pantheon Books.

The Meiji restoration, which followed Commodore Mathew Perry's visit to Tokyo Bay in 1853, is credited with transforming Japan from a feudal agricultural country into an industrial power capable of waging war on an international scale. The radical changes included introducing compulsory military service for men. Hane reveals that this "progress" came at the expense of the vast majority of the Japanese people, who remained subservient to the ruling class and whose lives did not improve.

Hough, Lt. Col. Frank O. et al. 1958. *Pearl Harbor to Guadalcanal: History of U.S. M.C.* Washington, DC: U.S. Government Printing Office.

See section dealing with the Japanese capture of Guam.

Houston, Jeanne Wakatsuki, and James D. Houston. 1973. *Farewell to Manzanar.* Boston: Houghton Mifflin.

A poignant memoir of life at the Manzanar internment camp.

Itō, Masashi. 1967. *The Emperor's Last Soldiers.* New York: Coward McCann.

Itoh's story of how he and his comrades survived as stragglers in the jungles of Guam.

Jones, Don. 1986. *Oba, the Last Samurai—Saipan 1944–45.* Shrewsbury, England: Airlife.

Captain Sakae Oba was a Japanese soldier who refused to surrender after Saipan was captured by the Americans in July 1944. He continued fighting for eighteen months, evading the efforts of 5,000 American troops to capture him, and only surrendered with his forty-six men when he received orders from his former commanding officer.

Josephy, Alvin M. Jr. 1946. *The Long and the Short and the Tall.* New York: Alfred A. Knopf.

The author was a marine war correspondent who took part in the invasion of Guam and the subsequent search for Japanese stragglers.

Kahn, E. J. Jr. 1962. *The Stragglers.* New York: Random House.

This book describes the stories of a number of Japanese stragglers on Guam, the Philippines, and other Pacific Islands, including a short history of Masashi Itoh and Bunzo Minagawa.

Keats, John. 1963. *They Fought Alone.* New York: J. B. Lippincott.

Story of Wendell Fertig and other American soldiers who refused to surrender to the Japanese and organized Philippine guerillas.

Keith, Agnes Newton. 1947. *Three Came Home.* Boston: Little, Brown.

This book tells the story of a family imprisoned in Borneo, mother and son in one camp, husband and father in another. The camp commandant orders Ms. Keith, a writer, to write the story of life in the camp. She writes one story, called "Captivity," for the commandant but secretly keeps hidden notes that become the true account of her captivity and survival.

Knox, Donald, 1981. *Death March—The Survivors of Bataan.* New York: Harcourt Brace Jovanovich.

This is the story of nearly 10,000 American troops who were captured and imprisoned by the Japanese in the Philippines, then transported to camps in Japan on rust bucket transport ships.

Krammer, Arnold. 1983. "Japanese Prisoners of War in America." *Pacific Historical Review*, vol. 52, no. 1, Feb. 1983.

A history of Japanese POWs held in the United States. Describes their psychological adjustment to captivity, use as workers, and escape attempts (none succeeded).

Lawson, Ted W. 1943. *Thirty Seconds over Tokyo*. New York: Random House.

The story of the Doolittle raid on Japan early in the war, by one of the pilots who flew the bombers.

Lewis, Lt. Col. George G., and Capt. John Mewha. 1955. *History of Prisoner of War Utilization by the United States Army, 1776–1945, DA 20-213*. Washington, DC: U.S. Government Printing Office.

Data and statistics on POW camps operated by the U.S. Army.

Lindholm, Paul R. 1978. *Shadows from the Rising Sun*. Quezon City, Philippines: New Day.

Story of a missionary who escaped the Japanese while hiding out in Negros Island, Philippines.

Lowe, Richard Barrett, Governor of Guam. 1959. Letter to Minister William Leonhart, U.S. Embassy, Japan, April 8, 1959.

This letter stated that it was unlikely that there were more stragglers on Guam.

Manchester, William. 1978. *American Caesar: Douglas MacArthur 1880–1964*. Boston: Little, Brown.

Biography of General Douglas MacArthur.

Manchester, William. 1980. *Goodbye Darkness: A Memoir of the Pacific War*. Boston: Little, Brown.

Describes wartime experiences in Okinawa and on Saipan Island and a postwar visit to the Philippines and Guam with a discussion of stragglers.

Maynard, Mary McKay. 2001. *My Faraway Home*. Guilford, CT: Globe Pequot Press.

The story of a young girl and her parents who fled when the Japanese invaded Mindanao. They survived in the jungle for two years and eventually were evacuated by submarine to freedom.

Morison, Samuel E. 1960. *History of U.S. Naval Operations in World War II*, vol. 14, *Victory in Pacific—1945*. Boston: Little, Brown.

Describes the victories leading up to the surrender of Japan.

Morison, Samuel E. 1963-1. *The Two Ocean War—A Short History of the United States Navy in the Second World War*. Boston: Little, Brown.

Describes the liberation of the Philippines and Guam.

Morison, Samuel E. 1963-2. *History of U.S. Naval Operations in World War II*, vol. 3, *The Rising Sun in the Pacific—1932–April 1942*. Boston: Little, Brown.

Details of the Japanese invasion of the Philippines and Guam.

Odo, Franklin. 2004. *No Sword to Bury: Japanese Americans in Hawai'i during World War II*. Philadelphia: Temple University Press.

There were more Japanese Americans (160,000) in Hawaii, home of the Pacific fleet, when Pearl Harbor was bombed than on the West Coast of the United States. Yet, they were not placed in internment camps. How does one explain this seeming inconsistency in U.S. policy? Odo relates the untold story of the government debate concerning their fate and how first-generation Americans of Japanese descent reacted to the crisis with public works and military service.

Onoda, Hiroo.1974. *No Surrender — My Thirty Year War.* Tokyo: Kodansha International.
Second Lieutenant Hiroo Onoda was trained as an intelligence officer in the Japanese army. At the war's end he refused to surrender and eluded capture for thirty years on the Philippine island of Lubang. He finally surrendered in 1974.

Palomo, Tony. 1984. *An Island in Agony.* Agana, Guam: privately published.
Tony Palomo, a journalist, was a ten-year boy when the Japanese invaded Guam. He provides a gripping firsthand account of life during the occupation and subsequent liberation of Guam.

Potter, E. B., ed., and Chester W. Nimitz. 1960. *The Great Sea War — The Story of Naval Action in World War II.* New York: Bramhall House.
This is a condensed version of naval actions during the Second World War that focuses on the most important engagements.

Prange, Gordon. 1982. *At Dawn We Slept.* New York: Penguin Books.
Chronology of events leading up to and during the Japanese surprise attack on Pearl Harbor.

Priestwood, Gwen. 1943. *Through Japanese Barbed Wire.* New York: D. Appleton-Century.
The story of this woman's escape from a Hong Kong prison camp to Chungking, China, a thousand miles away.

Sakamaki, Kazuo.1949. *I Attacked Pearl Harbor.* Translated by Toru Matsumoto. New York: Association Press.
The memoirs of the sole survivor of the five midget submarines that attempted to attack Pearl Harbor on December 7, 1941.

Sanchez, Pedro C. (ca. 1984). *Guam 1941–1945 — Wartime Occupation and Liberation.* Tamuning, Guam: PC Sanchez.
A short history of life on Guam during the Japanese occupation.

Savary, Gladys. 1954. *Outside the Walls.* New York: Vantage Press.
An American woman married to a French man manages to stay out of the Manila prison camps so she can aid the prisoners. Description of life in Manila under the Japanese occupation and during its recapture by American forces.

Sides, Hampton. 2001. *Ghost Soldiers.* New York: Doubleday.
This is the story of a daring raid behind enemy lines on January 30, 1944 by General Walter Kreuger's Alamo Scouts and the Sixth Ranger Battalion to liberate 512 POWs in the Cabanatuan POW camp near Manila.

Smith, Craig B. 1986. *The Diary of Sergeant Itoh*. Translated by Toshiko Lockwood. Los Angeles: Whirlwind Press.

The complete English translation of Masashi Itoh's wartime diary including his maps and drawings.

Smith, Craig B. 1987a. "A Guam Diary, part I," *Fortitudine—Bulletin of the Marine Corps Historical Program* 17, no. 2 (Fall 1987): 12–14.

The story of finding Sergeant Itoh's diary and its significance, part I.

Smith, Craig B. 1987b. "A Guam Diary, part II," *Fortitudine—Bulletin of the Marine Corps Historical Program* 17, no. 3 (Winter 1987–88):13–14.

The story of finding Sergeant Itoh's diary and its significance, part II.

Smith, Craig B. 1987c. "History," (in Japanese) *Focus Weekly Magazine*, no. 1 (Jan. 2): 24.

This article describes how his forty-year-old diary will be returned to ex-Japanese soldier Masashi Itoh who served on Guam.

Smith, Craig B. 1987d. "History," (in Japanese) *Focus Weekly Magazine*, no. 24 (June 19): 38.

This article describes the encounter between Craig B. Smith and Sergeant Masashi Itoh when they met in Guam for the return of Itoh's wartime diary.

Smith, Craig B. 1988a. "The Diary of a Lone Soldier," *Continental Islands* 7, no. 3 (1988): 47–50.

A short version of the story of straggler Masashi Itoh on Guam.

Smith, Craig B. 1988b. "Soldiers Time Forgot," *Soldier of Fortune Magazine* 13, no. 9 (Sept.): 50–83.

This article describes the American invasion of Guam, how Japanese stragglers avoided capture, why they refused to surrender, and the formation of the Guam Police Combat Patrol.

Smith, Robert R. 1961. *The United States Army in World War II—The War in the Pacific: Triumph in the Philippines*. Washington, DC: U.S. Government Printing Office.

This book documents Japanese army battle plans and American offensives leading to recapturing the Philippines.

Straus, Ulrich. 2003. *The Anguish of Surrender: Japanese POWs in World War II*. Seattle: University of Washington Press.

Describes the behavior of the 35,000 Japanese POWs taken by the Allies. Discusses uprising and escape attempts in Australia and New Zealand.

Tasaki, Hanama. 1950. *Long the Imperial Way*. Cambridge, MA: Houghton Mifflin.

This book details the life of an enlisted man serving in the Japanese army in China prior to Pearl Harbor.

Toland, John. 1970. *The Rising Sun*. New York: Random House. In two volumes.

This is a fascinating history, from the Japanese perspective, of the rise and fall of the Japanese Empire. Chapter 30 tells of the Japanese stragglers.

Tweed, George R. (as told to Blake Clark). 1945. *Robinson Crusoe, USN — The Adventures of George R. Tweed, RM1C, on Jap-Held Guam.* New York: Whittlesey House/ McGraw Hill.

Tweed was the only American military man to avoid capture when the Japanese invaded Guam.

War Relocation Authority. 1987. *Manzanar Relocation Center, Manzanar, California, 1942–1945.* Los Angeles: TecCom Productions.

A pictorial history of Manzanar. Includes copies of the original proclamation creating the War Relocation Authority.

White, W. L. 1942. *They Were Expendable.* New York: Harcourt, Brace.

This is the story of Motor Torpedo Boat Squadron 3, the group that enabled General Douglas MacArthur to escape from Bataan.

Declassified government documents. Unless noted otherwise, found in Box 19, accession no. 62A-2086. "Marine POWs," Federal Records Center, Suitland, MD. I accessed them courtesy of the Marine Museum, Washington Naval Yard, Washington, D.C.

- Muster Roll of Officers and Enlisted Men of the U.S. Marine Corps, Marine Barracks, Naval Station, Guam, from December 1 to December 31, 1941. This muster was prepared in Washington by Captain E. E. Barde after the fall of Guam and lists casualties known at that time.
- Ercanbrack, First Sgt. Earl B. 1945. "General Report of Commanding Officer, Independent Detachment of American Forces Held as Prisoners of War, Osaka Prisoner of War camp, Hirohata Sub-Camp, Hirohata, Japan, for the period October 6, 1943 to September 2, 1945." Describes general conditions in the camp, mistreatment of POWs, liberation of the camp, list of dead men and disposition of remains, and Muster Roll of Marines held at Hirohata. Memorandum dated November 12, 1945.
- Flournoy, Maj. Walter. 1945. "Prisoner of War Report." Memorandum dated November 5, 1945. Statement regarding his experiences in the Zentsuji POW camp. Highlights the difference in treatment received by the officers (who were not forced to work) compared to enlisted men.
- McMillin, Capt. George J. 1945. "Surrender of Guam to the Japanese." Memorandum dated September 11, 1945. McMillin was serving as governor of Guam and commandant of the Naval Station, Guam, on December 8, 1941. He describes the Japanese invasion, the surrender, his subsequent status as a POW, and includes a list of killed and wounded.
- McNeely, M. B. 1946. "Case of one (1) Japanese Straggler Killed in Target Area 342 Easy, by Guam Police Combat Patrol on December 25, 1946." Memorandum dated December 28, 1946, from the chief of police to the commanding officer,

Marine Barracks, Guam. This report describes the tracking down of one or more stragglers who had stolen a cow, the shooting of one straggler, and the recovery of a diary belonging to Sergeant Masashi Itoh. The file has photographs of the dead straggler and the straggler's hideouts. It also had Sergeant Itoh's leather-bound diary.

- Putnam, Lt. Col. Paul. 1945. "Prisoner of War Report." Statement regarding his experiences in the Zentsuji POW camp. Memorandum dated October 17, 1945. Putnam was captured on Wake Island and brought to Zentsuji on January 18, 1942. Detailed description of Zentsuji as it was transformed into an "officer's camp." Near the end of the war he was transferred to another camp at Rokuroshi in western Honshu.

- Spicer, Col. Donald. 1946. "Recognition of the Action at Guam, December 8–10, 1941." Memorandum dated July 11, 1946. Spicer describes the Japanese attack on Guam and the marines' response. (Also has a copy of Captain George J. McMillin's report dated September 11, 1945)

- War Department General Staff. 1944-1. "Prisoner of War Camp Conditions in Japan." Memorandum dated May 15, 1944. Originally classified "Secret." Washington, DC: Military Intelligence Division G-2. This document has sketches and descriptions of a number of POW camps. Some of the information appears to have been collected by debriefing Red Cross officials who visited the camps. The assessment has surprising details considering the date, but also contains propaganda errors, such as these statements regarding the Hirohata camp: "A surgeon visits once a week; a factory doctor calls daily. POWs are permitted to go for hikes in the country on Sundays."

- War Department General Staff. 1944-2. "Prisoners of War in the Philippine Islands." Memorandum dated September 20, 1944. Originally classified "Secret." Washington, DC: Military Intelligence Division G-2. This document has sketches and descriptions of POW camps. It also included a statement by First Lieutenant Michael Dobervich, U.S. Marine Corps, about his experience in Philippine POW camps and his successful escape from the Davao Penal Colony.

The following documents were personal communication from Garth G. Dunn to Craig B. Smith.

- Gibbs, John M. 1946a. "Prisoner of War Camps in Japan and Japanese Controlled Areas as Taken from Reports of Interned American Prisoners: Hirohata Camp-Divisional Camp of Osaka No. 12-B Japan." *Liaison & Research Branch American Prisoner of War Information Bureau July 31, 1946.* This report describes camp conditions, Japanese officers, food, mistreatment of prisoners, etc., in Hirohata.

- Gibbs, John M. 1946b. "Prisoner of War Camps in Japan and Japanese Controlled Areas as Taken from Reports of Interned American Prisoners: Zentsuji Headquarters Camp on the Island of Shikoku, Japan." *Liaison & Research Branch American Prisoner of War Information Bureau July 31, 1946*. This report describes camp conditions, Japanese officers, food, mistreatment of prisoners, etc., in Zentsuji.
- Sommers, Stan, ed. 1980. *The Japanese Story*. Marshfield, WI: American Ex-Prisoners of War. This document focuses on the maltreatment and medical condition and health issues of POWs, with emphasis on the Philippine camps and "hell ships."
- Young, J. R. 1942. *Diary-Book I, Dec. 8 1941 to May 9, 1942*. (unpublished). This document may be accessed in the Library Special Collections Division, University of Oregon. Young describes his capture on Guam and the first year at the Zentsuji POW camp.

Another source of information about Guam is the Micronesian Area Research Center (MARC), operated by the University of Guam.

- Satoh, Kazumasa. (no date). *Blood and Sands of Guam*. Translated by Iris K. Tanimoto-Spade. Agana, Guam: Micronesian Area Research Center. A series of letters (some death notes) and memoirs of Japanese soldiers stationed on Guam.
- Various maps of Guam including the World War II "Special Air and Gunnery Target" map used to track straggler locations.
- A-2 and G-2 "Periodic Reports" for the period December 7, 1944 to March 1947. These reports list the number of Japanese killed or captured. By August 1945, one year after the island had been declared secured, more than 7,000 additional Japanese soldiers had been killed.
- "The Guam Police Combat Patrol." (no author, no date). A document summarizing the operations of the Guam Police Combat Patrol from its inception until it was disbanded.

END NOTES

IHT IHT IHT

1. Brines (1944), 9–11, 275–291.

2. Straus (2003). See Chapter 3.

3. Tasaki (1950). This story of the life of an enlisted man in the Japanese army shows how the training and discipline of the ordinary soldier gave rise to brutality.

4. Daws (1994), 360; Fukubayashi (no date), 1–2; Knox (1981), xi.

5. See also www.mansell.com (accessed July 2011). This website is for the Center for Research for Allied POWs under the Japanese. It has a wealth of information about individual camps and the POWs held in each camp.

6. Toland (1970), 53–58.

7. Manchester (1978), 189.

8. Prange (1982), 371.

9. Manchester (1978), 201.

10. For the reader interested in more details concerning the Japanese attacks on Hawaii, Guam, and the Philippines, Agawa (1979), Dull (1978), and Morison (1963–2) present the Japanese view; Hough (1958), Morison (1963–2), and Morison (1960) provide an American perspective.

11. Dower (1986), 10–14. The Pacific War was characterized by bitter fighting with both sides claiming the other committed atrocities. Dower explains how racial stereotyping was one of underlying causes, and he shows how each side viewed the other before, during, and after the conflict.

12. See Prange (1982) for a discussion of the events leading up to the belated delivery of the Japanese Declaration of War.

13. Each of the sections that follow with quotations from Simon and Lydia Peters, Garth Dunn, and Mitzi Yoshinaga are based on my tape-recorded interviews with them.

14. Potter and Nimitz (1960), 193–195.

15. Itō (1967), 11.

16. Burlingame, Burl. (2002). "WWII's First Japanese Prisoner Shunned the Spotlight," *Honolulu Starbulletin*, May 11, 2002.

17. Spicer (1946) and McMillin (1945). Spicer describes the effort to repulse the Japanese attack; McMillin's memorandum dated September 11, 1945, describes the invasion and subsequent surrender.

18. Palomo (1984), 30.

19. Itō (1967), 191.

20. Ibid., 11.

21. Sakamaki (1949), 26.

22. Ibid., 27.

23. Palomo (1984), 109–119 and Tweed (1945). When the Japanese rounded up the American personnel, six sailors managed to escape to the interior of the island, where they were aided by friendly Chamorros. Nine months later, three of the Americans were found by a Japanese search party. They were beaten, made to dig a grave, and told to sit in it. Then they were bayoneted to death. One month later two more were found and shot on the spot by Japanese troops. The sixth man, George R. Tweed, managed to survive until July 1944, when he was picked up by a U.S. Navy destroyer. A number of Chamorros were beaten or killed on suspicion they had aided the Americans.

24. For additional descriptions of *Argentina Maru* and Zentsuji, see Boyle (1963), Brown (1982), Eads (1985), Flournoy (1945), Putnam (1945), and Gibbs (1946–2).

25. General Douglas MacArthur, his wife, son, and key staff members were evacuated from Corregidor on March 11, 1942 in a squadron of four PT boats commanded by Lieutenant John Bulkeley, thus evading capture by the Japanese. The PT boats took them to Del Monte Field, Mindanao, where they were flown to Australia. See White (1942) and Manchester (1978), 253–276.

26. Some of the Americans were able to avoid the Japanese, even though after a while the Japanese threatened to punish those who did not surrender voluntarily. See Lindholm (1978) and Maynard (2001). Maynard's story has many parallels to Simon and Lydia Peters. Her family lived at a gold mine in northern Mindanao. They managed to flee into the jungle to another remote mine site and had the good fortune to evade the Japanese for two years until evacuated by submarine.

27. The classic description of the Doolittle raid is found in Lawson (1943).

28. Epperson (2004), 15.

29. The *Gripsholm* was a Swedish ship hired by the U.S. State Department to carry Japanese citizens and diplomats back to Japan, and to bring American diplomats, correspondents, and other neutrals out of Japan and the occupied countries. The vessel sailed under the auspices of the International Red Cross. Passengers were taken to a neutral port where the exchange was made. Red Cross food and medicine packages delivered by the *Gripsholm* saved thousands of prisoners' lives, despite the fact that the Japanese pilfered many of the packages. The *Gripsholm* also carried out exchanges with Germany. See Brines (1944).

30. For more about the forced evacuations of Japanese Americans, see Adams (1944), Bosworth (1967), Girdner and Loftis (1969), and War Relocation Authority (1987).

31. For more about life at Manzanar, see Embrey (1972), Houston and Houston (1973), and the online version of Burton, Jeffery F. et al. (1999). *Confinement and Ethnicity: An Overview of World War II Japanese American Relocation Sites*. National Parks Service, Publications in Anthropology 74. Washington, D.C.: U.S. Department of the Interior. http://www.cr.nps.gov/history/online_books/anthropology74/index.htm.

32. For the underlying racism and trumped-up reasons for relocating West Coast Japanese Americans, see Drinnon (1987). Odo (2004) provides fascinating details of the wartime experiences of Japanese Americans living in Hawaii, including the "Varsity Victory Volunteers," young men who first volunteered to defend the islands, then worked on public works projects. Lewis and Mewha (1955) present a detailed account of POW labor utilization in the United States.

33. Sakamaki (1949), 50.

34. Ibid., 56.

35. Ibid., 74–78.

36. Ibid., 66–68.

37. Mr. Corcino remembered the Hughes family but did not know where any of the children lived. He also recalled Charles Baker, another American plantation owner married to a Filipina. He thought that the Bakers had moved to California after the war.

38. Keats (1963). Also see Dos Passos (1946), 224–239, who describes a trip to visit the guerillas accompanied by Lee Telesco.

39. War Department General Staff (1944–2). On April 4, 1943, Captain William Edwin Dyess, Lieutenant Michael Dobervich, and ten others escaped from the Davao Penal Colony Camp. After eluding the Japanese for forty days, they eventually made contact with Wendell Fertig and his guerila army. Some, including Dyess, were evacuated by submarine to Australia July 1943. Coincidentally, Dobervich was on the submarine *Narwhal* in November 1943, at the same time as Mary Maynard. See Maynard (2001), 223–133, for a description of their escape.

40. As the Japanese POW camp system expanded, base camps, sub-camps, mine camps, and others evolved. Roger Mansell, director of the Center for Research on Allied POWs under the Japanese, describes the camp system and has extensive details about each camp, the POWs who were held there, and general conditions in the camps. Refer to www.mansell.com (accessed December 2007).

41. Houston (1973), 63–65. The pro-U.S. internees belonged to a group called the Japanese American Citizens League (JACL) and were treated by the camp administration as representatives of the internees. As Mitzi noted, a JACL leader (later identified as Fred Tayama) was beaten by six masked men. Harry Ueno, a young cook who

was organizing a Kitchen Worker's Union, was accused of taking part in the beating and arrested. Ueno had accused the camp's chief steward (a Caucasian) of stealing sugar and meat from the warehouse and selling them on the black market. His arrest was seen by many internees as retaliation for his accusation. A crowd formed and divided into two groups, one to locate Tayama, the other to march on the jail and to demand Ueno's release. At the jail, the military police first tried to disperse the mob with tear gas and then the fatal shots were fired.

42. Note 29 describes the *Gripsholm*.

43. Mitzi was part of a generation where filial roles became blurred between the Issei (immigrant Japanese) and Nisei (second-generation or American-born Japanese). This tension was aggravated by strained circumstances of camp life with its lack of privacy, communal living, etc. See Yanagisako, Sylvia J. (1992). *Transforming the Past: Tradition and Kinship among Japanese Americans*, Palo Alto: Stanford University Press. 68–75, for additional information on this subject.

44. For other firsthand descriptions of life in the occupied territories and civilian internment camps, see Keith (1947), Savary (1954), and Priestwood (1943).

45. Ercanbrack (1945) and Gibbs (1946–1). First Sergeant Ercanbrack assumed command of the prisoners in the camp. After the war he provided a detailed report on camp conditions and prisoner illnesses and deaths.

46. War Department General Staff (1944–1). American intelligence officers had acquired a surprising amount of information about the POW camps in Japan before the end of the war. As this report shows, not all of the information was accurate.

47. Brown (1982). Brown, writing about Zentsuji camp, describes how the prisoners smuggled stolen food back into the camp. POWs used the same methods at Hirohata.

48. See www.mansell.com (accessed December 2007) for details on Hirohata camp prisoners, guards, and other information.

49. Epperson (2004), 29.

50. Smith (1987–1), 13.

51. Farrell (1984), 34–47, also see Sanchez (1984) and Palomo (1984).

52. Crowl (1960), 331–337.

53. Ibid., 337–377. In addition, Manchester (1980), 332–340, and Josephy (1946), 29–71, took part in the invasion of Guam and provide personal insights about the fighting.

54. See Josephy (1946), 93–144, for a description of the ongoing battles with the Japanese stragglers on Guam.

55. Smith (1986). See also Smith (1988–1) and Smith (1988–2), 54–55, for excerpts of the diary.

56. I interviewed Jack Eddy in Guam in April 1987. It was fascinating to hear him describe the ebb and flow of the battles on the beach, and the subsequent search for

the stragglers. He was stationed in the camp that Itoh surveyed with such longing from his jungle hideouts.

57. Early in the war the concept of "no surrender" was well known. See Brines (1944).

58. Josephy (1946), 116–135. He describes being on the "Peace Ship," a small green amphibious landing craft that cruised back and forth near coastal areas where stragglers were suspected of hiding. They were encouraged to surrender by a Japanese prisoner who volunteered to call to them over the ship's loud speaker system, and two other prisoners who went ashore to talk to any stragglers who appeared. On this trip, sixteen Japanese stragglers were rescued in this manner. Otherwise, they faced almost certain death by the patrols.

59. McNeely (1946). Based on this police report, it appears that the dates in Itoh's diary were off by one day. His entry of December 26 was actually December 25, 1946.

60. Greenfield (1959), 358–373.

61. For details about the rescue of the internees and POWs, see Chase (1975), 87–93, for Santo Tomas, and Sides (2001) for Cabanatuan, a prelude to the Santo Tomas and Los Banos raids. Dos Passos (1946), 150–157, gives a poignant description of what Santo Tomas was like a few days after it was liberated.

62. I interviewed Jane Wills on July 20, 1985. She told me about conditions in the Happy Life Blues Cabaret camp, and then the trip by boat to Manila, internment at Los Banos, and the dramatic rescue that occurred. See also Flanagan (1999).

63. Manchester (1978), 428–429.

64. Smith, (1961), 620–629.

65. Bailey (1981), 182, cites examples where prisoners were slaughtered by the Japanese the day the surrender was announced.

66. Ercanbrack (1945). See also Frank and Shaw (1968), 784, for a picture of the flag-raising ceremony at Hirohata.

67. Krammer (1983), 67, 76. Also see Lewis and Mewha (1955) for a history of U.S. POW camps.

68. Sakamaki, 92–93.

69. Ibid., 96–104.

70. Krammer (1983), 72.

71. Ibid., 80.

72. Ibid., 85.

73. Strauss (2003). See Chapter 8.

74. Kahn (1962).

75. Lowe (1959).

76. Details of my encounter with Sergeant Itoh in Guam are found in Smith (1987–2) and Smith (1988–2). For a Japanese-language version, see Smith (1987–3) and (1987–4). *The Pacific Daily News,* Agana, Guam, had various articles about Itoh,

stragglers, and the return of his diary every day during the week he was there, June 3–9, 1987.

77. Jones (1986).

78. Anon. "How Yokoi Was Captured," *The Guam Tribune,* April 18, 1986, 4.

79. Onoda (1974).

80. See http://www.timesonline.co.uk, April 20, 2006. After the war hundreds of thousands of Japanese soldiers were captured by Russian forces and forced to work. Many returned to Japan in the 1950s but a large number perished. Others, such as Uwano, may have married and disappeared into Russian society.

81. Itō (1967), 191.

82. Sakamaki (1949), 107.

83. Ibid., 109.

84. See case synopses from Judge Advocate's Reviews, Yokohama Class B and C war crimes trials, at http://socrates.berkeley.edu/-warcrime/Japan/Yokohama/Reviews/PT-yokohama-index.htm (accessed December 2007).

85. Goldstein, Richard. "Obituary: Kazuo Sakamaki, 81, Pacific POW No. 1," *New York Times,* Dec. 21, 1999.

86. Burlingame, Burl. "WWII's First Japanese Prisoner Shunned the Spotlight," *Honolulu Star Bulletin,* May 11, 2002.

ACKNOWLEDGMENTS

‖‖ ‖‖ ‖‖

A great many people have given generously of their time and assisted me in conducting research for this book. Many were complete strangers who welcomed me into their homes or offices and searched their memories and files for information concerning events that had transpired forty years earlier.

First, the book would not exist without the interest, support, and encouragement of Garth G. and Millie Dunn, Simon and Lydia Peters, Henry and Mitzi Yoshinaga, and Masashi and Taeko Itoh. My thanks also to Nancy Dunn, Lori (Dunn) Emery, and Masa (Yoshinaga) Stafford.

In Washington, D.C., Mr. Dan J. Crawford, head of the Reference Section, Marine Corps Historical Center, Washington Navy Yard, arranged a temporary office for me. He provided invaluable assistance in locating documents in the National Archives and arranged the necessary permission for me to return Sergeant Itoh's diary to him. Mr. Thomas E. Wilgus, reference librarian for military history, U.S. Library of Congress, was also helpful.

In Guam, Don and Carmen Farrell were my hosts, advisors, and opened many doors with their contacts. I gratefully acknowledge the support of Mr. Richard R. Williams, chief of staff, Guam Legislature; Mrs. Magdalena Taitono, head librarian, Maria Nieves Flores Library; and Al Williams, librarian, Micronesian Area Research Center. Captain H. J. Schmidle, U.S. Marine Corps, Guam, and a group of marine volunteers assisted in my jungle explorations searching for the stragglers' hideouts.

I am indebted to the following people for their help and guidance: Fred A. Aguon; LCDR Richard J. Bergren, COMNAVMARIANAS (U.S. Navy); James Butler; Jack Eddy; George G. Flores, one of the original members of the Guam Police Combat Patrol; John Leddy; Frank, Joe, and Paul Shimizu; Adolf Squambelluri; Reverend Mitsuzo Tani, head minister at the Queen of Peace Chapel (Japanese

War Memorial); Katsuo Tosa, consul general, Japanese Consulate, Guam; and Jesus Q. Uncangco, Guam Police Combat Patrol.

In the Philippines, Lee and Charlotte Telesco were my hosts in Manila and provided fascinating insights into life in the Philippines before, during, and after the war. Lee was intimately involved in liaison with the American-led guerrilla movement. I understand that his extensive collection of documents has been given to the Hoover Library at Stanford University. In Davao I was assisted by Ernesto Corcino, historian, and Ms. Maximina C. Dolendo, librarian, both at the Davao City Library; Bong Anacio Jr. of the Davao Insular Inter-Continental Hotel; Raphael "Jun" Mendoza; and Salesiano Tomado.

In Japan my friends at Kozo Keikaku Engineering Company helped me tremendously, especially Morimasa Saigusa, the president. Miss Mariko Era served as guide and interpreter for my visit to Hirohata. Mr. Akira Imai provided background information on Himeji during the war.

In California I was fortunate to locate Jane Wills and learn of her experiences when the Americans fled from Davao to Malaybalay, only to be captured there and returned to Davao to the prison camp. She also told of her family's harrowing trip to Manila by ship, then their imprisonment, first in the Santo Tomas camp and then in Los Banos.

I owe a special thanks to the following people: Toshiko Lockwood, who worked tirelessly to translate Sergeant Itoh's diary into English and also served as Japanese-language interpreter in Guam; John Lockwood, who provided professional photography services; Anne Elizabeth Powell, for encouragement and her usual insightful manuscript review; and of course, my wife, Nancy, who followed me once again into strange jungles and assisted in the research in ways too numerous to mention. My friends Seth and Yasuko Siegel helped with matters Japanese. To Carolyn Gleason and her fine staff at Smithsonian Books, and Lise Sajewski, editor, my deep gratitude for their excellent work and encouragement with this book. Many thanks to Thomas Fujita-Rony for his review of the manuscript, and to cartographer Rob McCaleb of XNR Productions.

One of my regrets is that with the passage of time I have lost contact with some of the persons described in the book, and others have passed away and will not see the final version—although they read the 1987 draft. Wherever they are, I hope they'll understand that I, like them, never gave up.

CREDITS

Portions of Chapter 22 were published previously in *Soldier of Fortune Magazine* and appear here with the permission of Robert K. Brown, editor and publisher. All maps were drawn by Rob McCaleb of XNR Productions, Inc. Pages 5, 216, courtesy of Garth Dunn family; pages 207, 211, John Lockwood; pages 12, 16, 161, 168, 175, 204, 209 courtesy of U.S. Navy; pages 40, 41, 42, 66, Simon Peters; pages 158, 163, 199, Craig B. Smith; pages 107, 120, 127, 189, Nancy J. Smith; pages 28, 129, courtesy of Mitzi Yoshinaga family; pages 85, 87, War Relocation Authority; and page 31, Wikipedia.

INDEX

卌 卌 卌

Bold page numbers are illustrations.